Philip Ruddock was commended for conviction and condemned for cruelty in his management of Australia's Immigration program between 1996 and 2003. As Australia's longest serving Minister for Immigration and second-longest serving Federal parliamentarian, he won praise in the 1970s and 1980s for his strong commitment to human rights and refugee resettlement but in the 1990s and 2000s drew sharp criticism for offshore processing and the mandatory detention of asylum seekers. A reserved man, Ruddock did not display his emotions when confronted with human tragedy or angry protests. His reserved manner led to allegations he was uncaring and callous.

This book is the first extended treatment of Ruddock's political career, focussing specifically on Immigration and the place of compassion in the development and administration of public policy. It will interest students of Australian politics, particularly the Howard era, and engage anyone committed to the exercise of moral virtues and ethical values in national life.

Philip Ruddock and the politics of compassion | Tom Frame

ISBN: 9781925826852

Published in 2020 by Connor Court Publishing Pty Ltd

Connor Court Publishing Pty Ltd
PO Box 7257
Redland Bay QLD 4165
sales@connorcourt.com
www.connorcourtpublishing.com.au

Printed in Australia

Cover and page layout by Graham Lindsay

Front cover image: The Mayor of Hornsby, Councillor Philip Ruddock, outside Sydney Town Hall, 24 July 2018, (AAP Image; Joel Carrett).

Back cover image: Outside the main entrance to the Baxter Detention Centre during Philip Ruddock's tour of the facility, 10 July 2002 (AAP image; Rob Hutchison).

Connor Court Publishing

PHILIP RUDDOCK
and the politics of
COMPASSION

TOM FRAME

Compassion proper to mankind appears,
which nature witnessed when she gave us tears.
of tender sentiments we only give
those Proofs: to weep is our prerogative;
to show by pitying looks, and melting eyes
how with a suffering friend we sympathise.
Nay, tears will even from a wronged orphan slide,
When his false guardian at the bar is tried ...

By impulse of nature (though to us unknown the Party be)
we make the loss our own; and tears steal from our eyes,
when in the street with some betrothed virgin's hearse we meet;
or infant's funeral from the cheated womb
conveyed to Earth, and cradled in a tomb.

The 15th satire of Decimus Junius Juvenal, circa 2nd century CE.
Translated into English by John Dryden, 1693.

CONTENTS

PREFACE

When researching or just browsing a new book there is much to be gained from asking about earlier works on the same subject. Who has written? When did they write? Why did they write? What did they conclude? No book is written in a vacuum. Each thought has a pedigree; every argument has a bloodline. An author claiming intellectual credibility will acknowledge his or her place in the continuing contest of ideas and where he or she has tried to advance the discussion.

When I started thinking about Philip Ruddock's public life and his contribution to national affairs and the possibility of a book, I found that his parliamentary career had been the focus of newspaper articles and magazine profiles but there was no extended treatment that attempted to link his personal convictions to his political outlook and professional achievements.[1] Although he is the second longest serving Federal parliamentarian in Australian political history, having served for over 42 years in the House of Representatives as the member for Parramatta, then Dundas and finally Berowra, his life has been overlooked by commentators and historians. The nuances of his character have passed unnoticed. His career was, however, far from dull or undeserving of attention apart from the policies he implemented and the decisions he made while exercising ministerial oversight of the nation's immigration program between 1996 and 2003. I then decided to write the book that had not yet appeared.

Ruddock's parliamentary longevity is surpassed only by William Morris 'Billy' Hughes who was a member of the House of Representatives for more than 52 years (1901–1952), including seven years as prime minister (1915–1923). There have been seven substantial studies of Hughes although no biography appeared during his lifetime.[2] The first and the largest, by LF Fitzhardinge, ran to two volumes that were published in 1964 and 1979. Hughes, who changed political allegiance five times, is certainly more 'colourful' than Ruddock who remained a steadfast member of the Liberal Party throughout his parliamentary career. Of the 69 parliamentarians who served in the four Howard ministries between 1996 and 2007, other than Prime Minister John Howard and the Workplace Relations and then Defence minister, Peter Reith, Ruddock prompted more commentary and attracted the most criticism.

There are passing mentions of Ruddock's parliamentary service in the memoirs of his Cabinet colleagues – John Howard, Peter Costello, Peter Reith and Tony Abbott. Howard wrote that Ruddock 'became a close and trusted colleague in my Government. Philip was an excellent Immigration Minister and Attorney General.'[3] Notwithstanding the tensions between them on immigration policy during the 1980s, when Howard asked his Cabinet colleagues ahead of the 2007 election whether he should remain as prime minister or resign after poor polling, journalist Peter Hartcher claimed that Ruddock was the only one who took a 'firm and consistent position that Howard should stay on as leader.'[4] Ruddock's actual recollection is a little different: he told colleagues that should Howard elect to remain leader of the Liberal Party, the prime minister's wishes should be respected.

Costello observed that Ruddock had 'become a special hate-object for journalists and critics on the left.'[5] He had, according to Costello, managed a difficult portfolio well and 'became something of a darling in the Liberal Party' by 2001. The references to Ruddock in Reith's published diaries were purely factual and few in number. Abbott praised Ruddock as 'one of the most effective members' of the Howard Government in a half page tribute to his colleague's 'prodigious administrative efficiency'. He thought it a 'terrible calumny to say that he had lost his conscience, let alone his liberal principles, in the administration of the government's border protection and national security policies.'[6] These general comments are courteous and concise.

Unsurprisingly, few Labor luminaries have offered any detailed assessment of Ruddock's parliamentary career. Kevin Rudd's expansive memoirs briefly castigate Ruddock for his role in the 2001 'children overboard' affair and alleged deception. Rudd criticises the Howard Government and targets Ruddock as 'never one with a sense of irony, let alone shame' for failing to deal with the exodus of refugees after the 2001 invasion of Afghanistan by a Western coalition of forces that included Australian personnel.[7]

There are occasional references to Ruddock in the Howard-era volumes by Paul Kelly and George Megalogenis with the now standard observation that Ruddock had been on the moderate side of the Liberal Party in the 1980s but by the 1990s was seen as one of the 'hard men' in the Howard Government. In *Faultlines*, Megalogenis quoted Ruddock's wife Heather as evidence of prevailing public hostility towards him:

> I'm often troubled by the public perception of him [Philip]. I find it quite hurtful when you might walk through a demonstration to go to a function and you've people shouting out: 'You're a mass murderer, you're a racist'. Blah, blah, blah. One thing he does not have is a racist bone in his body. Many faults he may have, but he is not a racist man.[8]

There are scattered references to Ruddock in other general works on the Howard years such as *The Land of Plenty: Australia in the 2000s* by Mark Davis and *The Year that Changed Everything: 2001* by Phillipa McGuinness.[9] Both works use Ruddock to substantiate the claim that the Howard Government responded to dire human need among asylum seekers with either callous indifference or convenient self-interest. Ruddock is portrayed as a 'grey man' lacking emotion who apparently could not see, or was unwilling to recognise, the pain and torment of those who came to Australia hoping to find a new life but were met with mandatory detention and possible deportation.

A little texture is added by polemical works such as Robert Manne's *The Howard Years*. After noting that Ruddock was considered one of the government's few remaining 'small-l liberals' in 1996, Manne alleged that 'not once did Ruddock express sympathy for or show understanding of the often terrifying political conditions from which those from Iraq, Afghanistan or Iran had fled'.[10] In a published collection of newspaper articles, Manne referred to Ruddock's concern for refugees as 'little more than moral cant – a debater's argument with the "bleeding heart" liberals he has come to despise'. He accused Ruddock of staging a 'long and highly personal campaign' with 'remorseless vigour, against the political refugees who have fled to Australia' from Afghanistan and Iraq. Ruddock had 'transformed our refugee regime' and 'thrown away, as if it were of no account, a noble post-World War II reputation for humane and decent treatment of political refugees.'[11]

One of few works willing to acknowledge his principles and to applaud his commitments was the thoroughly researched *Destination Australia: Migration to Australia since 1901* by Eric Richards. Ruddock is credited with taking a firm stand against discrimination within his own party in the late 1980s and against the racism associated with the rise of Pauline Hanson in the mid 1990s. Credited with being the 'most divisive' Immigration minister in Australia's history, Richards observes that Ruddock 'stood for mandatory detention of asylum seekers, border control and remotely located detention centres. But he also stood for a rigorous, generous and well-financed legal refugee program, for which he received less credit'.[12]

Most of the scholarly literature on immigration is empirical with evaluation of arrival and departure data, and assessment of settlement outcomes for those who become permanent residents. Commentary on the Humanitarian Program has concentrated on law and court proceedings or on political discourse and media reporting, the latter considering why segments of the electorate are opposed to immigration (either parts of the program or its totality) and are anxious about the nation's ability to absorb some people. Much of the discussion turns on the contention that the Howard Government, especially Ruddock, exploited negative community attitudes towards asylum seekers for domestic political gain. This remains a serious charge. It was made highly personal in the charge that Ruddock himself lacked any compassion for those whose lives were directly affected by his decisions.

Given that compassion was frequently cited as a criterion for judging Ruddock's performance, I am surprised that few Australian scholars have devoted much energy to discerning the place of compassion in political decision-making and in public policy. No Australian political scientist has emulated the work of Professor Clifford Orwin from the University of Toronto who studied the origins and expression of compassion in historical and contemporary affairs. Although I am critical of both works, few Australian writers have attempted analytical studies of the kind undertaken by Didier Fassin in *Humanitarian Reason: a Moral History of the Present*[13] or Ala Sirriyeh in *The Politics of Compassion: Immigration and Asylum Policy*.[14] The lack of scholarly attention to the practice of compassion is a notable omission in this field of inquiry.

Works on ministerial conduct such as *Motivating Ministers to Morality* by Jenny Fleming and Ian Holland and *Ethics and Political Practice* by Noel Preston and Charles Sampford have concentrated on acceptable standards of professional probity and personal integrity rather than describing the place and function of individual attributes and private convictions in the performance of public duty.[15] Scholars have written about the use and abuse of ministerial discretion but not in relation to the exercise of compassion either as a foundation for social good or as a reflection of the public interest.

By way of contrast, there are many works considering the recent history of refugee policy, critiquing the legal framework in which claims for asylum are assessed and featuring wide-ranging objections to Australia's treatment of those seeking protection. Journalist Margot O'Neill's, *Blind Conscience*, appeared in 2008.[16] The final chapter entitled, 'Why, Mr Ruddock?', drew on the author's extensive interview with the former Immigration minister. O'Neill discussed Ruddock's management of the refugee program and his own emotions, or apparent lack of them, in exercising oversight. I will refer to O'Neill's book later. More substantial and nuanced is Father Frank Brennan's *Tampering with Asylum: a Universal Humanitarian Problem*.[17] This insightful book is also empathetic. Brennan outlines the problems Ruddock faced as minister and acknowledges the legal and practical constraints that limited his options. Compassion is not dealt with specifically, either in depth or detail. It is plain, however, that Brennan believed the Australian Government should have been more compassionate in its treatment of asylum seekers. In reply, Ruddock asserted his department was compassionate to the extent that practicality and public opinion permitted. Father Brennan's critique will be addressed in chapter 10.

Several authors have written articles advocating a more humane approach to asylum seekers, foregrounding the need for compassion. They are largely polemical, not exegetical exercises. The authors want compassion to undergird Australia's refugee program but do not address the definitional problems or acknowledge the practical dilemmas associated with the place they want to afford compassion in public policy. These problems and dilemmas cannot be wished out of existence simply because the nation wants to appear more caring. If the philosophical and political issues are not taken seriously, the potential for inconsistency and incoherence in the application of compassion in public policy might lead to charges internationally of hypocrisy and insincerity. These charges are no more desirable than the present imputations of callousness and cruelty.

My interest in immigration is personal and professional. It is part of my own story and an enduring theme in my published work over the past 15 years. My adopted father, a Scotsman and a member of the Royal Naval Volunteer Reserve, was stationed in Australia when the Second World War ended in August 1945. Like many working men from the area around Glasgow, he sensed the probability of the region's industrial decline and decided to remain in Australia in the hope of a better life. He did not consider himself a migrant. Australia was part of the British Empire and he felt no need to ask permission to stay. He never returned to Scotland and did not see his parents ever again. At least half of our neighbours in Wollongong had come to Australia in the post-war migration program. They were from Italy, Greece, the Netherlands and Peru. I went to school with their children and was encouraged by my Labor-voting mother to call all migrants 'New Australians', the term coined by the first Immigration Minister, Arthur Calwell, in 1947. Multiculturalism was part of the life I knew as a child. I do not recall any of our neighbours being refugees until I reached my teenage years and encountered some of the Lebanese and Vietnamese refugees who had settled in the Illawarra. Later in life I met refugees from Czechoslovakia and East Timor, Afghanistan and Iraq. I have seen the inside of only one immigration detention centre. It was in Darwin. It resembled a medium security gaol and I recall being grateful that I could depart at the end of my visit.

I conferred with a number of senior Coalition ministers when writing this book, Ruddock and Howard most frequently. From a number of frank conversations, I have gained a clear sense of their views on immigration, especially the Humanitarian Program. I have also observed considerable diversity of opinion among senior Liberals. There were two consistent themes. First, the global movement of people is presenting Western governments with potentially intractable problems. Second, most politicians try to avoid drawing any public attention to immigration policy and practice. It is a subject that few nations manage well in terms of constructive debate, and I include the Scandinavian countries in this observation as they too host a range of opinions within their electorates, opinions not always expressed in a tolerant and respectful manner. In this book I have tried to outline the debate without giving inflammatory views a prominence to which they are not entitled. While I disagree with some of the things Ruddock said and did, I have tried to keep the focus firmly on how he saw the issues and why he responded as he did. I have endeavoured to avoid allowing my own views on immigration to drift into the foreground until the postscript.

Acknowledgements

I was assisted by a number of generous people in preparing the manuscript for this book. First and foremost was Philip Ruddock. He answered all of my questions and made no effort to embellish his legacy. He did not expect me to share his views. When I appeared unpersuaded by the necessity of what he said or did, he inquired about what I might have done had I been placed in similar circumstances. Philip's wife, Heather, was also helpful in clarifying the names of people and places, and other factual matters. Jeanette Farrell, his long-time secretary, explained why certain public documents and official reports were retained. Philip had earlier transferred the bulk of his papers to the Howard Library managed by UNSW Canberra. Steve Ingram, his former communications advisor at Immigration and chief of staff when Attorney General, shared many insights into the challenges of those years. Rick Forbes worked on many of Philip's local re-election campaigns and provided insightful perspectives on a wide range of subjects. Nick Cook, who is presently writing a general biography of Philip, generously shared the fruits of his research. Of Philip's cabinet colleagues, John Howard was always ready to explain the background to Coalition policy and, as always, to detect errors of fact about when Liberal Party thinking changed and where the impetus had come from. Now in his ninth decade, he remains mentally sharp and intellectually engaged. To get a sense of the Cabinet mood in the early years of the Howard Government I turned to my National Party friends, the late Tim Fischer, John Anderson and John Sharp, and when considering the middle years to David Kemp who also offered valuable insights on compassion in public policy. Bruce Baird helped me to understand why and how he, and a small group of others in the Liberal party room, opposed the Coalition's immigration policies. Rodney Cavalier, a former minister of the Wran and Unsworth Labor Governments in New South Wales, was his usual helpful self. My friend at the ANU, John Uhr, provided some leads for further reading in the area of compassion and politics. I spoke with a number of public servants who worked with Philip and I am especially grateful to Bill Farmer and Philippa Godwin for their recollections and insights into decisions and processes. My UNSW Canberra colleagues, Andrew Blyth, Annette Carter, Kus Pandey, Alan Wilson and Kathryn Stephenson, were willing to act as a sounding board for my ideas, and both Trish Burgess and John Nethercote read and improved draft chapters. My long-time colleague and friend Graham Lindsay very kindly typeset the manuscript and offered much helpful advice. This book is much larger than the one I had originally intended to write. I thank the publisher, Anthony Capello, for his goodwill and encouragement in being able to produce it.

Tom Frame
Old Parliament House
Canberra, ACT
1 November 2019

Endnotes

1   In saying there is no major work on Philip Ruddock I am excluding *Mr Ruddock Goes to Geneva* by Spencer Zifcak which was published in 2003 by UNSW Press. It is essentially a brief polemical tract that focusses mainly on Australia's attitude to the United Nations Human Rights Treaty System rather than on Ruddock's political philosophy and handling of the Immigration portfolio.
2   LF Fitzhardinge, *William Morris Hughes A Political Biography, Vol. 1: That Fiery Particle, 1862–1914, Vol. 2: The Little Digger, 1914–1952.* Angus & Robertson, Sydney, 1964 and 1979; WJ Hudson, *Billy Hughes in Paris: the Birth of Australian Diplomacy. Australian Institute of International Affairs*, Melbourne, 1978; Donald Horne, *In Search of Billy Hughes*, Macmillan, 1979; Malcolm Booker, *The Great Professional: A Study of WM Hughes*, Sydney, 1980; Peter Spartalis, *The Diplomatic Battles of Billy Hughes*, Hale & Iremonger, Sydney, 1983; Aneurin Hughes, *Billy Hughes: Prime Minister and Controversial Founding Father of the Australian Labor Party*, John Wiley & Sons, 2005; Carl Bridge, *William Hughes: Australia*, Haus Publishing, 2011.

3   John Howard, *Lazarus Rising: a Personal and Political Autobiography*, Harper Collins, Sydney, 2010, p. 56.

4   Peter Hartcher, *To the Bitter End*, Allen & Unwin, Sydney, 2009, p. 24.

5   Peter Costello with Peter Coleman, *The Costello Memoirs*, Melbourne University Press, Melbourne, 2008, p. 166.

6   Tony Abbott, *Battlelines*, Melbourne University Press, Melbourne, 2009, p. 44.

7   Kevin Rudd, *Not for the Faint-hearted, Volume 1: 1957-2007*, Macmillan, Sydney, 2017, p. 289.

8   George Megalogenis, *Faultlines: race, work and the politics of changing Australia*, Scribe, Melbourne, 2003, p. 146.

9   Mark Davis, *The Land of Plenty: Australia in the 2000s*, Melbourne University Press, Melbourne, 2008; Phillipa McGuinness, *The Year that Changed Everything: 2001*, Penguin Random House, Sydney, 2018.

10   Robert Manne (ed.), *The Howard Years*, Black, Melbourne, 2004, p. 32.

11   Robert Manne, 'What if the refugees were white?', *The Barren Years: John Howard and Australian Political Culture*, Text, Melbourne, 2001, pp. 176-79.

12   Eric Richards, *Destination Australia: Migration to Australia since 1901*, UNSW Press, Sydney, 2008, p. 329.

13   Didier Fassin, *Humanitarian Reason: a Moral History of the Present*, University of California Press, Berkeley, 2012.

14   Ala Sirriyeh, *The Politics of Compassion: Immigration and Asylum Policy*, Bristol University Press, Bristol, Bristol, 2018.

15   Jenny Fleming and Ian Holland, *Motivating Ministers to Morality*, Ashgate, London, 2001; Noel Preston and Charles Sampford, *Ethics and Political Practice*, Federation Press, Melbourne, 1998.

16   Margot O'Neill, *Blind Conscience*, UNSW Press, Sydney, 2008.

17   Frank Brennan, *Tampering with Asylum: a Universal Humanitarian Problem*, UNSW Press, Sydney, 2003.

INTRODUCTION

The media profile of Australia's longest serving Minister for Immigration, Philip Maxwell Ruddock, conceals more than it reveals. During countless press conferences and in media interviews, commentators noted that Ruddock was ready to listen and responded with reason but also appeared tough and uncompromising, unmoved by opponents' criticisms and unyielding to advocates' pleas. In personal encounters, Ruddock is always courteous and considerate. Constituents in the Federal electorates he served from 1973 to 2016 and, more recently, the ratepayers of Hornsby Shire in Sydney where he has been the Mayor since 2017, say he cares about people he does not know and is an advocate for the disadvantaged. Throughout a long life of public service, Ruddock has been attentive to personal sorrow and human suffering. A reserved man, he does not exude mood swings, and acknowledges success and accepts disappointment with equanimity. His even temperament is often interpreted as diffidence or even indifference to hardship. These interpretations are mistaken. His public statements are restrained, preferring reason over emotion. He does not play to the crowd or seek easy popularity. While he has a healthy self-view; he does not think too much or too little of himself. His usually gentle demeanour conveys neither humility nor hubris.

This portrait is drawn partly from his management of the nation's immigration policy, especially the provision of refugee protection, and his role in the promotion of human rights. Immigration is where he has contributed to national affairs for nearly 50 years and where his name is most widely known. This book draws on published sources, personal interactions and private papers held in the Howard Library at UNSW Canberra. I have examined hundreds of media releases and public speeches, listened to countless radio interviews and watched innumerable television discussions. Some of this material precedes the Howard Government and relates to his time in Opposition. After he ceased being the Minister for Immigration he still spoke about immigration, refugees and human rights. Indeed, he continues to devote a great deal of his own time to meeting ethnic communities and discussing the best ways to manage the global movement of people and the Australian nation's humanitarian program. Ruddock never wanted to be anything other than the Minister for Immigration and was not seeking another role when Prime Minister Howard asked him to become Attorney General in October 2003. Immigration and multiculturalism reflected his private commitments and embodied his professional aspirations. He would have been content to serve throughout the Howard years in one portfolio, not unlike Peter Costello at the Treasury and Alexander Downer at Foreign Affairs.

Those whose only acquaintance with Ruddock is derived from media reporting of public controversies associated with the Howard Government might not recognise the man I have described. Commentators who disliked his politics depicted him as a persistent journeyman whose demeanour was, they wrote, as warm as the welcome he offered to asylum seekers who defied his determined efforts to keep them away. Ruddock was disliked by many in the media because he was neither combative nor passionate when they thought he should have been both. His quiet and calm persona was mistaken for detachment and a lack of sympathy for people with dire needs in desperate circumstances. Rather than being lauded for drawing attention to the plight of oppressed people, critics claim Ruddock systematically abandoned the liberal principles that propelled him into public life and which initially marked him as one of few 'small-l liberals' in the Howard ministry. Ruddock is frequently accused of lacking what critics presume is the most necessary attribute of an Immigration minister – compassion. There is, however, a prior question: what part should compassion play in the management of the Australia's humanitarian program? If it has a role, did Ruddock show the degree of compassion that could be reasonably expected of him?

Competing views

The literature survey in the preface mentioned a number of works that were published between 1999 and 2007 when the Howard Government was still in power. Most of the authors accused Ruddock of promoting a cruel asylum seeker policy implemented with a management style that lacked empathy. More recent assessments (those published in the previous decade) are just as harsh and no less forgiving despite the authors having an opportunity (which none have exploited) to compare Ruddock's performance with that of his successors: Amanda Vanstone, Kevin Andrews, Chris Evans, Chris Bowen, Brendan O'Connor, Tony Burke, Scott Morrison, Peter Dutton and David Coleman. Those who followed Ruddock in the portfolio have done no better in the court of public opinion.

When Ruddock announced on 8 February 2016 that he was leaving Federal parliament, a number of journalists produced retrospectives for the national newspapers. Tony Wright, the *Sydney Morning Herald's* political commentator, referred to him as the 'unknowable hard man of the Parliament'.[1] Perhaps confusing hardness for discipline, and leaving readers to wonder what being a political 'wet' might entail, Wright began by observing that:

> it is all but forgotten now that Ruddock spent the entire first half of his more than 42-year career as a small-l Liberal 'wet', forever involving himself in the lonely business of concern for human rights, for those afflicted by war in Cambodia and other dreadful places; by apartheid in South Africa; by injustice across the world. He was a leader of Amnesty International's parliamentary group and was one of the very few Liberals who belonged to Parliamentarians Against Apartheid.

Wright's main contention was that John Howard shunned Ruddock during his first term as Opposition Leader (1985–1989) because 'it was generally believed, [Howard] couldn't stand him'. They had, according to Wright, little in common personally and had clashed over political principles, implying they had different values. The reason for this professional animus? Wright contended that Ruddock had:

> infuriated and publicly embarrassed John Howard when, in 1988, he and a tiny knot of fellow moderates crossed the floor and voted with the Hawke Government on a motion to oppose any form of racial discrimination in immigration. It was shortly after Howard had declared he was concerned Asian immigration was too high.[2]

When Howard returned to the Liberal leadership in January 1995, Wright asserted that Ruddock was tired of being overlooked for promotion and 'found ambition'. Wright alleges that Howard opportunistically exploited the situation by appointing a previously empathetic and compassionate man to a portfolio requiring a tough and resolute minister.

In short order, Ruddock became a hard-edged Howard insider – the immigration minister who enthusiastically embraced and broadened Labor's policy of mandatorily detaining asylum seekers. Under his watch, asylum seekers, including children, were locked behind razor wire in Australia's deserts. He railed against 'queue jumpers', introduced Temporary Protection Visas and was an architect of Howard's 'Pacific Solution'. Wright's commentary is damning of both Howard and Ruddock as well as being inaccurate as the following chapters will show.

According to Wright and those sharing this view, Howard shamelessly sought a compliant colleague eager for promotion; Ruddock sold out his personal principles for professional advancement. What is Wright's evidence for this serious charge? Some of Ruddock's Amnesty International friends demanded he cease wearing his member lapel badge while performing his ministerial duties and Ruddock's daughter Kirsty 'publicly turned against him' over his treatment of asylum seekers. Curiously, given his expansive claims, Wright also noted that

> Philip Ruddock had always kept his own counsel, and kept his motives close to his chest … He may have become the longest-serving federal politician in the land, but there seemed always something unknowable about him.

A man who disclosed little about himself publicly had apparently revealed enough for a journalist to conclude that vanity triumphed over values.

As one chapter in a long life of public service closed for Ruddock in 2016, another opened. He was appointed Australia's first Special Envoy for Human Rights. In her press statement, the Foreign Minister, Julie Bishop, noted:

> As a distinguished member of the Australian Parliament for over four decades, the current Chair of the Parliamentary Joint Committee on Human Rights, and a longstanding member of Amnesty International, Mr Ruddock is well-qualified to advocate and represent Australia's human rights views and record. As Special Envoy, Mr Ruddock will focus on advancing Australia's human rights priorities of good governance,

freedom of expression, gender equality, the rights of indigenous peoples, and national human rights institutions.[3]

The creation of such a position was widely praised and warmly welcomed. The choice of appointee drew cautious reactions and critical comment.

The Director of Advocacy and Research at the Human Rights Legal Centre, Emily Howie, said that any concerns about the appointee should not overshadow the important role the envoy could play.

> We shouldn't pre-judge Mr Ruddock's contribution. We have strongly opposed his positions on issues like asylum seeker policy in the past but recently we have appreciated his leadership on the abolition of the death penalty. This role has great potential.[4]

Lawyer and Jesuit candidate for the Catholic priesthood, Justin Glyn, thought that:

> human rights has been an issue dear to the new special envoy's heart, as evidenced during his work for Amnesty International in the 1980s and 1990s, even if the areas of immigration and refugee law subsequently marked a certain blind spot for him. Now, however, if he attempts to raise the human rights records of other countries (many of which are much grimmer than Australia's) he will be cheerfully ignored and have his own tenure as immigration minister thrown back at him in response. So he is unlikely to be a very successful envoy.[5]

One of the few lawyers to extend some latitude to Ruddock was Catherine Renshaw, Senior Lecturer in Law at Western Sydney University. She tried to separate public obligations from personal convictions.

> Ruddock is a professional. Even his enemies admit that he is disciplined, hard-working and committed. In politics, this translated into a steely determination to execute the government's policies regardless of the human cost, because he believed they were in Australia's long-term best interests. But, as a free agent – with a brief to independently promote a moral cause he believes in – it is possible (indeed likely) Ruddock will bring his discipline and determination to succeed to this entirely

different role. Strange things sometimes happen when politicians are unshackled from the constraints of politics.[6]

Others were not so sanguine. Lawyer and former Liberal staffer, Greg Barns, claimed that

> Philip Ruddock and human rights are not generally used in the same sentence these days except in the context of searing criticism about his role as immigration minister in the creation and expansion of cruel immigration detention centres in places like Woomera and Baxter in South Australia and Nauru during the early 2000s ... Under Mr Ruddock the mental and physical harm endured by asylum seekers was horrendous.[7]

Most damning was Spencer Zifcak, the Allan Myers Professor of Law at the Australian Catholic University, who made much of Ruddock's March 2000 appearance before the United Nations Committee on the Elimination of Racial Discrimination in its periodic review of Australia's compliance with the International Convention on the Elimination of Racial Discrimination.

> Mr Ruddock's performance was ... by any account, a dismal failure. His demeanour was arrogant and condescending. His arguments served only to harden the Committee's opinion that Australia, a nation whose human rights record had been admired, had joined the ranks of countries known routinely to violate the freedoms and entitlements of their citizens.[8]

Zifcak then turned his attention to Ruddock's time as Attorney General before concluding:

> The frank human rights violations of which Mr Ruddock has been guilty during the course of his long political career, and I have mentioned only a few, suggest two principal conclusions in relation to his appointment as Special Envoy for Human Rights. First, had he even a scintilla of insight concerning his record, he should courteously have refused the Prime Minister's offer of the position, regarding himself as particularly unsuitable. Secondly, the Prime Minister's judgment must

be called into question. He has just shot Australia's bid for a seat on the UN Human Rights Council in 2018 in both feet.[9]

Fortunately for Australia, these fears were exaggerated. His work as Special Envoy did not attract much favourable media attention but its primary objective was nevertheless achieved. Australia was elected to serve on the Council for a three-year period in October 2017. Ruddock's political past caused none of the difficulties and certainly provoked none of the dismay that the naysayers had forecast when he was appointed in early 2016. Hence, the need for a closer look at his character and his contributions.

Discerning a legacy

When determining the significance of an individual's place in history it is important to choose the best vantage point. When an assessment is made too early or too late, the necessary balance between the causes and the consequences of their actions might prove elusive. The circumstances in which a decision is made should not overshadow the outcomes in trying to determine whether the chosen course of action made a difference. Conversely, if evaluating the outcome of a decision is all that matters, there may not be due regard to the circumstances that made a decision easy or difficult to make.

Appraisals of Ruddock's political career have focused almost entirely on 1996–2003 and the Immigration portfolio. They have overlooked or ignored almost everything he said and did both before and after the Howard Government held office. A few scholars and a handful of journalists have acknowledged Ruddock's pioneering commitment to the parliamentary promotion of human rights, the need for a non-discriminatory immigration policy, the importance of multiculturalism to Australia's place in the world and the international campaign for abolition of the death penalty. But these commendable efforts in the 1970s and 1980s have been obliterated by the egregious sins he allegedly committed during the 1990s and 2000s. His detractors routinely rehearse his principal transgressions. First, falsely claiming that asylum seekers had thrown their children overboard in October 2001. Second, seeking to amend the *Migration Act* to deny asylum seekers the right to appeal decisions of the Immigration Department in the courts. Third, encouraging the 'Pacific Solution' for the offshore processing of refugee claims. Fourth, managing the amendment of the *Marriage Act* to ensure it remained exclusively between a man and a woman, thereby precluding same-sex marriage. And fifth, tolerating the United States military commissions established to prosecute detainees at Guantanamo Bay who had been captured during military actions in Afghanistan and Iraq, including Australian citizen David Hicks. The first three of these actions will be considered in the light of his personal beliefs and political commitments. But a note of caution is needed. Each of these matters is decidedly more complex than critics usually recognise.

My purpose is considering compassion in public administration and public policy, not offering an apologia for the Howard Government nor defending the actions of one man. But Ruddock's decisions and conduct require a fuller explanation that does justice to the difficult circumstances in which he was obliged to act. The exercise of political leadership is never as straightforward in practice as observers imagine it to be in principle. Philosophical principle collides with practical exigencies; parliamentarians are public officers not personal advocates; ministers must uphold the public interest against the conflicting demands of lobby groups; applying the law precludes certain actions and obliges others; precedents established in a worthy context can be exploited in less worthy ones; cabinet ministers are team members and not lone operatives; the media is not univocal or consistent in its reporting; and, public opinion is never static or fixed. That a policy seems harsh does not make it wrong, even morally wrong. Doing the right thing is not always the the most straightforward thing to do. Pursuing the best option may be precluded by legal restraints.

From my interactions with ministers and public servants over the past two decades there is a near universal lament that neither the press nor the people properly acknowledge the dilemmas and difficulties associated with many of the policies they are required to implement and the decisions they are obliged to make. Journalists and voters often overlook the public interest considerations that need to be considered when changing a policy, altering a procedure or spending public money. Organisational complexity is not an excuse for poor policy, bad decisions or rank incompetence. Frequently, a simple solution to enduring human need pursued on compassionate grounds is rarely a viable option. The difficulty will always lie in the detail and, lurking in the background, unintended effects and unforeseen consequences.

At first glance, the intention of Australia's humanitarian program – to provide protection to vulnerable people – appears uncomplicated. Its implementation, however, is highly complicated. It is naïve, if not reckless, to presume that people, even if appearing desperate and determined, will necessarily be honest, sincere and candid when their self-interest is at stake. Loopholes in procedures and inconsistencies in processes will be exploited. Precedents will be misrepresented and threats will be made. Public policy needs to be cognisant of the inevitability of dishonesty, insincerity and fraud. There is a place for scepticism. Good policy remains workable by imposing checks, balances and tests. Making intuitive judgements and reasoned decisions about the character and conduct of people, such as asylum seekers, requires both patience and practice. Hence, the complications of developing policies and drafting procedures that must deal with the reality of the human condition and the presence of flaws and frailties.

Ruddock held a difficult post in an extraordinary time. He confronted a range of challenges more demanding than those faced by his Labor predecessors Stewart West, Chris Hurford, Robert Ray, Gerry Hand and Nick Bolkus. The seeds of controversy arising from the complexities of managing the Humanitarian Program were already germinating when Ruddock was appointed to the portfolio in 1996. He did not create the problems; he inherited them. Some were produced by the actions and policies of the previous government; others were an unavoidable counterpart of the increasingly global movement of people. Ruddock did devise many of the solutions the Howard Government embraced and he must face the judgment of history as to whether they were effective, efficient and ethical. My analysis is focussed on whether these solutions could and should have been grounded in compassion.

A partial profile

Bad biographies are no more than identikit pictures. They are an approximation of features and usually not a close likeness. Even good biographies are essentially partial profiles. As it is impossible to consider the totality of a person's life, especially if they lived for a long time and possessed a 'colourful' character, the biographer must consider an individual from a particular vantage point or focus on only one dimension of their being. Most biographers avoid the inner life because its contours are difficult to discern and there is little corroborating evidence. Sometimes biographers are concerned with character assessments based on the experiences of those who interacted with their subject. Choices need to be made about focus and emphasis. The main area of interest could be private deeds or public decisions, words ahead of actions, or personal struggles not public battles.

Ruddock continued to hold elected public office as I was writing this book. Nonetheless, I felt it was an opportune moment to assess one component of his parliamentary career – immigration policy and practice. Those who worked with him are available and most were willing to share recollections and offer opinions. Ruddock himself was prepared to speak openly and candidly. Some of the official records relating to his ministerial service are now in the public domain. As there have been nine Immigration ministers since 2003, his administration can be compared and contrasted with those who came after him. Their tenure has been brief. The average incumbency has been less than two years. It is possible, however, to perceive the evolving place of compassion in the management of Immigration. As the portfolio encompasses a large and diverse range of activities, I am principally concerned with permanent immigrants and asylum seekers, the government's role in promoting immigration as a social good and providing services that optimise settlement outcomes for new arrivals. I am not interested in the management of overseas visitors or short-term, temporary migration, such as the entry of seasonal workers into Australia.

When Philip Ruddock became the Minister for Immigration,[10] three main groups were the concern of Australia's humanitarian program. The first consisted of people who were outside their own country seeking protection from persecution. The second were people in particularly vulnerable situations with close family ties or tangible community connections with Australia. The third component comprised people seeking relief from discrimination that was so severe it constituted a substantial violation of their human rights. The average annual intake within the Humanitarian Program in the 1990s was 12,000 people but the actual number of people accepted and resettled varied with the rise and fall of unauthorised arrivals seeking asylum.

The humanitarian intake must, therefore, be assessed in the context of the wider migration program. The annual average intake of permanent immigrants for the first half of the 1990s was 92,000 compared to previous decades: 107,000 in the period between 1945 and 1960; 130,000 in the 1960s; 96,000 in the 1970s (including the smallest annual figure recorded during the years of the Whitlam Government); and, 110,000 in the 1980s. These figures need to be considered against the steady increase in Australia's population over that period. By 1996, the annual immigration intake as a percentage of the total population was essentially half that of the late 1940s. The fluctuations reflected the state of the economy, especially the labour market. In 1996, 23 percent of the Australian population was born overseas. This represented an increase of 3 percent over the previous 25 years. During the Howard Government's term in office, Australia's annual population growth was 1.1–1.2 percent, lower than the world's overall population growth. Were immigration halted, the Australian population would still have increased because the birth rate exceeded the death rate by around 120,000 people annually.

Moreover, in the 1990s the *Migration Act* became, alongside the *Taxation Administration Act*, the most complex piece of Commonwealth legislation. When initially enacted in 1958, the *Migration Act* ran to 35 pages. By the end of Ruddock's tenure, it was nearly 500 pages in addition to many volumes of regulations. In the year he became the Minister, there were 673 applications challenging an Immigration decision filed with the Federal Court. The number rose to 914 in 1999–2000. Another three years later, there were an average of 70 applications filed each week with the courts and the Administrative Appeals Tribunal. By 2002, more than half of the cases decided by the Federal Court of Australia concerned immigration.[11] While the overwhelming majority of these applications were unsuccessful, the applicants remained in Australia until their extensive rights of appeal were exhausted. As the court processes were clogged and judgements were slow in coming, the length of detention became a moral issue as well as a political one.

Some of these cases raised important questions of principle about the nature of compassion: whether compassion could or should be reserved for exceptional cases and how compassion related to discharge of the nation's humanitarian obligations. In the absence of any emerging philosophical consensus, the law was amended to prevent compassion being a factor in the more difficult cases heard by the nation's courts and tribunals. The philosophical questions have remained unaddressed and political controversy persists despite several changes of government and the arrival and departure of numerous ministers. I have tried to deal with some of these issues in the pages that follow.

This book is divided into four parts. The first part deals with the period from Ruddock's birth in 1943 to his appointment as a Federal minister, the day before his fifty-third birthday. The second part considers the place and importance of compassion in government policy and practice, and identifies a series of problems associated with the expectation that compassion feature in ministerial deliberation and government decision-making. The third part examines Ruddock's administration of the Immigration portfolio from 1996 to 2003 and, briefly, his performance as Attorney General from 2003 until the defeat of the Howard Government at the November 2007 election. I will also consider the theory and practice of ministerial discretion, and whether the charge that Ruddock became a political chameleon who abandoned personal principles to fulfil professional ambition can be sustained from the available evidence. The concluding chapters contain some general observations of Ruddock's parliamentary service and the continuing place of compassion as an imperative for political action in Australian democracy. Some personal reflections appear in the postscript.

Readers need to remember that the Coalition's victory at the March 1996 ballot coincided with election of Pauline Hanson as the independent Member for Oxley and, a year later, the formation of her One Nation political party. Her complaints about the conduct of Australian politics and the power of elites resonated across the nation. Previous Australian governments had not been obliged to deal with a single-issue political party that was openly and vigorously opposed to immigration, especially Asian immigration, which then comprised 40–50 percent of the annual intake of new entries to Australia. Hanson's willingness to say publicly what many Australians allegedly thought privately, opened the way for much misinformed commentary on immigration policy and practice. The foremost complaints were quite similar to those that were current during the 1950s with the addition of a racial twist: Australia was not just being overrun by migrants, it was being 'swamped by Asians'. This claim was easy to make and, in the minds of some, difficult to refute. As the Minister for Immigration, Ruddock was required to explain and, more frequently, to defend the principal function of his department against public suspicion and political opportunism.

★ ★ ★ ★

This book is biographical but not a biography. Something answering the description of a biography would examine every aspect of Ruddock's public and private life. No such book presently exists.[12] I have looked at only one aspect – immigration. The treatment of his time as Attorney General is no more than a brief overview and deals with decisions that related to Immigration. I have concentrated on the exercise of compassion and not, for instance, on displays of legal acuity or organisational leadership. While there are dangers in trying to isolate one element of an individual's character – after all, we are integrated beings and an amalgam of everything we think and do – it is possible to deal with compassion as an insight into someone's view of humankind and an imperative for their interactions with other human beings.

I am offering a partial profile. In drawing attention to compassion as a consideration in Ruddock's administration, I am enquiring about the place and function of compassion more broadly. Does compassion have a place in public policy or only in the exercise of individual discretion? Is compassion a weakness or a strength, a liability or an asset in dealing with complex questions that require practical answers? Is a politician able to exercise compassion when the law and community expectation require actions and attitudes that seem callous or cruel? Can the exercise of personal values, such as compassion, be overwhelmed in the exercise of professional duties? After serving longer than anyone else in the Immigration portfolio, was Ruddock spiritually wounded, morally injured or existentially damaged by the experience?

I have tried to explore how a principled person addresses complex questions in demanding circumstances. My aim is neither to defend nor denounce Ruddock, although I believe he is largely misunderstood by those who abhor his convictions and condemn his conduct. Readers will inevitably come to their own mind about him if they have not formed some firm impressions already. In my view, there is more to be gained from assembling the factors he considered relevant to decision-making, and from understanding his thought processes, than attacking what we might assume are flaws in his character. There is a time for moral indignation when politicians say and do things that are contrary to the values expected of public officials by the people they represent. That time has ended. As more than a decade has passed since Ruddock relinquished the Immigration portfolio and ceased being the Attorney General, the priority needs to be assessing his decisions and interpreting their consequences as an evaluation of the past and a guide to the future.

The challenge is providing a more fulsome context for a balanced consideration of his political career and to invite a more realistic appraisal of the problems and the possibilities associated with giving compassion a central place in public policy. This means, in part, ignoring claims and criticisms that are purely political rhetoric. It is easy for opponents to condemn government policy because it lacks compassion. Most people in most circumstances can be more compassionate. Chastising someone for a lack of compassion is not difficult. As a charge, it is hard to deny given the exercise of compassion cannot be measured objectively against an agreed scale. Accusing a government of being heartless will produce a telling headline in the next day's newspaper. It plays to residual public prejudice against the state and enduring community dissatisfaction with political leaders. The electorate is apparently more virtuous than their representatives and capable of greater altruism.

But what can we reasonably expect of governments and ministers? Plainly, we do not want them to be heartless in rejecting any and every claim to empathy and kindness but we do not want them naively accepting any and every request for assistance and support. A government unmoved by human suffering and a minister who cares nothing for individual distress will harden society and see collective abandonment of qualities essential for individual flourishing and community growth. A society led by brutes devoid of feeling will be brutalised. By contrast, a government that too readily accepts tales of woe and a minister who too easily endorses assertions of disadvantage will weaken society by discouraging the exercise of responsibility and diminish the need for resilience. The absence of discretion and judgment will lead to systemic corruption and debase selflessness. In sum, we need governments and ministers with the wisdom to acknowledge the place and the limits of compassion in public policy. This study seeks to consider the performance of one government – the Howard Government – and one minister – Philip Maxwell Ruddock.

Endnotes

1   Tony Wright, 'Philip Ruddock: from wet to the unknowable hard man of the Parliament', *Sydney Morning Herald*, 8 February 2016, https://www.smh.com.au/politics/federal/phillip-ruddock-from-wet-to-the-unknowable-hard-man-of-the-parliament-20160208-gmonfm.html

2   Tony Wright, 'Philip Ruddock: from wet to unknowable hard man'.

3   https://foreignminister.gov.au/releases/Pages/2016/jb_mr_160208a.aspx

4   https://www.hrlc.org.au/news/establishment-of-australias-first-special-envoy-on-human-rights-a-step-in-the-right-direction

5   Justin Glyn, 'Ruddock appointment thumbs nose at human rights', *Eureka Street*, 14 February 2016.

6   http://theconversation.com/ruddock-as-human-rights-envoy-dont-scoff-too-soon-54409

7   Greg Barns, 'Four Australians with better human rights credentials than Philip Ruddock', Opinion, ABC News, The Drum, 9 Feb 2016.

8   https://johnmenadue.com/spencer-zifcak-special-envoy-on-human-rights-ruddock-what/

9   https://johnmenadue.com/spencer-zifcak-special-envoy-on-human-rights-ruddock-what/

10   The portfolio had several names during Ruddock's tenure, I will refer to it simply as 'Immigration'.

11   For an excellent overview of the evolution of immigration law during the first six years of the Howard Government see John McMillan, 'Immigration Law and the Courts', *Upholding the Constitution*, Proceedings of the Samuel Griffith Society, vol. 14, 2002, pp. 167–185.

12   At the time of writing (November 2019), the journalist Nick Cook was working on a general biography of Ruddock. I welcome its production as there are few autobiographies or biographies of the leading figures in the Howard Government. Only John Howard, Peter Costello, Peter Reith and most recently Richard Alston have written extensively about their role in national affairs between 1996 and 2007.

CHAPTER 1

A life in the making   1943–1973

Australia has produced few political dynasties. There have been several instances of a child following a parent or a grandparent into politics and making their mark. Australians who decide to run for public office tend to come from ordinary families where politics is an interest and not an obsession. While many parents who have enjoyed successful and enjoyable professional careers are gratified that one of their children has decided to follow in their footsteps, politicians are more sanguine if their child nominates such a choice. Politics is less of a career and more of a vocation – a calling to further the public interest in pursuit of the common good. It could be considered a calling because the rewards are hard won and largely intangible. Many politicians could earn more money in other walks of life. They would face less time away from their families, fewer hours in planes and nights in hotels, avoid highly personal criticism from the press and the people, and have the reassurance of greater job security. Elected office is arduous. Those who endure the hardships and deprivations that accompany this vocation are propelled by an abiding desire to make a difference – an objective that is sometimes beyond their reach.

Apart from some constitutional requirements and a few statutory provisions, there are no formal qualifications for elected office in Australia. An effective politician requires an array of abilities and aptitudes given the many and varied demands that are associated with the formal discharge of their official duties. Parliamentarians need to be leaders and managers, debaters and conciliators, listeners and speakers, initiators and responders. While many of these skills can be learned through experience and perfected by practice, the best parliamentarians possess the right temperament and have a natural sense of what is required of them. There are plenty of politicians elected to public office who do not possess this temperament. They are unlikely to be as successful as those who are able intuitively to read the mood of any place or people. Because temperament is a reflection of character and personality – something which is usually fixed from an early age – there is always merit when attempting to make sense of an individual's public life in looking at the circumstances of their birth and the circumstances in which they were nurtured. In close families the virtues that are esteemed by parents are embodied in the values they teach their children. This was certainly true in the Ruddock family.[1]

Service and sacrifice

Philip Maxwell Ruddock was born in the national capital at the then recently opened Canberra Community Hospital on 12 March 1943.[2] He nearly made history as an infant. The government announced that the first child to be born at the new hospital would receive £50. This was a considerable sum in 1943. Although his mother, Emmie, was the labour ward's first admission, Philip was the third to arrive in the new facility. He would become the first Federal parliamentarian to be born in Canberra. Like many people who exercise public leadership, family life would shape his evolving sense of service and devotion to duty.

Philip's father, Maxwell Stanley Ruddock, was born on 2 January 1914 at Marrickville in Sydney. Max's father, Stanley Gordon Ruddock, was born in Sussex, England, into a naval family. Stanley's father, Nathaniel, was stationed at the Queenstown Naval Base in County Cork when the southern Irish counties were still part of the United Kingdom. Stanley migrated to Australia and his brother, Nathaniel, moved to South Africa. Stanley married May Myers Cropper whose family were coachbuilders at Armidale in northern New South Wales. Stanley and May lived in Windsor where Stanley worked as a forestry officer for the state government. Max was the eldest of their three children. He attended Windsor Primary School (where he was Dux) and later won a scholarship to the highly regarded Fort Street Boys High School, a selective secondary school. To attend Fort Street, which was too distant for daily commuting, Max stayed with his maternal grandparents in Eastwood. This suburb was part of the original Federal electorate of Parramatta. It marked the beginning of the Ruddock family's enduring connection with the area.

Max's ambition was to study law at the University of Sydney. As the tuition fees were beyond his parent's financial means, he studied Economics on a Teacher's College scholarship instead. Max enjoyed university and was fully engaged in student activities including editing the student newspaper, *Honi Soit*, writing about socialism and attempting to introduce rugby league on the campus alongside rugby union. He was unsuccessful in the latter endeavour. Max graduated with a Bachelor of Economics in 1935. Three years later he completed a Master of Economics degree, an uncommon qualification at the time. Academically inclined, Max considered undertaking doctoral studies at Oxford University but decided to remain in Australia. Consequently, Penrith High School gained a highly credentialed economics teacher.

Max married Emmie Eileen Chappel on 24 August 1940 in St Jude's Church of England at Randwick in Sydney's eastern suburbs. Emmie had lived with her parents, Percival and Eileen Chappel, in Randwick. The couple met when Max's parents had moved from Windsor to the adjoining suburb of Bronte. Max became an Associate of the Federal Institute of Accountants in 1941 after topping the annual Australia-wide examination. Frank Crean, subsequently federal treasurer and later deputy prime minister in the Whitlam Government, was in the same cohort. By then, the Second World War was well into its third year and the need for uniformed men and women was growing.

Max was prevented from joining the armed forces by a rare hereditary neurological disorder known as Charcot-Marie-Tooth (CMT) disease. The disorder causes damage to the peripheral nervous system leading to muscle weakness in the body's extremities particularly the hands and feet. The onset of symptoms usually occurs in childhood or during teenage years. The legs are most commonly affected first. With time, the sufferer's legs become weaker and harder to control. Some people with CMT disease may be only slightly affected with high-sided shoes sufficient to deal with weakness in the legs and feet. Other people may need walking aids. The most seriously affected require use of a wheelchair. As he grew older, the affects of CMT made Max's life increasingly difficult. While he managed to become the Teacher's College tennis champion, war service was out of the question. He was then seconded to Canberra to serve as Senior Investigatory Officer and later Deputy Prices Commissioner under Sir Douglas Copland, positions he held from 1942 to 1948. His son, Philip, was born during this time.

Formative years

The Ruddocks lived in the suburb of Turner on what was then the northern edge of Canberra. Their house still stands with the large oak tree Max planted in the back garden continuing to provide shade. Philip's twin sisters, Janice Emmie May and Suzanne Emmie Eileen, were born on 21 December 1944. He attended kindergarten at Yarralumla Preschool followed by Ainslie Infants School. Owing to family illness, Max declined an offer of appointment as Secretary of the Commonwealth Grants Commission which was then located in Melbourne. Emmie was an only child and devoted to her mother Eileen. When Eileen was diagnosed with a terminal illness, the family returned to Sydney and settled on the northern edge of Sydney in the suburb of Pennant Hills. The house was near the railway line and the Elouera Bushland Reserve (now part of the Berowra National Park). Preserving trees and native flora became a passion for both father and son. Like many outlying Sydney suburbs, the Ruddock home was without sewerage until the adjacent suburb of Cherrybrook was developed for housing in the mid-1970s.

Philip attended Pennant Hills Public School between 1949 and 1954. Two other Federal parliamentarians, John Faulkner (Labor Senator, 1989–2015) and Andrew Leigh (Labor, House of Representatives since 2010), also attended the school. In the absence of a local state high school, Philip then went to Barker College, an Anglican secondary school in nearby Hornsby, from 1955 to 1959. Four other Barker College alumni have served in Federal parliament: Dr Bob Solomon (Liberal, House of Representatives, 1969–72), Mitch Fifield (Liberal Senator, 2004–19), Peter Garrett (Labor, House of Representatives, 2004–2013) and Rob Oakeshott (Independent, House of Representatives, 2008–2013).

After arriving in Sydney, Max decided to leave a promising career in the Australian public service for the private sector. He became a director of Jones Brothers (1948–1956), the manufacturing arm affiliated with David Jones retailers, then worked briefly as General Manager of Casben Swimwear (1956) before becoming a Public Accountant with the firm Stott & Underwood. He was also General Secretary of the Wheat & Wool Growers Association (1959–1962) and Secretary of the Wheat Industry Research Committee (1959–1963). In addition to his work and family responsibilities, Max stood as an Independent candidate for Hornsby Shire Council in 1952. He was elected and later served as Deputy Shire President (1955–1956) and Shire President (1960–1961). Despite being a financial member of the Liberal Party, Max was personally opposed to political parties contesting municipal elections, believing that community-based rather than party-based candidates were preferable in local government. During the Shire's fiftieth anniversary celebrations in 1956, Max disclosed his firm views on the matter in a message to ratepayers as Acting Shire President:

> Local government is concerned with the everyday problems of the citizens' lives and their homes. Councillors live among the citizens and are readily available for discussion and consultation. This is the way in which local government should continue. It should remain local. Trends towards council amalgamations and politics in local government are evident in some places today, but these trends are retrograde and should be resisted.[3]

The nine councillors, including the first woman to serve as a councillor, presided over the administration of 50,000 hectares of land, a substantial area on Sydney's suburban fringe. The long-running population boom necessitated the opening of new high schools including Normanhurst Boys, Asquith Boys and Asquith Girls, all established in the 1950s. Community life and churchgoing were also flourishing in what was becoming a materially affluent and an actively religious area of Sydney.

While the 1950s and the 1960s were decades of opportunity for self-starters and entrepreneurs to make the most of positive business conditions and labour market growth, this was also the era when organisations and associations were established across the country to promote mutual assistance and practical support for those whose needs were not met by the widening social safety net. Service clubs such as Rotary, Apex and Lions were formed by individuals who also belonged to trade unions and professional guilds to help those facing hardship and dealing with misfortune. Churchgoers, like the Ruddocks, were implored to support the charitable outreach of the Anglican Home Mission Society and the St Vincent de Paul Society in addition to overseas aid agencies that channelled resources to Third World and developing nations dealing with abject poverty and civil strife. Those who were relatively 'well off' were constantly exposed to human suffering within Australia and abroad, and urged to respond with compassion and generosity.

The adolescent politician

In addition to being active in his local church, Philip accompanied his father on weekend council duties. They visited ratepayers and talked about local government concerns: the state of footpaths, roads, kerbs and gutters, storm water drainage, local parks and bushland preservation. During these years, Philip learned much from his father. These lessons included the value and importance of public service. This was a highly influential time for Max's only son who seemed genuinely interested in many of the matters that occupied his father's attention, especially planning and development. It was this interest that involved Philip in his first political controversy.

In May 1959 the New South Wales government wanted to extend industrial zoning at Thornleigh. The subject area was then part of the Cumberland Planning Scheme and included a number of 'greenbelts'. Under the Scheme, land around Quarter Sessions Road was designated an industrial area. The State Labor Government wanted to extend industrial zoning further to the west. Philip noticed the area had been included in a Residential District Proclamation. It could not be re-zoned without removal of the proclamation. As a legislative instrument, parliamentary approval was required for that to happen. The Government was unable to secure approval, the green belt was preserved and a new residential suburb was created. Some months later Max was invited to name it 'Westleigh'. The suburb's central community space was later named 'Ruddock Park' to honour Max for 'saving' the suburb although it had been Philip who had identified the means of preventing further industrialisation.[4] Town planning and environmental protection were central in the formation of Philip's social and political views. As the area included many newly arrived migrant families, Philip was soon familiar with their concerns.

The travails of politics

While active in local government and still believing political parties were an unwelcome intrusion into local community affairs, Max hoped to become a Liberal parliamentarian. He sought pre-selection in the federal electorates of Bradfield (on the death of the long-serving former prime minister Billy Hughes) in 1952, Wentworth and Warringah in the mid-1950s, and Parramatta in 1958, as well as a number of state seats. He was runner-up on several occasions. Although a gifted speaker and a compelling debater, the disability that had prevented him from wearing military uniform during the

1940s also worked against him in pre-selections during the 1950s. 'Returned men' with war service, often lacking political experience, were often favoured over men like Max with extensive expertise in public administration. The 1958 pre-selection for Parramatta proved to be the most significant of his failed attempts.

Howard (later Sir Howard) Beale, the Liberal member for Parramatta, was appointed Australian Ambassador to the United States and resigned his seat in parliament in February 1958. When this safe seat became vacant and a by-election was required, Max emerged as the leading local candidate. Prime Minister Robert Menzies had his own man in mind. He wanted the eminent barrister, Sir Garfield Barwick QC, to secure pre-selection. Barwick lived in the adjoining suburb of Beecroft. Barwick had not played an active part in local branch affairs nor did he have war service. The closely fought pre-selection came down to two candidates: Barwick and Ruddock. Senator (later Sir) William Spooner, the Federal Minister for National Development and a very senior New South Wales Liberal, supported Barwick and worked quietly to promote his candidacy. Barwick, soon-to-be Commonwealth Attorney General and future Chief Justice of the High Court, had a narrow win: 27 votes to 23. Max was disappointed but not demoralised. As Barwick was a potential future prime minister and needed the support of Menzies and the party machine to succeed, Max had done exceptionally well to attract and hold so much local support.

After nearly a decade of trying and without any assistance from the General Secretary of the New South Wales division of the Liberal Party, John Carrick, over the previous decade, Max's political ambition was eventually fulfilled. He sought pre-selection as the Liberal candidate for the new state seat of The Hills. The electorate had a notional Liberal majority, taking in the northern and Liberal voting end of the seat of Blacktown. The electorate covered 51 square kilometres and included the suburbs of Pennant Hills and West Pennant Hills where he was well known and still a Shire Councillor. The pre-selection contest included Max and the Liberal member for Blacktown, Alfred Dennis. When Max prevailed, Dennis subsequently ran as an 'Independent Liberal'. After polling 56.28 per cent of the vote and defeating Dennis, Max was elected to the Legislative Assembly on 3 March 1962.[5] He continued to serve in local government until his term of office ended in 1965. By then, the incoming Askin Coalition Government ended 21 years of Labor rule in New South Wales. The slowly debilitating effects of CMT had, however, made it difficult for Max to walk without an aid. Disability did not impede his service to the state. Undaunted, he became known for strong local advocacy and careful policy deliberation.

Max's journey to successful pre-selection had a major influence on his son. Philip had learned that political opportunities usually come neither quickly nor easily. Consistency, commitment and collaboration were key to attracting stakeholders, securing support and ultimately achieving political appointment. At the age of 16 and before he was eligible to vote, Philip joined the newly formed Pennant Hills branch of the Young Liberals. The New South Wales State President of the Young Liberals was 21-year old, John Winston Howard, a member of the Earlwood branch. The two men first met in 1960. Few would have predicted that the younger Ruddock would be elected to public office before the older and politically better connected Howard.

Personal priorities
Philip was an unremarkable young man and there were no hints then that he would become a national figure. His experience at Barker College was mixed. With an emphasis on team sports, mainly rugby in winter and cricket in summer, he did not stand out. Part of the reason, although unknown at the time, was an eyesight convergence problem that impeded his ability to determine true depth of vision, a quality essential for dexterity in ball sports. He was also small in stature and among the youngest boys in his year. By way of contrast, he did very well academically and displayed a deep interest in politics. Although aged 16, his matriculation results were sufficient to gain him entry into Sydney University. Given his youthfulness, Barker's headmaster thought he should repeat the final matriculation year. Seeking the advice of Professor Niven White, Professor of Agriculture at Sydney University and Pennant Hills resident, Max was advised: 'it is better to be a little fish in a big pond than a big fish in a little pond'. Philip enrolled at the University of Sydney with the intention of studying Law. There was, however, one practical problem. As the minimum age for admission to the legal profession was 21, he would be too young to practice in the event his studies were completed in the minimum time. The answer was enrolling in a combined Arts-Law degree. It would effectively delay his graduation and lead to a broader education.

Reflecting his enduring interest in politics, Philip continued his involvement in the Young Liberal movement but was not among its leaders. His personal and professional priorities were clear. He wanted to do well at university and establish his legal career. Seeking political office could wait until he had established a firm vocational foundation in the event that a life in politics was beyond reach. As his father had known well, gaining pre-selection and winning an election depended upon a number of factors, most of which were beyond the aspirant's control. Philip had time on his side.

As a first-year undergraduate, Philip was influenced by Dr Harry Edwards, later foundation Professor of Economics at Macquarie University. Edwards lived in West Pennant Hills and on one occasion addressed the local Young Liberals branch at the invitation of his keen undergraduate. Edwards later joined the Liberal Party and won pre-selection for the safe Liberal seat of Berowra when Tom Hughes QC decided not to stand at the 1972 election after being dropped from the ministry in 1971. Among the field of 24 candidates for pre-selection in Berowra was John Howard.

As his studies continued, Philip was active in the Sydney University Liberal Club and the Anglican Church. In his first year at the Law School (then located in Sydney's legal precinct), Philip urged the Rector of St James' Church on King Street, Canon Frank Cuttriss, to conduct a weekly lunchtime service primarily for Law students. With his father's encouragement, Philip sought advice from two Askin Government ministers about serving his articled clerkship in law. John Maddison, the Justice Minister, and Ken McCaw, the Attorney-General, suggested he approach Douglas Murray, senior partner in the commercial law firm Berne Murray & Tout. He was offered a place in 1962 and was inspired by Murray's mentorship.

Murray, a successful solicitor, had undertaken a number of significant cases including the *Second Wagon Mound Case* (on foreseeability in tort law) and *Kades v Kades* on jurisdiction in custody disputes.[6] Both cases were argued at the Privy Council in London. Murray, who had first-rate people skills, told his clients they were entitled to expect the best possible advice delivered in the most timely manner. Murray implored his articled clerks to make decisions promptly and to back their judgment. After graduating with his Law degree in 1967, Philip remained at Berne Murray & Tout. He became an Associate in 1968 and Partner in 1970. The older partners were encouraged to have a 'next generation' lawyer in the firm when they accepted Philip although Murray sensed that politics might eventually draw his protégé away from the practice.

With his studies concluded and a legal career underway, Philip became more active in the Young Liberals and was elected New South Wales Political Vice President in 1970.[7] By this time he had met Heather Cramer, a South Australian Young Liberal, at the second Young Liberal national convention held in Perth. Heather was at Adelaide University studying Arts and Law. They shared similar interests and enthusiasm for political debate. To their friends and acquaintances, Heather seemed more suited to political activism. They were engaged in May 1970 and married in January 1971 at Scots Church in Adelaide before settling in the Sydney harbourside suburb of Neutral Bay. By then, Heather had completed an Arts degree at the University of Adelaide and was finishing her Law degree at the University of Sydney. The couple's first daughter, Kirsty, was born in February 1972 as Heather juggled motherhood, study and her own career. A second daughter, Caitlin, was born in April 1977.

Public duties and personal ambitions

As Philip approached his thirtieth birthday, his political outlook was taking a more settled form. He had been shaped by his father's experiences. Max was committed to the ideals of public service and the place of sound research in public policy. Persistence and determination would eventually prevail. Max believed in the virtue of hard work and the centrality of the family to human flourishing. He had a clear sense of the common good and knew the limits of party politics. Max demonstrated his sincerity through personal commitment and proved that physical disability could be transcended. He thought people ought to be treated fairly and respectfully, especially by public officials. Once elected to parliament, he contributed to party policy and government decision making with thoughtful and reasoned contributions. Max was interested in the machinery of government and was persuaded of the need for legal restraint on political power. He was a 'details man' who found satisfaction in promoting the orderly conduct of government. Disinterested in grand gestures or confected symbolism, Max's public persona was low-key and understated. He was disciplined in his approach to parliamentary business and restrained in the disclosure of his emotions. Debate was usually won by clear thinking rather than colourful oratory.

In his maiden speech delivered on 2 May 1962, Max decided to focus on the technically complex Local Government Amendment Bill. Drawing on his personal experience of local government and professional expertise in regulation of planning and development, Max spoke for nearly an hour on the need for clarity when it came to priorities for urban and suburban planning over the next century and the need to set limits on local government powers in the approval of development applications.[8] He contended that the Labor government's planning was short-sighted, narrowly conceived and usually indifferent to the environment and natural heritage. He also argued that local government was hampered by confusion and contradiction in its prerogatives to approve or deny developments with consequences that transcended well beyond the remit of local government. The availability of public transport and the prevention of pollution were state government concerns and yet, he contended, councils were creating problems that were the responsibility of parliaments to resolve.

Max wanted clear rules and concise regulations that reduced the need for individual interpretation and ministerial discretion. He called for the government's overall planning objectives to be made available and published so that all stakeholders could comment on deficiencies or duplications in the provision of services. In sum, he wanted a more comprehensive system with the roles and responsibilities of all parties better defined. If everyone knew their place in the process and received advice on how they could participate in pursuing the best outcomes, the government could ensure its policies and procedures were effective and efficient.

Max's maiden speech revealed a quintessentially Ruddock quality: an orderly thoughtful approach to complex administrative problems reduced the need for special pleading and would prevent the triumph of sectional interests. If the system within which decision-making took place was consistent and comprehensive, there would be greater transparency, less corruption and fewer appeals which would, in any event, tend to favour those with more resources. Further, Max believed that concentrating power in the hands of one person (or one office) was undemocratic and contrary to the public interest. He wanted to disperse power across the tiers of government so that the people's will was reflected in the enlarged participation of their representatives. Max was also concerned that the relevant minister's delegates, who were unelected, had too much power and that processes could be captured by agencies that were more concerned with enhancing their institutional prestige at the expense of the public interest. As elected officials answered to the people, he wanted them to make decisions when there were competing priorities and conflicting agendas. In the days before anyone was labelled an 'environmentalist', Max was also committed to trees and bushlands, watercourses and native flora. He was neither pro- nor anti-development. There was the need for balance and with the right systems and structures, a sustainable balance could be achieved. Max's erudition moved the Minister for Local Government, Pat Hills, to offer his congratulations on a speech that had 'tackled a most complex and involved matter' and which had given the government much to ponder.

There were aspects of Max's maiden speech that clearly influenced Philip's personal outlook and political temperament. If there were hurdles and setbacks in life, they were to be examined and a strategy devised to overcome them. Life can be hard and people are sometimes harsh. There was no place for self-pity and no point trying to be someone else. This was not a mindset of resignation but acceptance. If one door were closed, another would open. Life was full of unexpected opportunities and emerging challenges. It was important to do the right thing and to do it rightly. Max was a diligent local member and a conscientious contributor to the affairs of his party and the parliament. He wanted preferment but would not pursue it. Hard work would surely be recognised and potential would eventually be acknowledged. Scheming to depose of one's rivals and being obsequious in the hope of accelerated advancement was not the Ruddock way. Max would wait patiently and with dignity for an invitation to join the ministry. The father's example was not lost on the son.

With the retirement of Sir Robert Askin in January 1975, the new Premier, Tom Lewis, appointed Max to the post of Assistant Treasurer and Minister for Revenue. He later became Minister for Transport and Minister for Highways. After the Coalition lost the May 1976 election to the Labor Party led by Neville Wran, Max resigned his seat and left parliament on 26 May 1976. He died six days later, aged 62. In death, he was remembered for his honesty, determination and dedication to duty.[9] In reflecting on his father's time in office, particularly in Hornsby Shire, Philip later remarked: 'His record and passion for Hornsby is a demonstration of his enormous affection for this area – not to mention the fact that he was a great role model to me'.[10] Max had given his son a taste for politics and the possibility of doing some good through parliamentary service. Douglas Murray's suspicions were proved right. Philip decided in 1973 to pursue political office but few expected the sequence of events that followed.

Endnotes

1   Much of the factual detail in this chapter was provided by Philip and Heather Ruddock.
2   The present site of the National Museum of Australia.
3   The text of his message was reproduced in https://www.dailytelegraph.com.au/newslocal/hornsby-advocate/the-1950s-brought-new-schools-and-first-woman-politician/news-story/7e0b591e1c2b51b6cc42ed7d3685116e
4   https://www.playgroundfinder.com/playgrounds/361
5   http://www.tallyroom.com.au/archive/nsw2011/chil2011
6   https://casetext.com/case/matter-of-kades-v-kades-2
7   https://www.youngliberal.org.au/history
8   https://www.parliament.nsw.gov.au/hansard/Documents/HHP/Pre1991/Votes/indexes/Index%20-%2040th%20Parliament%201962-63-64.pdf
9   https://api.parliament.nsw.gov.au › api › daily › HANSARD-290296563-659
10 Jake McCallum, 'Local government election results: Philip Ruddock claims victory of Hornsby Shire Council in local government elections', *Hornsby Advocate*, 9 September 2017.

CHAPTER 2

The making of a liberal   1973–1984

There was nothing surprising in Philip Ruddock's decision to join the North Rocks branch of the Liberal Party in 1968. His father was a Liberal state parliamentarian and he had been a member of the Young Liberals since 1960. He became vice president of the Mitchell Federal Electorate Conference in 1971. This was the Federal electorate encompassing the state seat of The Hills held by his father since 1962. Ruddock became president of the New South Wales Young Liberals in 1971–72, a position that entitled him to concurrent membership of the Liberal Party State Executive. By 1973 he was federal chairman of the Young Liberal Movement and served on the Liberal Party Federal Executive.[1]

Ruddock was an emerging leader in the party's organisation when the Labor Party led by Gough Whitlam was elected to office after 23 years of uninterrupted Coalition rule on 2 December 1972. Despite Whitlam's personal popularity, the Labor Government had a very small parliamentary majority of 9 seats in the House of Representatives and did not command a majority in the Senate. Like his father, Ruddock had political ambitions and was starting to think about opportunities at the federal election expected in 1975. The seat of Mitchell which took in the suburbs of Baulkham Hills, Beaumont Hills, Bella Vista, Box Hill, Kellyville, Nelson, Winston Hills, Castle Hill, North Rocks, Old Toongabbie, Rouse Hill and West Pennant Hills, had been a swinging seat since it was first contested in 1949. When lost by the Coalition to Labor in 1972, the seat covered Westmead, Wentworthville, Northmead and The Hills areas. Considerable growth in The Hills district during the early 1970s suggested that a much safer Liberal seat would emerge at the next boundary redistribution expected before the 1975 election. Ruddock was intending to seek pre-selection as the Liberal candidate to win back the seat of Mitchell in 1975. He then owned 12 acres of land at Kenthurst and spoke about building a house there while retaining an apartment in Neutral Bay. There were, however, other options he had not considered.

The Liberal Party retained the adjoining Federal seat of Parramatta after the 1972 election. The margin was 359 votes after the distribution of preferences. The result surprised many senior Liberals who expected the seat to be won by the Labor Party candidate, Michael Whelan. In mid-1973, the sitting member and former Attorney-General and Minister for Foreign Affairs, Nigel Bowen QC, resigned from Parliament to accept judicial appointment. He became the President of the New South Wales Court of Appeal. Bowen had been in the House of Representatives for less than a decade when he was narrowly defeated by Bill (later Sir Billy) Snedden in a ballot for the Liberal Party leadership following the Coalition's election loss in 1972. Conscious his decision to leave politics would necessitate a by-election, Bowen thought delaying his departure until after the incoming Whitlam Government's 'honeymoon' period with the electorate had ended would give the Liberals a better chance of retaining the seat. Others in the party were not so sure. On the night that Bowen's resignation was announced, John Dowd, then a member of the Liberal Party State Executive, tried to convince Ruddock to nominate for pre-selection. Dowd's advocacy created a practical difficulty for the Ruddock family. Heather Ruddock wanted to complete her Law degree before her husband ran for public office. They had earlier agreed that Philip would seek pre-selection for Mitchell ahead of the 1975 election. A new plan was before them.

The unplanned pre-selection
The Parramatta electorate covered the suburbs of Parramatta, Harris Park, Rosehill and a small section of Merrylands in the south west, North and East Parramatta, Oatlands, Dundas, Carlingford and North Rocks to the north, Rydalmere and Ermington along the Parramatta River to the east and Eastwood, Epping and Marsfield (including Macquarie University) in the north east. The Labor Party, buoyed by the personal popularity of Gough Whitlam as Prime Minister, was quick to re-nominate its 1972 candidate for the seat, Michael Whelan, who had polled only five fewer first preference votes than Bowen (who was only victorious after the distribution of preferences). Ruddock had already concluded that only one winnable Liberal

seat would be created from the Mitchell and Parramatta electorates in the forthcoming re-distribution. He reasoned that the Liberal incumbent in one of them would have the stronger claim to the new seat. The call for nominations ahead of the Parramatta by-election would force his hand. Ruddock approached his father, Max, for advice: should he wait for Mitchell in 1975 or contest Parramatta now? There was a meeting of minds: nominating for Parramatta would be good practice for the Mitchell contest, assuming he finished the pre-selection ballot in the top six. The family was conscious that it took Max more than six attempts to gain pre-selection.

Some 30 candidates nominated. This was a large number for what was now considered a marginal seat. The nominees included Nick (later Sir Nicholas) Shehadie (then Deputy Lord Mayor and later Lord Mayor of Sydney), Rodney Purvis and Ross Vincent (barristers who became judges), John Spender and Maurice Neil (barristers who became Federal parliamentarians), Jim Cameron (a local state parliamentarian) and Peter FitzGibbon (Ruddock's predecessor as New South Wales Young Liberal State President). It proved a tight race despite its dour conduct. There were no glossy testimonials or promotional videos in those days. The candidates completed a nomination form and included whatever personal and professional information they felt was relevant. Ruddock decided not to contact pre-selectors directly; others did so on his behalf. The pre-selectors already knew him and would form their own view of his merits.

The Premier of New South Wales, Sir Robert Askin, personally preferred Shehadie whose wife Marie Bashir was later the Governor of New South Wales (2001–14). With his Lebanese background and public profile as a former rugby union international, the Liberal Party 'establishment' thought Shehadie could secure the large Lebanese vote concentrated at the Parramatta end of the electorate. The exhaustive voting process started early on a Saturday morning at the Wentworth Hotel in the city. Shehadie was expected to win easily after delivering a well-prepared speech. During question time with the pre-selectors, however, he seemed to struggle with answers. He was familiar with public appearances but pre-selectors were anxious that Shehadie might have difficulty with the intense media scrutiny associated with a high-profile by-election. As other candidates were eliminated, Ruddock performed well enough in question time to gather a sufficient number of votes to remain competitive. But the first timer was not very optimistic. Late in the day, six candidates remained and Ruddock was one of them. Despite concerns about the quality of his performance, the final ballot was between Ruddock and Shehadie. The votes were deadlocked 25–25. A further ballot was required. There was a result: Ruddock won 25–24. One vote was informal. The identity of the informal voter was never disclosed.

Why choose the youngest and perhaps least experienced candidate? The first and probably strongest reason was a desire for generational change. There was a growing appetite for renewing the Federal Parliamentary Liberal Party after its many years in power and the 1972 election loss. As the Young Liberal Federal President, Ruddock presented a fresh face to the electorate. A number of his fellow Young Liberals, such as Chris Puplick, and senior Party figures, such as John Dowd, actively promoted Ruddock among the pre-selectors. The second reason was more personal. Several branch members from The Hills conference who were on the pre-selection panel knew and esteemed Max Ruddock. They had met and liked his son and appreciated their shared commitment to the people and the electorate. The third reason was the long memory of Parramatta branch members. They had felt compelled to support Sir Garfield Barwick QC over Max Ruddock in pre-selection for the seat in 1958. Fifteen years later, they resolved to resist pressure from the party hierarchy and to select the candidate they wanted. That Max's son was standing for pre-selection highlighted this important principle. The father had again shaped the son's future.

The result shocked Philip, astounded Max and bewildered Heather. Just as surprised was the party organisation, especially the Federal Party President, Robert (later Sir Robert) Southey, and the Federal Opposition Leader, Bill Snedden. They had been expecting to greet Nick Shehadie as the newly endorsed candidate for Parramatta at a dinner being held that evening in the Sebel Townhouse Hotel at Sydney's Elizabeth Bay. Instead they were greeted by a beaming Max Ruddock still clad in his lawn bowling creams. The Labor Party was pleased with the outcome. The young Ruddock was largely unknown and considered a less competitive candidate than the high-profile Shehadie. As neither of the final two contenders for pre-selection then lived in the electorate (Ruddock had at least grown up in the adjacent area to the north, that was once part of the Parramatta electorate), Labor might try to depict them as self-serving interlopers.

Philip Ruddock prepared for his first big political contest on 22 September 1973. It was an extended campaign prompting the usual exhaustive media coverage that accompanies a critical by-election. The Liberal Party branches were well organised and highly dedicated. Their footprint was large. Party members belonged to every significant community group within the Parramatta electorate. Volunteers drawn from all over Sydney descended on the campaign headquarters located on Bridge Street in Epping. They were all keen to prevent the seat from falling to Labor. The Liberal Party also needed a victory to revive its corporate spirit. Max's state parliamentary colleagues in both the Liberal and National parties provided the 'X' factor. Premier Askin together with his ministers and backbenchers were active throughout the electorate. The campaign's supporters included a young Tim Fischer. Max had befriended the newly returned Vietnam veteran when he arrived at the state parliament in Macquarie Street in 1971 as the Country Party member for Sturt.

For Snedden, success in the Parramatta by-election was crucial to his future as Opposition leader. A good result would demonstrate his appeal to the electorate after narrowly securing the leadership by a single vote over Bowen (who did little to promote his candidacy) on the fifth ballot. Snedden needed the Liberals to retain the seat and preferably with an increased majority, and invested a considerable amount of time on the campaign trail. Opposition frontbenchers, such as Doug Anthony (Leader of the Country Party), Phil Lynch (Deputy Leader of the Liberal Party) and Andrew Peacock (a former Liberal minister), also made appearances. The opinion polls were tight until the Federal Budget was unveiled in early August 1973.

The Liberal campaign received a boost when the Whitlam Government announced its decision to build Sydney's second airport at Galston in the Federal electorate of Berowra. Residents familiar with the Galston area were astonished because the area featured rolling hills and deep valleys. In any event, the flight path of incoming aircraft would track over the elec-torates of Parramatta and Mitchell. Norm Bolitho, who attended Pennant Hills Primary School with Ruddock and was then living in Galston, drove a vehicle rigged with loudspeakers on the roof playing a recording that was intended to replicate jet engine noise on take-off. The locals were given an audible sense of what was looming. Max Ruddock led the protest from The Hills district at a local Galston rally. Speaking subsequently as a guest of the Castle Hill Agricultural Show, Prime Minister Whitlam made it clear that Galston airport would be built whether the residents liked it or not. In snubbing local opinion, the Labor Party appeared to be indifferent to the prospects of its own candidate. Les Johnson, Minister for Housing in the Whitlam Government, later confided that when Cabinet was considering Sydney's second airport, the Prime Minister sought suggestions for the best Liberal electorate in which to build it.

As by-elections usually go against the party in power with the casting of local protest votes against the national government, Labor figures contin-ued to believe their candidate had a chance in Parramatta despite fears of a new airport in Galston. The Labor strategists were badly mistaken. In the first poll to include voters aged between 18 and 21 after the *Commonwealth Electoral Act* was amended, the Liberals won convincingly with a swing of 6.6 per cent. Ruddock polled 33,506 first preference votes which represented 52.6 per cent of the electorate. There was no need for preferences to be distributed. Bowen had only managed 28,463 votes in 1972 despite being a senior government minister and a well-known candidate. In contrast to his predecessor, Ruddock made contact with the growing ethnic communities in the electorate and assured them of the Coalition's support for their busi-nesses and its appreciation of their contributions to national development. Most notable of the statistics was a 7.3 per cent swing against Labor. The outcome signaled dissatisfaction with the Whitlam Government and the depth of anger at the proposed airport. Ruddock had amply repaid the party's investment in his candidature and campaign. Within days of the result being declared, he was in Canberra being sworn-in as the newest federal parlia-mentarian. Harry Edwards, Ruddock's former economics lecturer and the Liberal Member for Berowra, together with Michael MacKellar, the Liberal Member for Warringah, escorted Ruddock into the House of Representatives chamber for the administration of the oath of allegiance.

A faction of one

Ruddock was not part of a new 'class' of parliamentarians with whom he shared a common experience of winning the same election. He was on his own. In 1973 there was no orientation program for new members or their spouses. The Opposition Whip, Max Fox, was not interested in helping his new colleague absorb the procedures of the parliament to which he had just been elected. Ruddock would have to learn by experience and find his own way around the cluttered building. Fox's initial conversation was concerned with finding Ruddock a suitable committee to join and ensuring he had a desk. Ruddock would share a small room in the over-crowded south-east wing of Parliament House with two other Liberal backbenchers, Ian Wilson from South Australia (whose father had held the seat of Sturt before him) and David Hamer from Victoria (a former senior naval officer and brother of that state's premier). In their modest room there was not even space for a single visitor seat and there was no privacy when making or receiving telephone calls. In sitting weeks, the meeting rooms and wide corridors of Parliament House were usually buzzing with conversations and negotiations. The construction of a new building to accommodate the federal parliament was still a decade and a half away from completion.

Ruddock sensibly retained a very experienced electorate secretary in Dorothy Still. She had worked for a succession of Federal parliamentarians since the 1940s, including his immediate predecessor Nigel Bowen. She was the solitary staff member in Ruddock's electorate office but knew the area and the people well. Her local knowledge had been invaluable to Ruddock's predecessors who had never devoted much time to local matters. Garfield Barwick entered parliament and several months later became Attorney-General and a Cabinet minister. He had the External Affairs portfolio added to his duties after 1961. His successor, Nigel Bowen, was appointed Attorney-General in 1966, Minister for Education and Science in November 1969, Attorney General again in 1971, and then Foreign Minister in 1971–72. Still's mantra was simple: as most people contacted a parliamentarian's office only once in their lifetime, they need to have a positive experience.

As maiden speeches are customarily uncontroversial and heard without interruption, Ruddock restricted his remarks to the importance of Parramatta as an historical locality and commercial centre in the nation's continuing evolution.[2] He highlighted the poor environmental condition of the Parramatta River and connected its degradation to the need for a Federal Department of the Environment to preserve Australia's natural heritage. Ruddock also drew attention to Parramatta's historic buildings and the need for careful management. He believed they were also at risk. He called for the creation of a Parramatta River Commission that would include municipal representatives, public servants and scientific experts to give advice to government on remediation and development. The wrong approach, he believed, was for the Commonwealth to impose its wishes on local authorities. The Commonwealth should facilitate good processes but not force practical solutions when it did not have a clear mandate to intervene. The Commonwealth could helpfully fund the development of university courses on environmental law to promote community awareness and improve local decision-making.

The tenor of his remarks resembled the tone of his father's maiden speech a decade earlier: the government needed a comprehensive plan, transparent procedures and targeted funding. The Ruddock approach to public administration – an ordered system that was undergirded by clear rules and informed by the best thinking – was on view. His attention then turned to the Whitlam Government's commitment to relocating federal administration from urban to regional centres as he offered the familiar liberal critique of expansive government.

> Regionalisation appears to be seen by this Government as a means whereby it can achieve its objectives of bringing about an egalitarian society. Unfortunately, these objectives do not bring about equality but rather debase the quality of life and bring down people and their environment to the lowest common denominator.[3]

In reply, the Labor member for Robertson, Barry Cohen, complimented Ruddock on his speech which, he said, was 'delivered with great aplomb and a feeling of confidence'. He also commented on the new member's suggestion that guards ought to patrol the Parramatta River and thought they might be called 'Ruddock's Raiders'. This moment of mirth could not obscure the extent of Ruddock's firm commitment to the environment nor the strength of his convictions about urban development. The notion that the Liberal Party would always side with developers against conservationists overlooked Ruddock's advocacy of natural heritage and the need for responsible building and construction, especially in areas adjacent to waterways. The new member for Parramatta was not a reactionary or a conservative; he was a man of liberal instincts with broad sympathies.

In this and in relation to a host of other issues, Ruddock's colleagues learnt that he was equally interested in local matters as national affairs when they had a bearing on everyday life. Ruddock would never deprecate electorate concerns. They, too, were important and worthy of close attention. Not surprisingly, his first question without notice was directed to Tom Uren, the Minister for Urban and Regional Development, in the Whitlam Government. The question concerned road access to the proposed Galston airport.[4] More than four decades later, the location of Sydney's second airport was finally confirmed at Badgery's Creek, in Sydney's south-west, a considerable distance from The Hills district.

Managing conflict, building trust

Ruddock spent the remainder of 1973 consolidating his support within the electorate and connecting further with local communities. He also needed to fulfil a campaign pledge to reside in the electorate. During the October long weekend, the Ruddocks bought a house at Oatlands overlooking the golf course and started living there early in 1974. The Ruddocks were a united team. Heather represented her husband at school speech days and community events. Campaigning and electorate commitments made it difficult for her to balance family life and academic study. Nonetheless, she graduated with her Law degree in March 1975 but was unable to complete her postgraduate articles. Heather was admitted to the New South Wales Bar in December 1976 as a non-practising barrister.

When Prime Minister Whitlam called a double dissolution election on 11 April 1974, the Ruddock's decision to live at Oatlands and connect with community groups paid dividends. The new Labor candidate was the long-serving Mayor of Parramatta, Barry Wilde. He proved to be a much stronger candidate than Whelan, having been a member of the Parramatta Council since 1959. He joined the Labor Party in 1949 and was well-known among its members. When the result was declared, Ruddock's margin was reduced to 1,829 votes after the distribution of preferences although there was a 3.3 per cent swing in his favour. [Wilde became state Labor member for Parramatta the following year.] The Liberal vote at the North Rocks and

Carlingford booths (both areas overlapping The Hills state electorate still held by his father), ensured Ruddock's survival. The election also promoted a refreshing of the local party organisation. New branches were formed and the local business community was engaged more actively. By 1975, the Parramatta Liberals were greater in numbers and stronger in resolve.

In Canberra, simmering leadership tensions in the Liberal Party had become acute. When he became leader at the end of 1972, Snedden had pledged to lead a more progressive Liberal Party but critics doubted he had the intellectual capacity to match Prime Minister Gough Whitlam or the strength of personality needed to lead a divided Coalition back to government. In November 1974, and with the Coalition still doing poorly in the polls, the young and ambitious member for Wannon in western Victoria, Malcolm Fraser, unsuccessfully challenged Snedden for the leadership.[5] Fraser, a former Cabinet minister and prominent conservative, had played an active part in John Gorton's downfall as prime minister in March 1971. Fraser was first elected to parliament in 1955 and had been Minister for the Army (1960–68), Education and Science (1968–69) and then Defence (1969–71). He contested the ballot for the party leadership after the 1972 election but his transparent ambition and utter ruthlessness unnerved some of his colleagues who opted instead for Snedden. In 1974, Ruddock was too new and too junior to play any role in the resolution of the party's leadership tensions. He managed to convince both Snedden and Fraser he had supported neither of them in the leadership spill. Avowing factional strife within the party did not help Ruddock's political career. He was owed no favours when promotions were being considered but, conversely, he owed no-one else any support. By the time Fraser challenged again in March 1975, Snedden's position was untenable. On this occasion Fraser prevailed. Ruddock supported Fraser because he stood the greatest chance of defeating Whitlam.

Deciding on a much more aggressive stance towards the Whitlam Government in the light of what was known as the 'Loans Affair', the Coalition used its majority in the Senate to block a number of budget bills which provided the necessary funds for many public programs, including the salaries of public employees. Fraser's aim was to force the Labor Government to an early election that he confidently believed the Coalition would win.[6] After a month of political gridlock and the Government's money bills no closer to being passed, the Governor General, Sir John Kerr, dismissed Prime Minister Whitlam and appointed Fraser 'caretaker' Prime Minister on the condition he call an election; in the event, Fraser advised a double dissolution. At the election held on 13 December 1975, Ruddock defeated the Labor candidate (and future Hawke Government minister) John Brown. He was re-elected with 56.7 per cent of first preference votes and 59.2 per cent of the two-party preferred vote. He had won three elections in three years and won them convincingly. The party knew it had an able campaigner with a dedicated support team.

The long anticipated electoral redistribution planned for Sydney's north-western suburbs was announced in 1977. The electorate of Parramatta combined the largely working-class area around the business district which voted Labor and a larger amount of adjacent territory that traditionally returned a non-Labor vote. The only time Labor had held the seat was 1929–1931, a short period that coincided with the worst years of the Great Depression when the Scullin Labor Government held office. Albert Rowe, a board member of the Printing Industry Union, was unexpectedly elected after the 10,000-vote majority enjoyed by the Nationalist member Eric Bowden was turned into a 4,511-vote majority for Labor. The 1977 redistribution split the electorate almost in half. Much of the wealthier eastern half was absorbed into what would become the comfortably safe Liberal seat of Dundas. Most of the western half, including the Parramatta local government area that remained pro-Labor, formed a notionally marginal Labor seat that retained the name 'Parramatta'. The reconfigured electorate of Parramatta was anchored, however, in traditionally pro-Labor territory in western Sydney.

Ruddock won the Liberal Party nomination and successfully contested the new seat of Dundas at the 1977 election. He secured 53.8 per cent of first preference votes and 60.1 per cent of the two-party preferred vote (gaining a slight swing of 0.01 per cent). John Brown, who stood as Labor's candidate in Parramatta in 1975 became the new member and would hold the seat of Parramatta for the next 13 years. Ruddock would be the only member for Dundas. The electorate was abolished as a separate division in another redistribution that was completed in 1993.

Acquiring confidence and discerning conviction

Ruddock had met the Liberal Party's expectations. He was popular in the electorate and diligent in parliament. There was, however, a large Coalition backbench (one that would become even larger after the 1977 election which handed Malcolm Fraser the largest parliamentary majority in Australian history) and Ruddock was not among those considered for a ministerial post in the new Fraser Government. He was still one of the Coalition's youngest parliamentarians at 32 years of age. There was worthwhile work to done from the backbench and he was genuinely driven by a spirit of public service. The party wanted him to gain more experience and parliamentary committees were the best available vehicles. Max Fox had earlier arranged for Ruddock to replace Robert 'Duke' Bonnett, the retiring Liberal member for Herbert, on the House of Representatives Standing Committee on Aboriginal Affairs. Ruddock remained a member of the Committee until February 1983, including serving as its chair from April 1976 to February 1983. His mentors were Bill Wentworth, the Liberal member for Mackellar who voted against his own party more times than any other Federal parliamentarian in history, Gordon Bryant, the Labor member for Wills, and Les Johnson, the Labor member for Hughes. Each had served as Minister for Aboriginal Affairs in different governments, they were all deeply committed to Indigenous issues and promoted a spirit of bipartisanship in their work. The Committee dealt with a series of important land title claims during this period and encouraged a greater sense of partnership between the parliament and Indigenous people in pursuit of better policy outcomes.

Ruddock had not revealed any particular ambitions when he entered parliament in 1973. There were no specific causes to which he was personally wedded and no grand plans that he was striving to fulfil. Like most new parliamentarians he wanted to serve the people of his electorate and was hopeful of securing a ministerial post in due course. Improving conditions for Indigenous people, promoting respect for human rights and ending discrimination against refugees and migrants were campaigns he embraced at the invitation of parliamentary colleagues on both sides of the political divide. In each instance he was moved by concern, if not compassion, for people whose welfare was imperiled and whose interests needed advancing. He gained a reputation for caring about marginalised and disadvantaged people, especially when they were not well served by institutions or policies. He recognised the potential of legal remedies but favoured approaches that provided services and afforded protections that did not require individual advocacy.

While his more ambitious colleagues were seeking roles on the prominent Public Accounts, and Foreign Affairs and Defence committees, Ruddock was content with his work in Aboriginal Affairs. He was personally energised by the committee's deliberations. He oversaw the publication of many key reports including those examining alcohol problems in the Northern Territory and, more generally, Aboriginal health, education and the 'outstation' movement that involved relocating Aboriginal people from towns to remote outposts on traditional tribal lands. Professors Bill Stanner and Janice Reid, both anthropologists, and Professor Max Kamien, who specialised in remote primary care, were the committee's influential expert advisers. Professor Fred Hollows, an ophthalmologist concerned with eye disorders in Aboriginal communities, advocated broadening the committee's remit beyond alcohol abuse to general health issues. During 1976–77, Ruddock was concurrently a member of the Joint Select Committee on Aboriginal Land Rights in Northern Territory and later served as the parliamentary representative on the Council of the Australian Institute of Aboriginal Studies between February 1978 and April 1983.

After Dundas was confirmed as a safe Liberal seat and finding the demands of his electorate were not overwhelming, Ruddock accepted an invitation from the Attorney General, Senator Peter Durack, to chair the Joint Select Committee on Family Law in October 1978. The committee's main task was reviewing the recently enacted *Family Law Act* which had replaced the *Matrimonial Causes Act*. The Act was devised by Labor's controversial Attorney General, Senator Lionel Murphy, and was considered highly progressive and possibly even 'ahead of its time'. Despite pressure to restore a fault-based divorce system, Ruddock was determined to have the committee focus on custody and maintenance arrangements for children (now known as 'contact' and 'support') and to ensuring the Family Court's jurisdiction was clear. The review noted that Family Court orders did not necessarily include financial support for families with the burden of such support passing to the welfare system and, ultimately, being borne by the taxpayer. In 1980, the committee recommended the establishment of a national maintenance enforcement agency. After the Hawke Labor Government came to office and another review was completed, the Child Support System was eventually established on 1 June 1988.

The man who speaks for minorities

Ruddock was also gaining a profile in the promotion of multicultural affairs. He had been active in this kind of work since his teenage years. The Parramatta electorate remained ethnically diverse and a good place to enlarge an understanding of migrant concerns that had been growing since the 1950s. Attracting the Lebanese vote was considered important in the 1973 Parramatta by-election. Early in his campaign, Ruddock met the Lebanese community (mostly Christian Maronites) at the home of John and Therese Isaac in The Park, a prominent street overlooking Parramatta Park and the city centre. If the community were disappointed that Nick Shehadie was not the Liberal candidate, it was not evident from the warm reception they extended to Ruddock. Community leaders, such as Karim Kisrwani and Joseph Baraket, campaigned for the young Liberal candidate and became enduring political supporters and lifelong personal friends. [Ruddock's friendship with Kirsrwani would be the focus of a Senate inquiry in 2003–04, a matter dealt with in chapter 8.] Other community groups gathered around places of religious worship. The Greek community was concentrated on the Greek Orthodox Church; the Jewish community were drawn to the Parramatta Prayer Hall; the Chaldean Assyrians focused on their church in Ermington; the Italians, many of whom were originally market gardeners, were plentiful in Marsfield alongside an emerging Chinese community.

His interest in the administration of multicultural affairs and his experience with constituents led him inevitably into immigration policy and the plight of refugees. The Lebanese civil war, which began in April 1975 and brought widespread death and destruction, had generated a number of serious immigration issues that affected the entire Parramatta community. Ruddock became familiar with the plight of Vietnamese refugees after Ian McPhee, the Immigration Minister in the Fraser Government between 1979–82, asked Ruddock and the Labor member for Prospect, Dr Dick Klugman, to assist with the Vietnamese refugee resettlement program in Cabramatta. In 1981, Ruddock led a Parliamentary Delegation to India and Pakistan where he visited a large Afghan refugee camp outside Peshawar in the North West Frontier province. He addressed a tent gathering attended only by men who seemed more interested in receiving weapons to fight the occupying Soviet forces than in their prospects for refugee resettlement. As the delegation's leader, Ruddock needed to explain that Australia was not a great military power and that aiding and abetting anti-Soviet forces was not the purpose of his visit.

The following year Ruddock and his wife visited the Traiskirchen Refugee Centre near Vienna in Austria at the request of the incoming Immigration Minister, John Hodges, who was appointed to the portfolio in May 1982. The centre accommodated Eastern European refugees fleeing communist countries like Romania through Hungary. When they visited the camp kitchen the Ruddocks discovered that some of the produce, such as vegetables, had also come from Romania. The main revelation at Traiskirchen was that many Romanian residents were escapees from gaols and mental institutions. The Romanian dictator, Nicolae Ceausescu, frequently 'cleaned out' these institutions by allowing the inmates to escape. This practice was inspired by Fidel Castro's policy in Cuba with many 'unwanteds' making their way to the United States.

Complementing his commitment to Indigenous people, migrants and refugees, Ruddock promoted greater protection for human rights. He had founded the bipartisan Parliamentary Amnesty Group with Labor parliamentarian Tony Lamb in 1974. Liberal Senator David Hamer from Victoria was elected the inaugural Chair and Ruddock was the group's first secretary. Bill Wentworth, his Indigenous affairs mentor and the most prominent anti-communist in Federal parliament, was insistent that Liberal members should support the organisation because, in his words, Amnesty International 'hated the [communists] as much as they hated right wing dictatorships'. The group's first campaign gathered momentum in January 1975 after Dr Dick Klugman and Ruddock visited Jakarta and made enquiries about political leaders who had protested against Japanese investment in Indonesia the previous year and were being tried for promoting political instability. During the latter 1970s the group took up the cause of many prisoners of conscience including those in the Soviet Union where the treatment of Jews was a particular source of concern, in South Africa where the minority apartheid regime continued its dominance, and in Central and South America where military juntas and

Marxist dictatorships were oppressing opposition groups. Ruddock became the group's chair in 1986 after the death of Liberal Senator Allan Missen.

By 1983, there were few parliamentarians as familiar or as committed to social issues than Philip Ruddock. Over the previous decade he had taken the time and the effort to understand systemic problems and to have a sense of where and when government could make a positive and lasting contribution. It was not work for which he received public appreciation or political recognition. These fields of government activity had not yet attracted the concern of those now referred to as 'progressives'. But those who interacted with him realised he found satisfaction in raising the standing of distressed and disadvantaged people rather than furthering his parliamentary career and ministerial prospects. The reward was in the 'doing' rather than the 'being' and a spirit of compassion propelled his efforts to pursue change.

Well-regarded by colleagues, Ruddock had not even risen to the rank of parliamentary secretary when, John Howard, elected to parliament nine months after him, was appointed to the Fraser ministry late in 1975 as Minister for Business and Consumer Affairs. Howard became a senior minister in 1977 when he was appointed Treasurer (the youngest since 1904) and then deputy party leader in 1982 (succeeding Phillip Lynch). Nearly five years younger than Howard, Ruddock was still on the backbench and seemed destined to stay there. The times did not suit him whereas they plainly suited Howard. Ruddock's interests were not those of the dominant faction within the Liberal Party; his temperament had not marked him out as a parliamentary warrior; and, his political philosophy had not endeared him to factional heavyweights. Ruddock was quiet and serious. He did not draw attention to himself and did little to enhance his profile. After a decade in parliament, it was conceivable that Ruddock would only be remembered as a conscientious backbencher and diligent committee member who cultivated a strong local following and maintained a healthy electoral margin. The years to come would be even more difficult, in terms of advancement, for a man of his mood and mindset.

Travail of the moderates

By the early 1980s, the Liberal Party comprised a number of incipient factions. There was nothing new in the existence of sub-groups within a party that was wary of being ideologically doctrinaire. The factions were referred to broadly as the 'wets' and the 'dries'. The party's founder, Sir Robert Menzies, intentionally chose the name 'Liberal' rather than the alternatives. He wanted to avoid any suggestion that the new party resembled the conservative and anti-Labor United Australia Party (UAP) that was dissolved in 1944. The Liberal Party would be neither conservative nor radical. It was liberal in its instincts and imperatives, eschewing ideological rigidity in favour of shared values that allowed party policy to reflect changing practical realities. There were, however, members thought to be 'on the Left' of the party and there were those 'on the Right' who were divided over domestic and international issues. On the domestic front, those on the Left were more committed to liberalising laws relating to censorship, Sunday trading, marriage and the selection of migrants who were still drawn mainly from English-speaking European nations. On the international front, when the white minority regime in Rhodesia led by Ian Smith issued a universal declaration of independence from the British Government in 1966, those on the Right of the Liberal Party formed an unofficial 'Rhodesia lobby' in support of white rule. The Right were also more committed to the continuing conflict in South Vietnam which was soon to become the most divisive conflict in the nation's history.

With time, the titles evolved with those on the Left known as the 'moderates' while those on the Right were labeled 'conservatives'. In relation to economic policy, they were also known as the 'wets' and the 'dries' despite the titles being poorly defined and practically imprecise. There was, however, no single issue that defined their affiliation because Liberal parliamentarians had differing attitudes and widely diverging views on the role of government in the conduct of business, the regulation of industry and the provision of welfare. The Coalition was unlike the Labor Party which had institutionalised its internal divisions with formally appointed factional leaders. The animosity that existed between the members required careful negotiation whenever a joint statement was required.

While every party has its ideologues and some will always be more ardent in expressing their convictions than others, it was difficult segregating most Liberal parliamentarians into the 'wet' and 'dry' camps or, even less accurately, sorting them into representatives of the 'Left' and the 'Right' of a party that referred to itself as a Centre-Right party seeking to balance the Centre-Left Labor Party. Some parliamentarians were liberal on economic policy but conservative on social issues. Many preferred to be known simply as Liberals because the differences between the 'wets' and the 'dries' were not as firm nor were the policy distinctions as forceful as those professed by the Left and Right factions of the Labor Party. During the early to mid-1970s, however, the perceived dominance of conservatives led those sometimes referred to as 'small-l liberals' to abandon the party. In South Australia they formed the Liberal Movement led by Steele Hall and, federally, a small number followed Don Chipp into his newly formed Australian Democrats.

The New South Wales division of the Liberal Party was reasonably united until the 1970s. There was internal tension when an Eastern European 'captive nations' faction led by refugees from countries dominated by the Soviet Union tried to extend their influence within the party organisation. This faction, organised by Lyenko Urbanchich, were known as 'the Uglies'. Their ambitions were resisted by traditional party operatives led by John (later Sir John) Carrick, Sir Robert Cotton, Sir John Atwill and John Howard. The 'moderate' group consisting of Michael MacKellar, John Dowd, Don Dobie and Peter Baume also opposed them. Ruddock was associated with the moderates who were more of a fellowship than a faction.

By the 1980s, Malcolm Fraser was said to be one of the last liberals of the Menzies tradition still active in the Liberal Party. On a range of issues, such as multiculturalism, Fraser openly sympathised with the 'wets'. He remarked in a 1980 statement:

> The key elements of multiculturalism can be simply stated. They are based on both realism and idealism. The starting point is the recognition and appreciation of the fact that the Australian population is derived from a wide variety of ethnic and cultural backgrounds, and that these backgrounds are important to the way Australians see themselves … multiculturalism is concerned with far more than the passive toleration of diversity. It sees diversity as a quality to be actively embraced, a source of social wealth and dynamism.[7]

Fraser's critics were willing to accept his liberal views on social questions, they were less sanguine when it came to his dithering when dealing with the ailing Australian economy and the conduct of international diplomacy. In April 1981, the Minister for Industrial Relations, Andrew Peacock, resigned suddenly from Cabinet over Fraser's alleged intrusions into the work of his department.[8] The two men had clashed over a range of matters including Australia's continuing recognition of the ousted Kampuchean government led by Pol Pot. While Minister for Foreign Affairs, Peacock, his department and most Liberals had urged Fraser to 'de-recognise' the regime which had been overthrown during an invasion from neighbouring Vietnam after appalling human rights abuses. Fraser refused. Knowing he had the support of the majority of his parliamentary colleagues, Fraser called a leadership ballot and won decisively: 54 to 27. With the Coalition's election loss in March 1983 and its replacement by a Labor government that appeared to be much more comfortable with economic reform closely attentive to market forces, a more descriptive form of liberalism began to emerge.

After Fraser's departure, the 'wets' concentrated on preserving individual freedoms and liberties, protecting the vulnerable from exploitation, advancing the cause of social justice and promoting environmental responsibility. They claimed a lineage from the nation's second prime minister and classical liberal, Alfred Deakin, but shunned a formal organisation to promote their views. An inventory of the notable 'wets' included Peter Baume, Max Burr, Fred Chaney, Harry Edwards, David Hamer, Robert Hill, Ian Macphee, Alan Missen, Chris Puplick, Peter Rae, Baden Teague, Ian Wilson and Philip Ruddock. Occasionally they would be joined by Bob Ellicott, the Minister for Home Affairs, who was concerned about the Government's human rights law reform agenda and who urged Fraser to support the legislation required to establish the Australian Human Rights Commission.[9] Ruddock had affirmed his place among the 'wets' shortly after entering parliament when he voted in favour of former prime minister John Gorton's motion calling for the decriminalisation of 'homosexual acts between consenting adults in private'. Andrew Peacock had supported it; Paul Keating had voted against it.

The leader of the 'wets' in the late 1970s was Peter Baume from New South Wales;[10] in the 1980s it was Ian Macphee from Victoria. Baume has been described as 'a small l Liberal in the Deakinite tradition, representing the ameliorative and interventionist strand of the Liberal Party'.[11] He facilitated an informal group known as the Liberal Forum which held open meetings and published discussion papers which Baume edited. He was personally troubled by the prominence of privatisation and deregulation in the party's policy agenda. Baume fought against any hint of racial preference in the management of immigration and opposed his own party over the sponsorship of sport and cultural events by tobacco companies.[12] The other leading 'wet', Ian Macphee, was instrumental in promoting multiculturalism while serving as Immigration Minister in the Fraser Government. He oversaw the migration of large numbers of Indochinese refugees to Australia, backed a family reunion scheme and was involved in establishing the Special Broadcasting Service (the SBS).

Senator Graham Richardson, one of Labor's foremost factional warriors, thought the 'wets' were mixed parliamentary performers. Baume, he said, was a 'man of honour [and] very, very capable' but was left to languish on the backbench by a party that never appreciated his abilities. He considered Fred Chaney's performance as Opposition Leader in the Senate to be 'reasonable but unspectacular'. While he had little personal acquaintance with Ruddock, Richardson thought the member for Dundas 'never could cut the mustard' because he was from Sydney's North Shore and was too accustomed to mixing with privileged people.[13] Ruddock did not care what others thought. He maintained productive relationships with colleagues but was always a faction of one. If he were advanced, it would be on the basis of ability rather than networking.

A ministerial appointment – just

A ministerial reshuffle in May 1982 following the leadership spill that saw Fraser defeat Peacock prompted media speculation that Ruddock might be appointed Minister for Aboriginal Affairs given his extensive experience and emerging expertise in the portfolio. It remained speculation as the post went instead to Ian Wilson, the member for Sturt in South Australia. Ruddock was entitled to be disappointed as Wilson had not shown consistent interest in Indigenous affairs. After the Fraser Government was defeated at the March 1983 election, Ruddock was in line for the shadow ministry. The new Opposition Leader, Andrew Peacock, was a regular visitor to the electorates of Parramatta and then Dundas. He knew Ruddock and liked him. When Peacock moved to the Industrial Relations portfolio early in 1981, he arranged for Ruddock to be appointed Parliamentary Representative on the Australian Council of Trade Union Training. His prospects for promotion seemed good.

Peacock selected a large Opposition front bench of 30 shadow ministers. Ruddock was the last selected and the most junior. He had been a member of parliament for ten years; the average length of service before ministerial service in the 1970s was 12 years. He became Shadow Minister for the Australian Capital Territory (ACT) and Shadow Minister Assisting the Opposition Leader on Public Service Matters. These appointments drew on his committee work and his experience as parliamentary representative on the Australian National University Council from 1976. For the first time in his political life, Ruddock could make the most of his standing as the only Federal parliamentarian who had been born in Canberra. Ruddock quickly became well known for providing the local ABC news bureau with stories suitable for the separate Canberra news bulletin which would be broadcast at 7.55am, just before the national current affairs program – *AM*. As his parliamentary colleagues also listened to *AM* after the 7.45am radio news, Ruddock influenced a captive audience and gained a public profile through his active media presence as the shadow minister prior to introduction of self-government for the Australian Capital Territory in 1988.

The Shadow Immigration portfolio had been given to the outspoken Tasmanian Liberal, Michael Hodgman. Known among friends and foes as the 'mouth from the south', Hodgman was ill-suited to the portfolio and proved a poor choice. After Professor Geoffrey Blainey delivered a controversial speech in Warrnambool calling for Asian immigration to be slowed,[14] Hodgman accused the Hawke Government, during a parliamentary debate in May 1984, of making 'a substantial reduction in British and European migration ... and altering dramatically the traditional proportions of Australia's successful immigration policies'. After claiming the end to bipartisan support for immigration, Hodgman pledged a Coalition government would restore 'balance' to the program.[15] Hodgman contended that anger with the Hawke Government's immigration policies amounted to five per cent of the primary vote in certain parts of the country and could be translated into the Coalition gaining 12 marginal seats at the next election. Macphee questioned his own colleague's interpretation of the data on incoming migrants before lamenting that 'this debate has fueled some anti-Asian sentiment and that is tragic for this country'. Ruddock tried to counter the alarm and to dissipate the anger directed at the Coalition by Hodgman's statements. The most effective speech during the debate was delivered by John Howard on 23 August 1984.[16] Still, the Coalition had inflicted damage on itself and observers wondered how long Hodgman would remain in the role.

When the Shadow Cabinet finally settled the details of the Opposition's Immigration policy, Ruddock asked Hodgman about the progress he had made on the party's ethnic affairs policy. Ruddock thought that one policy could not exist without the other. If Australia was accepting migrants into the community it also needed a policy that promoted the interaction of their cultures when they became citizens. A ruffled Hodgman was both incredulous and unimpressed. He had expended all the goodwill he could muster securing his colleagues' agreement on the party's immigration policy. Peacock quietly asked Ruddock to prepare a paper for consideration the next shadow cabinet meeting. Most of the work had been done. While performing his shadow ministerial duties earlier in the year, Ruddock had a chance meeting with a local Liberal Party branch member in Canberra, Nea Stathopoulos, who suggested the Territory needed an ethnic affairs policy given the large number of migrants who were residents and the substantial community of overseas students that Canberra hosted. When Ruddock agreed, she handed him a completed document that reflected months of work on her part. After the episode with Hodgman, Ruddock returned to his office, located an amended draft of the document prepared by Nea Stathopoulos and replaced every reference to the 'ACT' with 'Australia'. The Coalition now had an ethnic affairs policy and Ruddock was its champion.

Prime Minister Bob Hawke then called a surprise election in December 1984.[17] Most voters could not see why they needed to go to the polls early. It looked like pure political opportunism on Hawke's part although the actual purpose was to bring elections for the House of Representatives and the Senate into alignment. Despite the Prime Minister's personal popularity, there was a 2 per cent swing against Labor whose parliamentary majority was reduced from 25 to 16 seats. Peacock had again performed well in Dundas. There was now a strong chance that the Coalition might be returned to government at the next election. Having consolidated his position as Liberal leader, Peacock decided to refresh his shadow cabinet with several promotions and some new faces. Ruddock was appointed Shadow Minister for Immigration and Ethnic Affairs. After more than 11 years in parliament, he had responsibility for influencing an area of government policy on matters that meant much to him personally and professionally.

Endnotes

1   Ruddock later served on the State and Federal Executives between 1982–1985 and the State Executive 1994–1995 as the Leader's representative when Shadow Cabinet Secretary.

2   Philip Ruddock, maiden speech, 20 November 1973.

3   https://parlinfo.aph.gov.au/parlInfo/search/display/ display.w3p;db=HANSARD80;id=hansard80/ hansardr80/1973–11-20/0086;query=Id:%22hansard80/ hansardr80/1973–11-20/0114%22

4   https://parlinfo.aph.gov.au/parlInfo/search/display/display. w3p;query=Id:%22hansard80/hansardr80/1973–11-20/0087%22

5   https://trove.nla.gov.au/newspaper/article/110789997

6   See http://guides.naa.gov.au/malcolm-fraser/chapter3/3.4.aspx

7   https://archives.unimelb.edu.au/explore/collections/ malcolmfraser/resources/postparliamentspeeches/ inaugural-address-on-multiculturalism-to-the-institute-of-multicultural-affairs

8   https://australianpolitics.com/1981/04/28/peacock-resigns-from-fraser-government.html

9   Malcolm Fraser with Margaret Simons, *Malcolm Fraser: the Political Memoirs*, Miegunyah Press, Melbourne, 2010, p. 404.

10   https://press.anu.edu.au/publications/series/anzsog/dissident-liberal

11   https://biography.senate.gov.au/baume-peter-erne/

12   Dissatisfied with the direction in which the Liberal Party was headed, Baume resigned his Senate seat in 1991 to become the Professor of Community Medicine at the University of New South Wales.

13   Graham Richardson, *Whatever it Takes*, Bantam, Sydney, 1994, p. 188.

14   http://www.multiculturalaustralia.edu.au/library/media/Timeline-Commentary/ id/115.The-Blainey-debate-on-immigration-

15   This debate is covered in Anthony Moran, *The Public Life of Australian Multiculturalism: Building a Diverse Nation*, Palgrave, Cham, 2017, p. 68

16   CDP (Reps), 23 August 1984, p. 276.

17   https://electionspeeches.moadoph.gov.au/speeches/1984-bob-hawke

CHAPTER 3

The making of an advocate   1984–1995

When Philip Ruddock became the Opposition spokesman on Immigration in December 1984, he was well acquainted with the portfolio's main challenges and well versed in the positions that distinguished Liberal policy from that of the Labor Government. Unlike many ministers and shadow ministers who were without previous experience of the complexities and controversies associated with their portfolios, Ruddock had been part of discussions and had contributed to debates about immigration throughout the previous decade. He was not only committed to developing creative policy and compassionate procedures, he found working with migrants and their community associations particularly fulfilling.

Establishing a tradition

Despite the importance of large-scale migration to Australia's national development, few Immigration ministers have ever been in the post long enough to have an influence on either the department or the policies it implemented. The first minister, Labor's Arthur Calwell, served from July 1945 to December 1949 – four and a half years. In terms of political temperament, Ruddock had most in common with the nation's second minister, Harold Holt, who served in the Immigration portfolio from December 1949 until October 1956. Holt was the first Liberal to hold the post and the longest serving Immigration minister for the first 40 years the office existed.[1] Other than 'Alick' (later Sir Alexander) Downer who held the portfolio for over five years (1958–63) in the Menzies Government and Michael McKellar for nearly four years (1975–79) in the Fraser Government, none of the other Immigration ministers has served for more than three years. There was also considerable turnover in departmental heads with only Sir Tasman Heyes (1946–61) and Sir Peter Heydon (1961–71) serving for extended periods.

Prior to the creation of a separate department in 1945, managing immigration was one of many responsibilities handled by the Minister for Home Affairs (1901–32) and later the Minister for the Interior (1932–47). It had proven to be a demanding task politically as it involved balancing manpower needs with economic expansion and contraction. From Federation in 1901 to the outbreak of war in 1939, Australia's net gain from immigration was just under 60,000 people with an annual average increase of 15,000. Most immigrants arrived in the three years before the Great War of 1914–18 and during the 1920s. During two periods – 1901–05 and 1931–35 – the Australian population actually decreased.

With the end of the Second World War in 1945, Australia needed to expand its economic base to fund major new infrastructure projects, further its industrialisation and provide for national defence. One answer was to increase population through a large-scale immigration program. The first minister, Labor's Arthur Calwell, coined the slogan, 'Populate or Perish'. The initial immigrant arrival rate was slow owing to a shortage of ships when the war ended. But by 1947 the number of new arrivals exceeded departures by 12,000. In 1948 the figure was 48,000. By 1949 it was 149,000. In the five years between 1945 and 1950, the number of new arrivals exceeded the entire population of Tasmania at that time. Although there was initially bipartisan support for the conduct of the Immigration program, it is mistaken to think the Labor Party supported a large annual intake of immigrants and promoted a progressive multicultural policy and to believe that the Coalition opposed both. For decades, the reverse was actually true.

Labor Party policy acknowledged the importance of immigration to Australia's economic development but was concerned that immigrants might take the jobs of locally-born workers or be willing to accept lower wages; argued that the cultural homogeneity of the nation needed to be preserved by giving priority to British migrants; and contended that assimilation and absorption of new arrivals was preferable to a multi-racial society which would inevitably lead to internal tension and civil strife. Similarly, a 1946 policy platform committed the Liberal Party to preserving the 'ideals of the White Australia Policy' with the Victorian State Council claiming two years later that its maintenance was 'vital to the existence of a free Australia'.[2] The policy also called for 'fostering a spirit of neighbourliness and friendship with Australian immigrants, thereby countering any tendency to congregate in small communities of their former nationality'.

When he became the Immigration minister in the newly-elected Menzies Government in 1949, Holt prohibited use of the term 'White Australia policy' because it was offensive to Australia's neighbours. It was replaced with the term that Holt's predecessor, Arthur Calwell, had begun to use – 'the restricted immigration policy'. Holt explained that Australia's Asian migration policy 'rested on a frank recognition that important differences of race, culture and economic standards would make successful assimilation of Asians unlikely. There was no racial superiority in this approach'.[3] When asked by a reporter from the Singapore *Straits Times* about the 'White Australia Policy', Holt replied: 'We don't call it that. I have tried to administer Australia's immigration policy with commonsense and humanity during my term of office'.[4] The policy was not, he stressed, either a colour or an economic bar.

Holt was widely criticised for his decision in 1952 to accept German immigrants although he had earlier stated publicly that he was willing to consider their applications to settle in Australia. Holt responded to his critics: 'By accepting as migrants to Australia some of the selected Germans of Western Europe, Australia would be helping ease the strains on the seething occupied zones of Europe. It would be making a humanitarian gesture and a real contribution to the spread of justice and goodwill in the world'.[5] Holt also provided assurances over the following three months that no former Nazi party officials or soldiers would be permitted to enter Australia and that accusations of previous Nazi affiliation would be thoroughly investigated. He also made it clear that he would not make exceptions in dealing with 'prohibited migrants' such as those who were 'stowaways' or came to Australia illegally. Holt considered wartime refugees who wanted to remain in Australia 'a special case' and worthy of separate consideration. Australia had accepted more than 7000 refugees from Nazi Germany in the 1930s and took nearly 200,000 European refugees after the Second World War. The Chifley Labor Government had been reluctant to recognise a 'general right of asylum' when the United Nations (UN) Universal Declaration of Human Rights was being drafted in 1947–48 but the Menzies Coalition Government signed the 1951 UN Convention Relating to the Status of Refugees on 22 January 1954.

Within two years of Holt's appointment to the Immigration portfolio, the press detected a clear distinction in the management of immigration under the Coalition.

> The difference now is that instead of the merciless rigidity with which Mr Calwell administered the immigration laws there will be under Mr Holt a prudent exercise of a ministerial discretion that was always permissible ... The deportation campaign pursued against a handful of wartime refugees and others was rapidly convincing [the new Asian nations] that the White Australia Policy was not a justifiable national measure of self-protection but an expression of racial superiority. The new minister's humane and balanced approach ... should repair much of the harm done.

While Immigration was now increasing at a sustainable rate, the Labor Opposition attacked Holt for by-passing the 'White Australia Policy' by allowing too many 'Chinese and other Asiatics' into the country. The secretary of the New South Wales Branch of the Labor Party claimed that Chinese were 'breaking down labour standards'.[6] Notably, there was no specific quota for refugees in the Immigration program and no specific arrangements for dealing with people who claimed to be refugees. As Australia was usually willing to take as many people as it could to further economic growth, the only objection to refugees was their race or ethnicity.

In his nearly seven years as minister and helped by the highly successful Colombo Plan which focused on enhancing economic and social growth in the Asia-Pacific region, Holt maintained Calwell's better initiatives with more tact and diplomacy than his predecessor could usually muster.[7] There were few disagreements with the Opposition and bipartisanship was the norm. The main difference was that while Holt said publicly he upheld the White Australia Policy, he had privately begun to dilute and erode it by generous application of ministerial discretion. Holt relaxed the policy through changes to the eligibility requirements for citizenship: extending eligibility for citizenship to non-European spouses of European immigrants; allowing the non-European wives of Australian servicemen to become Australian citizens; admission of immediate relatives as Australian citizens and the grant of indefinite work permits to allow qualified people to remain in the country and to allow non-European immigrants resident in Australia for 15 or more years to become citizens.[8] After Holt took office, 'with the exception of a few minor cases, the 1950s were almost entirely free of incidents related to the White Australia Policy. Most Australians, due very largely to Holt's more flexible attitude to the subject and new immigration legislation enacted in 1956 and 1957, believed that the general tenor of the policy was changing.'[9] Holt presented a caring and compassionate public face, and won for himself and the Liberal Party personal and electoral popularity with non-British migrants. The mood he created persisted well beyond his departure from the portfolio in 1956.

Immigration in the Fraser years

Two decades later, the Fraser Government's handling of immigration was consistent with the performance of previous Coalition governments. By this time the Liberal Party's policy platform emphasised the importance of immigration 'to the continuing economic expansion of the country', the need to match annual intakes to the 'absorptive capacity' of the nation, the value of encouraging 'persons of British stock' to settle in Australia and the entitlement of every nation 'to decide its own immigration policy according to its own circumstances.'[10] There was also recognition that it was wrong to treat migrants as an industrial workforce without attending to their entitlements as citizens and their specific needs as ethnic groups. The Liberals' policy was to be guided by the principles of 'humanity, equity and compassion'. While immigration was a means to an end – national development and population growth – the 'humanitarian and compassionate aspects' would not be subordinated to short-term fluctuations in the economy. The New South Wales and Victorian branches of the Liberal Party had their own ethnic councils and advisers and the Lewis Coalition Government in New South Wales was the first to establish a Ministry for Ethnic Affairs in 1975. In the same year, Misha Lajovic, a Slovenian migrant, was pre-selected as a senate candidate for the Liberal Party and was subsequently elected. In response to Labor claims his pre-selection was tokenistic, he argued that 'the Liberal Party is interested in migrants not only as voters, but as active participants in forming their policies – not only on immigration, but on all the issues which concern today's society'.[11] He did note, however, the failure of the Liberal Party to create stable migrant branches, noting that many migrants did not want to participate as migrants but as members of the general community.

To ensure there was a real 'contest of ideas', in 1975 the Coalition re-established a separate Department of Immigration and Ethnic Affairs after the Whitlam Government merged Immigration with Labour (which had lost National Service in December 1972). Fraser was personally committed to multiculturalism and was heavily influenced by his trusted adviser, Petro Georgiou (later appointed inaugural director of the Australian Institute of Multicultural Affairs and Federal member for Kooyong) who worked closely with a unit established in the Department of the Prime Minister and Cabinet to develop policy initiatives. The responsible ministers, Michael MacKellar (1975–79) and Ian McPhee (1979–82), were considered fair-minded and effective administrators. MacKellar made a point of being available to the leaders of ethnic communities and was proactive in the use of ministerial discretion. His aim, according to James Jupp, was

> less an attempt to bypass the Anglo-Celtic bureaucracy than a means of developing a politico-cultural form which would maintain the patron-client role between the Minister and the 'leaders' and maintain the power and influence of the latter group in their own communities.[12]

After the number of migrants admitted to Australia had fallen from 185,000 under the Coalition Government led by Prime Minister John Gorton (1968–71) to 50,000 under the Whitlam Labor Government (the lowest number since the Second World War), the Fraser Government restored the program to its former level with numbers rising to 120,000 in 1982. The Whitlam Government adopted a non-discriminatory policy and claimed to have 'buried' the White Australia Policy but immigration became more multi-racial under the Fraser Government which also established the Special Broadcasting Service (SBS) in 1978 and the Australian Institute for Multicultural Affairs in 1979. In April 1982 and just before McPhee relinquished the portfolio, the Coalition introduced a new migrant selection system making more generous provision for family migration with sponsors being required to guarantee accommodation and employment for their relatives. Cabinet endorsed an annual intake of 115,000 to 135,000 migrants for the ensuing three years (1982–85) and a refugee and special humanitarian intake of 24,000 for 1982–83.

By January 1983, however, economic recession and growing unemployment had cut the estimated intake for that financial year to 90,000. Fearing that migrants were taking jobs away from local born workers, there was increasing community concern about the number of newly arrived skilled tradesmen and the longer-term consequences of unrestricted migration from New Zealand which then accounted for around 20,000 arrivals each year.

The Fraser Government was also confronted with the management of refugees. After taking a very large number of displaced people between 1945 and 1950, the annual intake of refugees had not been sufficiently large to prompt a wholesale review of policy or practice in the 1950s. In 1963, shortly after the Dutch relinquished its colony of West Papua, thousands of people fled to Papua New Guinea (PNG), an Australian trust territory, when Indonesian military forces occupied the territory and prevented the assertion of West Papuan independence. Australia built a camp on Manus Island to accommodate those who could not return home but the West Papuans were not granted refugee status or permitted to enter the Australian mainland because entry to the Territory of Papua New Guinea did not bring an entitlement to enter Australia. [They remained stateless until finally granted PNG citizenship in 2017.] By the 1970s, the end of colonialism, the proliferation of civil war and the rise of oppressive dictatorship in various parts of the world had displaced many people and created a new refugee problem to which the Fraser Government needed to respond. Its response was uneven.

When the long-running Vietnamese civil war ended in April 1975, those who supported the defeated Saigon regime fled Communist reprisal and repression when the country was reunited. After more than 180,000 people left Vietnam, an orderly international refugee resettlement program was devised with a number of South-east Asian nations processing applicants in refugee camps in Hong Kong, Malaysia, Thailand, Philippines and Indonesia for resettlement in the United States, Canada, France and Australia. This arrangement was the forerunner of later offshore processing arrangements. On this occasion, the program was conducted largely free of political controversy. Having fought to preserve the territorial integrity of South Vietnam, and as the most prosperous nation in the region, Australia was obliged to help its former allies and their families seeking refuge abroad. Australia agreed to resettle 56,000 Vietnamese refugees. Of that number, some 2,059 Vietnamese arrived in Australia by boat between 1976 and 1981.

The Fraser Government sent immigration officers to offshore camps to process applicants. The first wave consisted largely of educated South Vietnamese, many of whom had served in the Saigon government. Those on the Labor side of politics were not well disposed towards their arrival, believing they were likely to oppose Left wing political parties and to favour the Coalition. The Leader of the Opposition, Gough Whitlam, had referred to them disparagingly as 'Asian Balts' who would take jobs from Australian workers and, in being fiercely anti-communist, probably vote for the Liberal Party. Their settlement outcomes proved to be positive in Australia and elsewhere with a substantial number of women from a Vietnamese background achieving higher degrees and senior academic positions. Labor's fears were misplaced as the Vietnamese enriched Australian society and contributed to its economic growth.

The Fraser Government's response to the Lebanese civil war was less successful.[13] Shortly after winning office, Fraser and MacKellar were lobbied by a group of influential Maronite Christians led by the prominent menswear retailer Reuben F Scarf. They were concerned for the safety of relatives in Lebanon which had descended into civil war after April 1975. People attempting to escape the bloody conflict between rival Muslim and Christian factions would be not accepted into Australia under the existing regulations. They needed to be categorised as refugees although they were not fleeing persecution. The Fraser Government allowed this to happen, easing the usual requirements relating to skills, language and existing family ties within Australia. Many who wanted to come in 1976 were Muslims from poorer rural areas seeking to exploit the 'Lebanese Concession' in their quest for a better life rather the Christians from the war-torn cities trying to evade politically motivated violence.

The Department of Immigration soon conceded that it was unable to verify the claims of those seeking relocation to Australia and management of the individual caseload exceeded its resources. Australia lost control of the program. Late in 1976, Cabinet decided to end the program and apply the usual rules to all applications from Lebanon. Over the next 15 years, some

30,000 Lebanese came to Australia as 'refugees' from the civil war although the Sunni Muslims from northern Lebanon settled primarily in the Sydney suburb of Lakemba while Shia Muslims originally from southern Lebanon lived mainly in the nearby suburb of Arncliffe. MacKellar concluded that the 'Lebanon Concession' was a mistake. The previously and mainly Christian Lebanese community in Australia was fractured and those who came with few skills were marginalised, alienated and some were eventually radicalised.

It was only after the resettlement of refugees became a pressing problem that the Liberal Party started to consider the principles that might undergird its policy. In 1980, two members of the Federal Executive Philosophy Sub-Committee, Sir Robert Southey and Senator Chris Puplick, produced a thoughtful treatise entitled *Liberal Thinking*. They explained that

> Liberals have always supported the freest movement of people and ideas across all frontiers and between all nations. The opportunity and ability of people to emigrate freely are a matter of fundamental importance to liberals. The corollary is that liberals believe in the development of open and compassionate systems of immigration which serve to give homes and refuge to displaced and emigrant persons, while achieving a balance between their needs and the needs of the recipient communities.[14]

While a liberal state was entitled to be 'selective about those it welcomes', they argued that 'policies based upon compassion and a sense of international responsibility are to be favoured over those based upon artificial constraints of numbers or race'.

Immigration in the Hawke-Keating years

Immigration was not an issue in the foreground when Australians went to the polls in March 1983. The economy was doing poorly and the labour market lacked vitality. The country was divided between those whose fortunes appeared to be improving and those who thought disadvantage was deepening. The electorate rejected the Fraser Government and gave the Labor Party, led by the newly ascendant Bob Hawke, a resounding victory. Stewart West was the new Minister for Immigration and the only member of the party's Left faction in the Hawke Cabinet. West, a former union official from the Illawarra region south of Sydney, was elected to Federal Parliament in 1977 after the death of the sitting member and former Whitlam Government minister, Rex Connor. He had no previous involvement in Immigration matters but feared, as a more traditional socialist trade union leader, that skilled migration would harm the prospects of local workers. West immediately lowered the skilled intake from 41 to 17 percent of all admissions. At the same time he began increasing family reunion-based migration from 29 to 49 percent of the annual intake. His stated aim was to address the Coalition's 'significantly moderate previous bias' towards young and white, affluent and English-speaking applicants. He wanted to 'give the battlers a better chance' of settling in Australia.[15]

Consistent with the Labor Government's policy of 'looking north' and Prime Minister Bob Hawke's later insistence that Australia is 'part of Asia', the new government also set a migration target of 80–90,000 for 1983–84 including 20,000 refugees. New Zealanders would continue to have unrestricted entry while the arrangement remained in Australia's national interest. Citizenship qualifications were steadily eased. The residence period needed for citizenship was reduced from five years to two and the English language requirement was wound back from adequate to basic. In terms of accepting refugees, West wanted the emphasis to be more on political solutions to the 'push factors' – the reasons that people fled their homes – than on resettlement being the preferred solution.

After the November 1984 election which saw the Hawke Government's majority in the House of Representatives nearly halved, the Leader of the Opposition, Andrew Peacock, decided to reshuffle his shadow ministry. His decision to appoint Philip Ruddock to the shadow immigration portfolio made sense. In the first instance, Michael Hodgman had not been effective in the role over the previous 20 months partly because West made no attempt to confer with his Opposition counterpart in the hope of widening bipartisan policy agreement. Ruddock was a confident parliamentary performer who might better hold Labor's new Minister for Immigration, Chris Hurford, to account. While Hurford had no previous experience in either Immigration or ethnic affairs, Ruddock could draw on his experiences during the Fraser years and on the policy expertise he had gained from long service in oversight and advisory committees. As he had a safe seat, he could devote more time to portfolio matters than those of his colleagues who were continually obliged to promote themselves and their achievements in their local electorate.

Ruddock was also helped by Hurford's 'open door' policy and willingness to communicate with the Opposition.

Ruddock continued to make his mark by gaining first-hand knowledge of portfolio issues, especially the challenges of refugee resettlement. He and wife Heather visited Pulau Bidong, an island camp in North East Malaysia, early in 1985. The centre was essentially a Vietnamese village. Arriving in a naval vessel, the dockside featured a large welcome banner in English and a sign hanging from a window bearing the words, 'Will We Ever Find Happiness'. On the same trip the Ruddocks travelled with a World Vision group to the Thai-Cambodian border to visit a United Nations refugee camp established for Cambodians.

On returning to Australia, Ruddock called for an increase to Australia's intake of Indochinese refugees. This action outraged the Victorian President of the Returned Services League (RSL) of Australia, the outspoken Bruce Ruxton, who referred to Ruddock as a 'little commie' and called on him to be sacked. Ruxton claimed

> We have more than enough political division in Australia without importing any more. Until the Government can get its act together and substantially screen them all, it is just plain stupid for Mr Ruddock to call for any increase. We don't like to use the term white Australia policy, but in these circumstances I can see no alternative.[16]

This was one of Ruxton's many forays into immigration policy. His notorious views were ignored by politicians but received plenty of media coverage. Peacock did not respond to his call for Ruddock's sacking. With the help of World Vision, Ruddock continued to visit Cambodia and Vietnam with the blessing of his party leader.

At this time he was also introduced to 'Initiatives of Change' (formerly known as Moral Re-Armament) and the conferences it was hosting in the Mountain House at Caux, Switzerland, where second-tier people-to-people diplomacy was being attempted between political opponents in Cambodia. These negotiations were being conducted after the Vietnamese had ousted the dictator Pol Pot at a time when stories of the 'Killing Fields' were beginning to attract worldwide attention. Ruddock had made contact with many of the survivors who had settled in the suburb of Cabramatta. The small Cambodian diaspora in that part of Sydney consisted mostly of young adults often without parents or siblings. Every survivor had a heartbreaking account of survival under the Khmer Rouge regime from 1975–1979.

Over the next few years Ruddock also visited a number of other refugee camps to gain a fuller sense of the emerging refugee problem and the impact the growing global movement of people was having. Vietnamese refugees were illustrative of emerging challenges. Apart from former political prisoners escaping the country after being released from their 10 year stay in re-education camps, Vietnamese boat arrivals at the designated regional processing centres in the mid-1980s started to present themselves as economic migrants rather than political refugees. The United States needed persuading that its policy of regarding all departures from communist countries as refugees was flawed. In June 1989, the Americans finally agreed to the Geneva 'Comprehensive Plan of Action' for Indochinese refugees. The Vietnamese regional processing centres would be closed and those who could not establish they were refugees would be returned to their country of origin. At the Galang camp in Indonesia there were ugly scenes as unsuccessful claimants were deported and the centre was closed. The Indonesians were highly sensitive to the adverse publicity created by the closures. This may have been the source of their later reluctance to host offshore processing centres.

As the second wave of Indochinese boat arrivals commenced in 1989 with people mostly from Cambodia, southern Vietnam and China, Ruddock gained a personal appreciation of both the issues which these raised and the proposed solutions. He also became aware of the 'grey line' that separated people who were political refugees from those seeking economic opportunity. Ruddock believed the 1951 United Nations Refugee Convention was under stress and in need of review. The document had been drafted at the height of the Cold War with those fleeing communist regimes, particularly in Eastern Europe, mostly in mind. The United States had already rethought its position in relation to the Vietnamese caseload with the Comprehensive Plan of Action. The foremost problem was the people smuggling industry that was emerging and exploiting a wider group of fragile states and authoritarian regimes.

The bipartisan consensus that had accompanied the handling of immigration was also starting to unravel, partly because the program's objectives were unclear and the value of its outcomes was being questioned. Ethnic communities were united in distrust of Hurford whom they felt had downplayed the importance of multiculturalism and unacceptably changed the selection system for preferred migrants. Unpersuaded by the direction in which the department was heading and the policies it was pursuing, Hawke replaced Hurford with Mick Young in February 1987. Young served as shadow spokesman for Immigration in 1976 but had contributed little to the policy debates in the 1980s. This did not greatly matter because Hawke, who had strong views on immigration, took the initiative and appointed the 'Committee to Advise on Australia's Immigration Policies' to give the program clearer direction. The Committee was to report by March 1988. Chaired by the former Australian ambassador to China, Stephen FitzGerald, the Committee's report noted that the purpose of the Immigration program had not been well explained by officials nor properly understood by the public.

> Over time, the need for a strategic rationale for immigration was lost. The immigration program came to be driven by its own momentum and by external stimuli, rather than by planned initiative within defined national objectives. Policies became reactive, tentative, short-term and disconnected, both internally and from the mainstream of government policy. The economic rationale for immigration became diffuse, unsupported, unresearched, and under some administrations almost unnoticed.[17]

The report argued for greater weighting for economic factors in choosing the most suitable immigrants and appeared to suggest that multiculturalism's moment had come and gone. The Hawke Government was also deeply concerned about 'unregulated population flows' from Southeast Asia and the possibility of waves of refugees 'on a massive scale – beyond the ability of civil or military authorities to prevent'.

Within the Australian community there was appreciable concern about the Immigration program. Aside from enduring low-level prejudice against new arrivals, growing unemployment led almost inevitably to widespread complaint that immigration should cease because local-born Australians were unable to find work. Refugees and migrants were in need of advocates and, in some instances, apologists. Among Coalition parliamentarians, there was no stronger advocate than Ruddock. He was more familiar with immigration issues than any other Australian parliamentarian, including the complexities of responding to the world's growing refugee crisis. But he had to manage the contest of ideas within his own party and immigration was clearly an area of dis-ease and division.

Testing the limits of bipartisanship

Immigration was yet to become a hot political issue. There was a spirit of bipartisanship although the occasional high-profile case involving an alleged lack of compassion or a double standard was exploited for short-term political gain. The Liberal Party's approach to immigration had always been generous. Migrants were needed to expand and augment the workforce and there were few objections from the electorate over the number of migrants entering the country. The key policy differences between the Coalition parties and Labor over the previous four decades were industrial relations, economic management and national security – not immigration. When the Fraser Government lost office in March 1983, few Liberal parliamentarians had much experience of opposition and those who retained their seats knew little about immigration. Whereas the incoming Hawke Government had many members who had known only opposition, the longer serving Liberal members had experienced the Whitlam years and regarded them as an aberration after 23 years of unbroken Coalition rule from 1949–72. Liberal Party strategists hoped, and probably believed, they would be returned to power in 1989 or thereabouts. After two terms, they presumed, Labor would have either lost momentum or lost its way. But it was the Liberal and National parties that were unable to maintain focus and sustain unity. A lack of experience in managing opposition was soon apparent. The Coalition parties were divided over policy while leadership tensions were never far from public view. Immigration would become a contentious issue and one that divided the leadership aspirants.

Ruddock had supported Andrew Peacock who assumed the party leadership after Malcolm Fraser resigned following the March 1983 election defeat. Although he had known Howard for 20 years and they were both from New South Wales, Ruddock was much nearer in his political outlook to Peacock who won the party room ballot for the leadership 36–20. Howard retained the deputy leadership of the Liberal Party which he had secured in 1982.

Following a period of tension in which Peacock accused Howard of working against him, another party room ballot returned John Howard to the deputy leadership in September 1985 after Peacock tried to have him replaced. Peacock interpreted the outcome as a vote of no confidence in his leadership and immediately resigned. Howard was subsequently elected leader of the Liberal Party, defeating Jim Carlton 57–6. The new leader then dispensed with the Peacock-appointed members of the outer ministry, replacing them with his own supporters.

After less than 12 months as shadow spokesman for Immigration, Ruddock returned to the backbench. The Liberal member for Mitchell and Howard supporter, Alan Cadman, took his place. Ruddock and Howard were never close personally or professionally. Neither owed the other any favours. Although Ruddock had been in parliament slightly longer, they were usually considered contemporaries with Howard advancing within the party more rapidly. Ruddock accepted his 'dumping' with characteristic good grace. He had known disappointment before and knew it to be a passing emotion. Senator Fred Chaney offered Ruddock some sound advice: 'how you handle disappointment is a key to your future'. Ruddock was not a factional warrior. He played no part in either promoting or exploiting leadership tensions between Peacock and Howard. As a backbench parliamentarian once more, he continued to engage with culturally diverse communities believing that building trust required an enduring personal commitment to their welfare. To diversify his experience of domestic issues and public administration, Ruddock served on the Public Accounts Committee and the Foreign Affairs and Defence Committee between 1985 and 1989. He was also appointed a Deputy Speaker.

The philosophical differences between Ruddock and Howard became public and plain during a debate in 1988 that has continued to reverberate. A controversy over immigration policy that threatened to expose deep divisions in attitude to race among Liberals began in March 1984 when the well-known Australian historian, Professor Geoffrey Blainey, Dean of the Faculty of Arts in the University of Melbourne, addressed a Rotary gathering at Warrnambool. Neither Blainey nor the audience thought his talk would be memorable. In remarks later reported by the Melbourne press, Blainey claimed that over the last few years – especially in the last year – we have given powerful preference to Asian migrants. More than half (of) our immigrants are now from Asia and many come from a peasant background, which is very different to the typical Asian immigrant of recent years ... It is almost as if we have turned the White Australia policy inside out.[18]

Blainey was concerned that Australia could not absorb the present level of Asian migration without creating new problems for the preservation of social harmony. By this time, the proportion of voters favouring a racially discriminatory immigration policy had fallen significantly. In 1971, a poll found that 73 percent wanted to exclude mainland Chinese or to admit just a few to 33 percent holding that view in 1987. Some 43 percent of Australians conceded they were a 'little prejudiced' when it came to immigration.[19] The Warrnambool Rotary address sparked what became known as 'the Blainey debate' with both Peacock and Howard accused of exploiting community division in order to reintroduce a racially discriminatory immigration policy. A number of Chinese Australians were concerned about attitudes in some sections of the Australian community to Asian migration.

In July 1984, the shadow spokesman, Michael Hodgman, had claimed the electorate objected to the Hawke Government's pro-Asian immigration policies and predicted the Coalition would gain a dozen marginal seats. Ruddock instantly recognised the implications of this deeply alarming development for newer arrivals in Australia. They naturally wanted to avoid resentment at their presence. This debate also worked against the Coalition's political self-interest. Working professionals and business people predominantly from Hong Kong were more likely to be Liberal Party voters. The Shadow Cabinet resolved in August 1984 to continue the Coalition's commitment to a non-discriminatory immigration program. Howard delivered a speech in a House of Representatives debate calling for restraint and tolerance in debate on Asian immigration. He was widely praised and his views almost universally applauded.

One Australia, political controversy and party dissension
Howard had taken a leading role in reaffirming 'the policies of the former Coalition Government which were humanitarian and liberal in the truest sense of the word'.[20] But immigration remained contentious within the

Coalition party room, views diverging about both the rate and the composition of the annual migrant cohort. There was also concern on the Labor side about drifts in the direction of policy. Howard, too, noted that FitzGerald had identified the 'clear and present need for urgent immigration reform'. The report's authors felt the community did not understand the philosophy of multiculturalism, believing it was divisive. Howard thought multiculturalism was problematic and called for its abolition. In launching the Coalition's immigration and ethnic affairs policy, 'One Australia', Howard proposed a new vision that 'requires of all of us a loyalty to Australia at all times and to her institutions and values and her traditions which transcends loyalty to any other set of values anywhere in the world'. This policy was part of the larger *Future Directions: It's Time for Plain Thinking* manifesto released in December 1988. Ruddock had not contributed to the policy. He had not even seen the details before its release.

On 1 August 1988, Howard introduced the policy in an interview with talkback radio host John Laws and expressed a preference for immigration policy to be biased towards skilled applicants rather than family reunion. In this sense, he was simply echoing a recommendation of the FitzGerald Report but was placing himself in a difficult position. His remarks could have been interpreted as contemplating a return to the White Australia Policy. Later the same day, answering a question during an ABC Radio interview about the increased rate of Asian migration to Australia, Howard remarked:

> I am not in favour of going back to a White Australia policy. I believe that, if it is in the eyes of some in the community ... too great, it would be in our immediate term interest and supportive of local cohesion if it were slowed down a little, so that the capacity of the community to absorb [it] was greater.[21]

These concerns were soon echoed by the National Party leader, Ian Sinclair, and by the shadow Finance spokesman, Senator John Stone of Queensland. On 17 August, Howard reiterated his position: 'I do not intend to alter one inch the stand I have taken ... I do not intend to alter my position on this issue'.[22]

'One Australia' was formally launched on 22 August. The Liberal premiers of New South Wales and Victoria, Nick Greiner and Jeff Kennett, both opposed the policy together with former Liberal prime minister, Malcolm Fraser. The

Hawke Government seized an opportunity three days later in the House of Representatives to exploit obvious divisions in the Coalition with a motion that opposed any reference to race in the selection of immigrants. Prime Minister Hawke commented: 'I do not accuse [John Howard] of racism or of being racist. In a sense, sadly, I make the more serious charge, I make the more damning indictment, of cynical opportunism, in a cynical grab for votes'. Hawke described the previous commitment to bipartisanship on immigration as 'the triumph of compassion over prejudice'. The Labor Party was clearly playing politics as the Government had no intention of changing its policy and was not under any pressure to do so. But there were limits to playing politics and unnecessarily dividing the community. Such a contentious issue was one of them. Having drawn the electorate's attention to divided opinion within the Coalition, Labor urged the Opposition not to insist on the matter being debated along party lines. Ruddock expressed his angst about the Opposition's approach to what was clearly an exercise in what is now called 'wedge' politics. He shared these concerns with Howard and others. Ruddock also sought the advice of former Immigration ministers Michael MacKellar and Ian Macphee, both of whom were still in parliament. They agreed that a non-discriminatory Immigration program was a fundamental principle for the Coalition and that its preservation needed not merely defending but actively promoting.

An amendment was moved supporting the Opposition's policy commit-ments in non-discriminatory terms. All Opposition members supported the amendment. Howard opposed the Government's motion and called for a formal division. Ruddock crossed the floor to vote with the Hawke Government. This was a defining moment in his political career. He was not naturally combative but on this occasion he would not shy away from conflict or controversy. Too much was at stake. Macphee and Steele Hall (former Premier of South Australia, senator for South Australia and then Liberal member for Boothby) also voted with the Government. MacKellar and Ian Wilson (a former Minister for Aboriginal Affairs) abstained. In explaining his position, Ruddock said he wanted to give

> an unambiguous and unqualified commitment to the principle that, whatever criteria are applied by Australian governments in exercising their sovereign right to determine the composition of the immigration

intake, race or ethnic origin shall never, explicitly or implicitly, be among them. I could not in conscience vote against that proposition and I could not be silent on that matter. For that reason, I felt obliged to vote today in favour of the motion. For me it was a very significant step.[23]

This was the first time in 15 years that Ruddock had voted against his own party.

Commentators suggested that the disagreement merely reflected the divide between Peacock-Howard supporters. The Moderates siding with Peacock and those with more conservative views with Howard. But this was not how Coalition members voted. A number of party hardliners proclaimed that Ruddock should lose party endorsement for his disloyalty. As pre-selections were about to be called for the next Federal election, the threat was real. He won a contested preselection 41 votes to 6. Those who knew Ruddock well, especially those in culturally diverse Australia, thought he had simply demonstrated his deep commitment to a non-discriminatory immigration policy and acted consistently with his own political principles.

This rupture became a defining moment in Australia's immigration policy, establishing a principle embraced by every subsequent government. While it was a lonely journey for Ruddock in 1988, he understood why people from all over the world wanted to come to Australia and how they could help to build a stronger, more prosperous nation. In the year of the Bicentennial celebrations, Ruddock noted that the small number of involuntary arrivals who came to New South Wales from Britain in 1788 had been supplanted by a large contingent of voluntary arrivals from all over the world in 1988.

Ruddock knew that voting with the Government in August 1988 would drastically reduce the likelihood of his return to the shadow ministry in any capacity. Howard had, indeed, been embarrassed and Ruddock was part of its cause. The others who had voted with the Government on this occasion had already occupied leadership positions. They were essentially in their twilight years with much less to lose than Ruddock who had yet to experience ministerial office. Of the four dissenters, Ruddock is usually the only name recalled. The immigration controversy and the persistence of poor polling diminished Howard's hold on the Opposition leadership. He did not lead a united team. Tensions were simmering and discontent was rife.

Notwithstanding that he had performed credibly in the 1987 electoral defeat and shown he could contend with Hawke, a movement to replace Howard with Peacock quietly gathered momentum in the first few months of 1989. Howard knew his handling of Asian immigration was mistaken. His words were ill-chosen and the emphasis misplaced. The damage had been done.

Howard dramatically lost the leadership to Peacock in May 1989 after a party room coup. Senator Chris Puplick believed 'the debate about immigration, racism, multiculturalism and "One Australia" was the most significant factor in leading to the eventual replacement of Howard by Peacock'.[24] The debate also allowed the Hawke Government to avoid a good deal of opprobrium from ethnic organisations that disliked the emphasis on skill as a weighted factor in the immigration entry score which was a feature of recent amendments to the *Migration Act*. Labor could take the moral high ground by asserting its enduring support for a non-discriminatory policy and its formal commitment to multiculturalism.

Changing political fortunes
With Peacock's return to the Liberal leadership, Ruddock was again shadow spokesman for Immigration. He was a known Peacock supporter but was not among the plotters who had worked surreptitiously for months to undermine and oust Howard. In an interview with the *Canberra Times* in November 1989, Ruddock stressed that there would no change to the Asian intake under a Coalition government. He stressed that

> The Coalition does not have a view on whether there are too many people of any racial or ethnic origin. We have a view that when people come to Australia they should give their first loyalty to this nation. We offer to those who have settled here a tolerant and compassionate community.[25]

Ruddock faced the voters in the March 1990 Federal election aware that he had taken a stand on immigration and multiculturalism. He secured 49.4 percent of the primary vote but suffered an 8 per swing that was spread across four other candidates. First preferences for the Labor candidate, Richard Talbot, were also down 2.7 percent. On a two-party preferred basis, the swing against Ruddock was only 1.7 percent. He remained the sitting member of a very safe Liberal seat. Despite a solid performance by Peacock, the Hawke Government retained office in what was Labor's fourth successive election victory. Peacock resigned as Liberal leader and was replaced by John Hewson who retained Ruddock in the Immigration portfolio with the added responsibility of ethnic affairs. The local *Northern Herald* newspaper claimed that his 'highly public stand against apartheid and discriminatory immigration has marked him not simply as a compassionate politician, but a maverick in the now hard-line conservative Liberal Party'.[26]

As the Opposition spokesman over the next few years, Ruddock had another opportunity to shape his vision for Australia's immigration policy. With more than a million applications annually, he thought that migrants should be selected without reference to country of origin, race, ethnicity, culture or religion and believed they needed as Australian citizens to make a firm commitment to parliamentary democracy, the rule of law, equality of the sexes, freedom of speech and association and tolerance of others. He argued that if the benefits of culturally diverse immigration were understood and experienced by all Australians, public support for the Immigration program would be overwhelming. He was willing to work closely and cooperatively in a spirit of bipartisanship with the Minister for Immigration, Senator Robert Ray, to overhaul the *Migration Act*. [The major amendments to the Act, particularly codification of ministerial discretion, are covered in chapter 10].

As the extent of this exercise was being determined, Ruddock continued to focus on refugee and humanitarian resettlement. By now the second wave of Indochinese boat arrivals as well as people smuggling by the 'Snakehead' gangs from the Fujian region of China to Australia, Europe and North America started to test the boundaries of the Refugee Convention. The Hawke and Keating Labor governments feared losing control of the nation's capacity to accommodate arrivals following a new wave of boat arrivals after 1989, the first since 1981. In 1992, the Keating Government introduced mandatory detention for all persons entering Australia without a valid visa while the claims of such people to remain were processed and health and security checks completed. The main target of this policy had been the Cambodians who were starting to arrive by boat. Despite public assertions to the contrary, the policy was intended to be punitive and to serve as deterrence. What became known as 'border security' was emerging as a contentious national issue. Ruddock supported Labor's stance.

The critical question was (and remains) how to determine whom to resettle when there are millions of displaced people in the world all seeking a new home and a better life. Hard decisions and tough choices had to be made in determining where the most pressing need resided. Ruddock developed a consistent view as the shadow minister. He thought that refugee resettlement should be an orderly process that identified those in greatest need of protection and gave priority to them. This identification should be undertaken in collaboration with the United Nations High Commissioner for Refugees (UNHCR) and the International Organisation for Migration (IOM). One of the impediments he identified was the indifference of other nations to the plight of refugees, evidenced by the absence of any mention of refugees in the Vienna Declaration on Human Rights drafted in 1993.

> I am angry about the extent to which there is an expectation here that we have obligations to honour, not only the letter and the spirit, but also provisions that people imagine go well beyond the letter and spirit, when the rest of the world has absolutely minimal commitment to doing anything about refugees at all.[27]

He argued during a hearing of the Joint Standing Committee on Migration held on 12 October 1993 that, given the 'lack of seriousness with which the rest of the world seems to treat international documents', Australia should 'try to set a positive international example'.

Ruddock was now a well-known and vigorous advocate for personal freedoms and human rights. During a parliamentary debate in November 1985 on a proposed Australian Bill of Rights, Ruddock claimed that his 'concern for fundamental human rights I would put against the concern of any other member in the Parliament. My record of protection of human rights not only in this country but also in relation to the affairs of other countries would stand scrutiny, I suggest, with that of any other colleague'. Instead of introducing a bill of rights, Ruddock thought the better approach was promoting 'vigilance' among judges, parliamentarians and the people. He also rejected any attempt 'to describe the concern for abuses of human rights as an interference in the internal affairs of other states'. The international community had a duty to judge those nations that denied their citizens 'basic and fundamental human rights'.[28]

His membership of the Parliamentary Group of Amnesty International had prompted him to address the political rights of Polish trade unionists in September 1982; the cultural rights of ethnic Hungarians residing in Romania in November 1985; the entitlement of Khmer refugees to be physically safe following the closure of the Khao-I-Dang camp by the Thai Government in December 1986; the inadequacy of arrangements for Kampuchean and Laotian refugees in other camps on the Thai border in February 1987; the harassment and restriction of movement endured by Ukrainians within the Soviet Union in March 1988; the right to independent, sovereign nationhood for Lithuanians, Estonians and Latvians in May 1990; the plight of the Kurdish minority in Iraq and of Kuwaitis during the short-lived Iraqi occupation in December 1990; the sufferings of those displaced by civil war in the former Yugoslavian Federation in November 1991; the intimidation and systemic violence waged against the East Timorese people by Indonesian security forces in November 1991; the suppression of those practising the Buddhist faith in Vietnam in August 1992; and the torture and imprisonment of Tibetans by the Chinese Government in October 1992.

He was concerned with the shape of compassion and how it should be conveyed through public policy. How was Australia to demonstrate it was a good international citizen? How would the Commonwealth manage the nation's borders while dealing humanely with unlawful arrivals? How would the Commonwealth fund refugee and humanitarian resettlement when the budget was already in deficit? And, critically, how would the Government foster and maintain the necessary public support for such a program? Ruddock was able to devote considerable time to these questions because he occupied the safe seat of Dundas. But things were about to change.

Ahead of the Federal election scheduled for 1993, an electoral redistribution in New South Wales abolished two Sydney electorates – Dundas (which was a safe Liberal seat) and Phillip (a safe Labor seat). Ruddock faced political uncertainty for a second time. A small part of Dundas would be returned to Parramatta. As the 1990s boundaries were very different to the 1970s, the redrawn electorate of Parramatta was more marginal than in 1973. Most of Dundas was moved to the adjoining seat of Bennelong, held by John Howard since 1974, making it more marginal. The remainder of Dundas was allocated to Berowra which was still represented by Dr Harry Edwards. The so-called

'Moderate' faction within the New South Wales Division of the Liberal Party, led by the state police minister, Ted Pickering, urged Ruddock to stand against Howard in Bennelong in the hope that Howard might nominate for the potentially safer seat of North Sydney, then held by the Independent Ted Mack. There was little love for Howard among the 'Moderates' within the state party machinery. When Howard decided to remain in Bennelong, Ruddock faced the prospect of being without a winnable seat. Edwards then announced his retirement from parliament. Ruddock had strong connections with Berowra. He had grown up in Pennant Hills and attended primary school there. He completed his schooling at Barker College in Hornsby which was also in the electorate. Many in Berowra also remembered and revered his late father as the local state parliamentarian. Overcoming internal party tensions, Ruddock secured nomination in Berowra and his political future again looked assured.

Continuing electoral disappointment

The Coalition led by John Hewson was expected to win the election held in March 1993 and to secure a substantial parliamentary majority. Some of the pundits were calling it the 'unlosable' election. Labor's most electorally successful prime minister, Bob Hawke, had been deposed by his former Treasurer, Paul Keating, in December 1991 after an unsuccessful bid for the leadership five months earlier. Keating had cited poor polling as the reason for his challenge but he was initially unable to revive Labor's fortunes. The Government was increasingly unpopular and, after ten years of Labor rule, the electorate appeared committed to change. Keating's own net approval rating, according to Newspoll, was minus 25. Few prime ministers had ever rated so low. But the Coalition managed to alienate a large section of the ethnic vote after Hewson restated those sections of the FitzGerald Report critical of the influence wielded by ethnic organisations on the Hawke Government. Community leaders were considered Labor Party agents who could be dismissed because they would probably never vote for the Coalition. The Coalition's detailed policy statement, *Fightback!*, chided the Government for allowing too many immigrants into the country at a time of economic austerity notwithstanding the positive benefits flowing from immigration, and pledged that a Hewson Government 'will substantially reduce immigration to a level significantly below the Government's current predictions'. Hewson was subject to personal abuse as support for the Coalition among southern European and Asian migrants ebbed away. Pollsters claimed that losing the ethnic vote would not alter the election outcome. The net effect was to make the Liberal Party look racist and xenophobic.

As polling day neared, the Coalition's campaign started to unravel around its plan to introduce a broad-based consumption tax. The result was completely unexpected. The Government was returned to office after increasing its primary vote – the first time an incumbent government had achieved that feat since 1966. Labor gained two seats while the Coalition lost four. There were two independents, Phil Cleary in Wills and Ted Mack in North Sydney. Paul Keating referred to the election result as one 'for the true believers'. This was, he remarked, the 'sweetest victory of all'. In the electoral division of Berowra, Ruddock had increased the Liberal vote by 3.44 percent. Although there was a small swing of 0.5 percent to the Labor candidate on a two-party preferred basis, Ruddock had secured 62.2 percent of the vote after the distribution of preferences. Berowra would remain among the safest Liberal seats in the country.

Fightback! was largely blamed for the defeat coupled with a poorly run election campaign. Some commentators concluded that 1993 would be the last time a major party would be courageous enough to provide a blueprint for reform well before an election. [The surprise defeat of the Bill Shorten-led Labor Party in the May 2019 poll was in many respects likened to the 1993 election.] *Fightback!* had given Labor a large political target. Inevitably there were calls for Hewson to resign. He had lost an election that most thought he should have easily won. Recriminations flowed freely in a party devastated by its fifth straight election loss. Hewson, despite his leadership being fatally damaged, refused to go. He managed to persuade enough of his colleagues that he remained their best option and retained his position. There was no attempt to heal the rift with the ethnic communities. Ian Macphee, who had left Federal parliament at the 1990 election after losing pre-selection in the seat of Goldstein to Dr David Kemp, claimed the Liberals' decision to walk away from bipartisanship on Immigration policy under Howard and Hewson was

> going to haunt the Liberal Party, not because of any ethnic lobbies, not because of an ethnic vote, but because young Australians, regardless of

their ancestry, feel comfortable with the society we have got and don't understand the vibes that come from those who don't understand it.[29]

Ruddock's preference was to remain in Immigration which would have sent a strong signal to ethnic communities who appreciated his empathy and goodwill. Hewson, however, asked Ruddock to take on the Social Security portfolio to broaden his experience of domestic policy. The new Immigration spokesman was Senator Jim Short from Victoria. A sensible appointment, it was welcomed by ethnic communities. It certainly made practical sense. As the new Minister for Immigration, Nick Bolkus, was a senator, there was merit in having his Coalition opponent in the same house. Short had been active in developing Coalition immigration policy and had close ties with the Vietnamese and Baltic communities. He had supported independent nationhood for Latvia, Lithuania and Estonia during the era of the Soviet Union. In 1986, Short had established his electorate office in the culturally cosmopolitan Melbourne suburb of Brunswick. He would serve as deputy chair of the Joint Standing Committee on Migration and worked with the Labor Government to achieve bipartisan agreement when possible. As shadow spokesman, Short projected strong and positive affirmation of the migration program while drawing attention to alleged disorganisation in the Department of Immigration, the administrative problems created by unpredictable interpretation of the *Migration Act* and Regulations by the courts, and what he considered 'a more and more legalistic framework' for the development of immigration policy.

Learning from the past

The Coalition still struggled to present a united front to the press and the people on Immigration. Early in 1994, Hewson used Howard's 'anti-Asian' immigration remarks of August 1988 to demonstrate he had heard and heeded the community's views. Howard, plainly angered, told a gathering of Sydney's Asian leaders in May 1994 that his remarks of six years earlier were misrepresented by the media. The Liberals' credibility among migrant communities was still threadbare. The National Party had not made things any easier. In August 1993, party leader Tim Fischer responded injudiciously to a media question with the stark pronouncement: 'I think multiculturalism in all its facets should be reviewed'. He then called for the migrant intake to be reduced. The resulting controversy was deeply distressing to Ruddock who felt the understanding he and Jim Short had generated within the migrant community could not overcome lingering suspicion that the Coalition was anti-immigration despite Short's energetic advocacy on behalf of Chinese students who sought to remain in Australia after the Tiananmen Square massacre in June 1989.

Despite his designated role as Shadow Minister for Social Security, Ruddock remained active in immigration matters, especially where human rights were concerned. His widely known commitments led to an invitation to monitor the first South African democratic elections in April 1994. The Australian delegation also included John Cain, the former Labor Premier of Victoria, and Janine Haines, former Senator and Leader of the Australian Democrats. Ruddock attended a number of political rallies with his colleagues including a huge gathering in the Athlon Football Stadium to hear Nelson Mandela. On the day of the election, Ruddock monitored polling booths in the Cape Flats. People had queued for more than 24 hours before polling began. Those in the queues were adamant: having waited all their adult lives for the right to vote, waiting a few more hours to cast a ballot was a minor matter.

The following year Ruddock visited Lebanon for the first time. The main purpose was to attend the re-opening of the Australian Embassy in Beirut on 18 July 1995. The embassy was closed in 1984 when the security situation deteriorated with the worsening of the civil war. During the next eleven years, Australia's relations with Lebanon were handled by the Australian Embassy in Damascus, with the Ambassador accredited to both Syria and Lebanon. In 1994, a temporary Australian Government Office, staffed by locally engaged officials, was established in the Mayflower Hotel at West Beirut. The embassy was formally re-opened by the Minister for Foreign Affairs, Senator Gareth Evans, and the Minister for Immigration and Ethnic Affairs, Senator Nick Bolkus. Ruddock and Short represented the Opposition. Joined by wife Heather, he was accompanied by a large Lebanese contingent who travelled throughout the country apart from those areas under continuing Israeli occupation. The visit included the renaming of the main road through the village of Kfarsghab in North Lebanon. A number of villagers from Kfarsghab had settled around Parramatta and were acquainted with Ruddock as their local Federal parliamentarian. To honour this connection, the road was officially renamed Parramatta Road, complete with the City of Parramatta logo.

By this time, the Liberal Party's leadership had endured considerable upheaval. Hewson had been replaced as Leader of the Opposition by Alexander Downer in May 1994. Ruddock remained Social Security spokesman. Although Downer made it clear that he was 'very dedicated to a non-discriminatory immigration policy', his decision to exclude the Immigration portfolio from the Shadow Cabinet was yet another miscalculation. The Federation of Ethnic Communities Council interpreted the move as evidence Downer was 'not supportive'. Goodwill was unnecessarily lost. After poor polling and little sign the Coalition's support would recover, Downer relinquished the leadership of the Liberal Party to John Howard in January 1995. In contrast to 1985, when he was discarded by Howard, Ruddock was retained in the shadow ministry in the Social Security portfolio and had his responsibilities expanded to include senior citizens.

After 13 years in government, Paul Keating led the Labor Party into the Federal election held on Saturday 2 March 1996. As the campaign drew to a close, the Coalition looked set for a substantial victory. Keating was personally unpopular and the electorate had become tired of Labor in power. The government and the nation were about to change.

Endnotes

1   There is a detailed discussion of the creation and early evolution of the Department of Immigration and the work of the first four ministers in Tom Frame, *The Life and Death of Harold Holt*, Allen & Unwin, Sydney, 2005.

2   Quoted in DM White, *The Philosophy of the Australian Liberal Party*, Hutchinson, Melbourne, 1978, p. 150.

3   Address delivered at the Second Citizenship Convention, 1951.

4   *Straits Times*, 22 January 1952.

5   *Argus*, 14 September 1950.

6   *Tasmanian Truth*, 26 December 1953.

7   Geoffrey Bolton, *The Oxford History of Australia*, Oxford University Press, Melbourne, 1990, p. 77.

8   Alan Watt, *The Evolution of Australian Foreign Policy*, Cambridge, 1968, p. 202.

9   HI London, *Non-White Immigration and the 'White Australia' Policy*, Sydney University Press, Sydney, 1970, pp. 17–18.

10   Quoted in DM White, *The Philosophy of the Australian Liberal Party*, p. 175.

11   Misha Lajovic, 'The major political parties and ethnic affairs' in James Jupp (ed.), *Ethnic Politics in Australia*, Allen & Unwin, Sydney, 1984, p. 40–41.

12   Andrew Jakubowicz, 'State and ethnicity: multi-culturalism as ideology', in James Jupp (ed.), *Ethnic Politics in Australia*, p. 22.

13   The Lebanese 'concession' has been the subject of considerable commentary. See https://thesydneyinstitute.com.au/blog/1970s-lebanese-commission-led-to-an-immigration-debacle/ and for more recent analysis https://www.theaustralian.com.au/commentary/opinion/1970s-lebanese-commission-led-to-an-immigration-debacle/news-story/0d504285023bc42b79c70b3b70f93c2e

14   CJ Puplick and RJ Southey, *Liberal Thinking*, Macmillan, Melbourne, 1980, p. 131.

15   Quoted in Rachel Stevens, *Immigration Policy from 1970 to the Present*, Routledge Studies in Modern History, Routledge, New York, 2016.

16   'White Aust. Policy 'needed'', *Courier Mail* (Brisbane), 21 June 1985.

17   Stephen FitzGerald (Chairman), *Immigration: A Commitment to Australia*, Report of the Committee to Advise on Australia's Immigration Policies, AGPS, Canberra, 1988, pp. 13–14.

18   The initial reporting and subsequent commentary on Blainey's speech are covered in great detail in https://www.standard.net.au/story/726448/blaineys-speech-still-proves-to-be-the-fuel-of-much-fiery-debate/

19   Survey results quoted in Andrew Norton, 'Towards a new Australian settlement?', in JR Nethercote (ed.), *Liberalism and the Australian Federation*, Federation Press, Melbourne, 2001, p. 240. A valuable longitudinal assessment of polling on attitudes to immigration and race is Murray Goot, 'Public opinion and public opinion polls', in Andrew Markus and MC Ricklefs (eds), *Surrender Australia: Geoffrey Blainey and Asian Immigration*, Allen & Unwin, Sydney, 1985, pp. 49–62.

20   John Howard, CPD (Reps), 23 August 1988.

21   Andrew Markus, *Race: John Howard and the Remaking of Australia*, Allen & Unwin, Sydney, 2001, pp. 85–89.

22   Quoted in https://speakola.com/political/bob-hawke-affirming-immigration-policy-1988

23   See David Adams, 'Political Review', *The Australian Quarterly*, vol. 60, no. 4, Summer, 1988, pp. 499–515.

24   Chris Puplick, *Is the Party Over? The Future of the Liberals*, Text, Melbourne, 1994, p. 112.

25   *Canberra Times*, 17 November 1989.

26   *Northern Herald*, 19 April 1990.

27   Philip Ruddock, Joint Standing Committee on Migration Inquiry into Detention Practices, *Hansard*, 12 October 1993, pp. 783–84.

28   CPD (Reps), 20 October 1988, p. 1977.

29   http://www.multiculturalaustralia.edu.au/doc/macphee_1.pdf

CHAPTER 4

Politics and compassion

A range of expectations are imposed on immigration ministers. They are urged to show compassion when dealing with their department's clients, especially those who seek entry to Australia within the Humanitarian Program. The rules and regulations governing entry are complex and their application is often complicated. There is controversy whenever people are denied entry for what might seem heartless reasons. When government policies fail to take account of specific circumstances or procedures work unintentionally against a particular person, there are calls for the minister to override administrative hurdles and overrule officials with an exercise of compassion to alleviate actual or potential suffering. The objective is drawing attention to a situation in which a reasonable person, on being made aware of the facts, would be moved to act in a manner that is consistent with respect for human life and regard for human dignity. In such instances, the minister is asked to respond as the average citizen would respond when confronted by the dire needs of a desperate person. If a departmental functionary will not see reason or if legal remedies are elusive, the last resort is an appeal to the personal sensibilities of the minister and the presumption that he or she is capable of showing compassion.

To some people, compassion trumps other values because curtailing suffering and alleviating pain is always and everywhere the most pressing obligation imposed on individuals. Compassion is a conscious refusal to remain indifferent. To overlook the suffering of another person is to deny their humanity; to ignore their pain is to trivialise their predicament. The place of compassion is unavoidable in any discussion of the plight of asylum seekers. Mere mention of the word conveys a respect for human decency and communicates a regard for human dignity. The word is used so frequently and with such conviction that it implies a clear sense of what is meant and what is required. But this is far from true. Is compassion a sentiment or a principle? A mood or a mindset? A feeling or an attitude?

Many depictions of compassion are synonymous with charity and kindness or moral imperatives producing ethical obligations. Others suggest that someone feels pity but acts compassionately. Compassion has been included on many inventories of virtue and in statements of moral responsibility. Defining compassion is not a mere academic exercise. Given the word's powerful resonances, the claims that are often made about what compassion demands, and noting the prominence of compassion in continuing debates about immigration policy and practice, there is a need for clarity on what it means and consensus on what it requires.

Defining compassion

Like many words, 'compassion' has meant different things to different societies at different times. In the medieval era, compassion was a religious virtue synonymous with benevolence. In the eighteenth century it was often referred to as a 'moral instinct' evoking sympathy and secular notions of 'humanity'. A consistent theme was the transcendence of self. Philosophers of this period, such as Thomas Hobbes, Bishop George Berkeley, Adam Smith, David Hume, William Wollaston, Francis Hutcheson and Benjamin Franklin, began to consider the question of personal self-interest and wondered whether genuine compassion was ever possible. They asked whether human beings were capable of complete selflessness and, therefore, true benevolence. Self-interest could be transcended because, some believed, part of human nature made people aware of, and attentive to, suffering. Conversely, if human beings were without what was called 'fellow feeling' they were little more than monsters. Compassion was an important marker of the ability and the capacity of human beings to care for others.

By the nineteenth century, a less laudatory view of compassion gained currency. The German philosopher Friedrich Nietzsche thought compassion typically emanated from pointless guilt about the plight of others.[1] To show others pity was effectively to treat them with contempt. It was better to encourage people to acknowledge their disadvantage and recognise their difficulties in the hope they would struggle and ultimately prevail against them. Others thought compassion was an indulgence that swayed reason and subverted justice.[2] It ought, therefore, to be resisted because it prompts emotion and elicits charity, potentially obscuring the real problem and the best solution.[3]

Modern references to compassion are highly personalised. They imply a temperament marked by sensitivity, thoughtfulness and consideration in contrast to character that exudes callousness, indifference and apathy. The emphasis is on showing generosity of spirit. Compassion is, then, the antithesis of meanness and heartlessness. A number of world religions, such as Buddhism, do not see compassion as an action but an experience of entering into a deeper sense of the truth of human reality. Given its evolving use and much ambiguity about what it demands, there is a need for definitional clarity if compassion is to be considered a legitimate factor and a realistic imperative in the conduct of an immigration program.

To begin with its origins, the English word 'compassion' is derived from the Latin, *com*, meaning 'with' and *passio*, meaning 'suffering'. Literally understood, compassion means suffering with another. The suffering involves a person feeling pain which might be physical or emotional, and the suffering could be common or shared, caused by the same factors or derived from the same source. Some accounts of compassion suggest it is essentially an expression of love and a response to sadness. In effect, compassion is not a distinct emotion but a product of more deeply held or strongly felt emotions. An alternate account suggests it is a distinct emotion that can be differentiated from love and sadness because the sufferer may not be known personally and the source of their suffering may not produce sadness. Yet another explanation sees compassion as embodying empathetic distress. A person enters the experience of another, shares in their suffering and is affected by it. There is much to commend the conceptual distinction that Hannah Arendt drew between *compassion* as direct attention to individual suffering and *pity* as an abstract consideration for the suffering of the masses.

The common feature in each of these accounts is the involvement of emotion. Compassion involves and, indeed, relies upon human feelings especially in response to undeserved misfortune. It might even provoke scrutiny of what caused or contributed to the misfortune and whether anyone is complicit. There is a sense in which compassion, because it is based on a feeling, is spontaneous and often surprising. It is an immediate and unscripted reaction to the unfortunate and their plight. Simone Weil once remarked that compassion for the afflicted is a 'more astounding miracle than walking on water, healing the sick or raising the dead.'[4] Because compassion is more a reaction than a response, it is not contrived and cannot be compelled. Compassion is not a mental exercise which is the eventual outcome of a careful sifting of evidence. Compassion comes from the heart. It is putting oneself imaginatively in their place and acting in a manner that seeks to end their suffering or to alleviate their pain. This might also be understood as sympathy followed by an action. Without any action, there is only sympathy. A person is compassionate when their sympathy obliges a response.

Compassion cannot be measured on a scale. It is not experienced in half measures. Someone is compassionate or they are not. We do not tend to speak to 'calculated compassion'. Because compassion consists of an object, is conscious of context and is informed by conscience, what moves one person to be compassionate may barely influence or arouse another. A person's capacity for compassion reflects their own experience and is less likely to be felt if the suffering and pain were either self-inflicted or caused by foolishness or selfishness. People who have brought suffering upon themselves are more likely to attract pity – a form of empathy lacking an imperative to act – than compassion.

Compassion is significant in that it usually excludes self-interest and extinguishes self-will. The compassionate are no longer concerned foremost with themselves; they are seized by the needs of others and how they might be met. The deepest form of compassion involves trying to enter the sufferings of another and to discern their pain. The American ecologist, Lynn White, suggested that compassion 'actualises love in time and space'; it drives a feeling to become an action.[5] He characterised compassion as 'showing reverence actively' towards other people, acknowledging their dignity and respecting their uniqueness. It is an expression of 'comradeship' with other living and sentient beings. Compassion may not always lead to alleviation of suffering because there may be other emotions bearing values that need also to be taken into consideration. But compassion precludes indifference. Some accounts of compassion make it a last resort. If a person is not moved by prejudice, intolerance and injustice, he or she may be moved by suffering to feel compassion for those in pain.

There is, however, a line of thinking that contends compassion is always tinged by some sense of the compassionate individual gaining something for themselves in showing compassion, if only personal satisfaction that they cared for a person in need. In other words, when I profess to be concerned about others, I am actually disguising concern for myself. Others are helped in the hope or expectation that they will help me. These theories need to overcome the phenomenon of altruism – actions that appear to be inconsistent, if not antithetical, to the pursuit of personal self-interest. Real compassion transcends selfishness in that the compassionate feel they should care and are thus inclined to care, notwithstanding the personal cost. It also assumes that a personal acquaintance with the sufferer and their pain. It is not a generalised sensation that exists as a permanent state; its focus is a person and their situation and an immediate response.

Compulsive compassion?

Can a person be too compassionate? Replicating the suffering of others or pursuing vicarious pain are not more fulsome or even alternate expressions of compassion. The person feeling compassion and the person for whom compassion is felt are (and remain) separate and distinct beings. The compassionate might feel intensely for the them but they do not feel *their* pain. Feeling compassion might involve accepting or incurring a measure of pain or even suffering but it is not the pain or the suffering of the other. Charles Birch, the noted Australian geneticist who also wrote on theological subjects, argued that

> it is possible, by a certain distancing of ourselves, both from our own feelings and from those of the other, to enter into a relationship of feeling with another in which both maintain their own integrity in a larger whole that is enriched by their contrasts.[6]

Conversely, seeing compassion as sharing in the sufferings of others or solidarity with their pain might also be a means by which the expression of compassion is curtailed. Bishop Butler noted in 1726, in his 'Second Sermon on Compassion', that the intensity of feelings associated with compassion might lead some people to 'industriously turn away from the miserable'.[7] The celebrated German writer, Johann Wolfgang von Goethe, was very susceptible to severe compassion and made avoiding suffering and pain one of his rules of life. If there were less sympathy in the world, there would be less trouble, he mused.[8] Other people take solace or find satisfaction in the suffering of others. Those who think the virtuous deserve their good fortune might find vindication in the misfortune of others and could refuse to show compassion and reject an urging to intervene. Suffering and pain are seen as recompense or punishment for weakness or stupidity and any mediation goes against the grain of natural forces. It is also possible that those who have never faced suffering or endured pain may feel favoured or superior, making it less likely they could ever feel or show compassion.

By contrast, when human suffering is so severe or widespread that it exceeds the remedies at hand, the response is sometimes resignation rather than compassion. As the mind can experience mental exhaustion, so the heart can be beset by compassion fatigue. There is a sense, then, in which an understanding and experience of compassion is bound to adherence to a larger story about what it means to be human and of what human life consists. This larger story will not necessarily attract consensus about when and how compassion should be felt or needs to be shown.

Similarly, if compassion is generated by fear or dread – if this could happen to someone else, it could happen to me – it is likely that self-interest has managed to creep back into the equation with the attendant concern that compassion is more likely to be expressed when the suffering being observed is potentially universal and not unique to one individual or circumstance. There is, too, the possibility that compassion could be a disguise for gaining and exercising control by making others grateful or reliant to the one who addressed their suffering and alleviated their pain. There may be a sense of debt or obligation that could be exploited by someone willing to manipulate vulnerable people. While the origins of compassion might be altruistic and noble, its outcomes could be selfish, self-serving or even malicious. The emotional health and well-being of the person confronted by suffering and pain are, therefore, relevant to expression of compassion.

Compassion clearly relies upon imagination. We try to place ourselves in the position of others and gain a sense of what they might be feeling as an exercise of imagination. This is an imprecise activity that is inclined to miscalculation inasmuch as it involves my life experiences, the life experience of others and our knowledge of the circumstances shaping specific experiences. We estimate (or guess) what an experience might be like for others in light of our knowledge of suffering and pain. It is pure approximation. What one person might consider tolerable, another will deem intolerable because their experiences and expectations are different or the specific circumstances that made a particular experience intolerable might not have been properly understood. Compassion is, then, shaped by perspective and influenced by context. Within any society, there will be different expressions and experiences of compassion. This is because, as Clifford Orwin has noted,

> Imagination is idiosyncratic, shaped by our own past and dominated by our own present. It therefore bestows its favours by rules which must seem egocentric. The evils to which it responds are principally those we know or fear for ourselves – not because pity is in the end self-pity, but because the more thoroughly we grasp some evil, the more deeply we sympathise with its victims.[9]

Thus, it needs to be recognised that compassion could be misguided or exaggerated. Compassion is not a precise feeling because no two circumstances and no two sufferings are the same. This is acutely the case when compassion is felt for people who are entirely different from ourselves in terms of how and where they were raised, where they live and what they consider normal or familiar. We assume that other people would or should feel like we do, and proceed on the basis of what seems to be similar. It is difficult to stand in the shoes of others and even more difficult to walk in those shoes. When Westerners feel compassion they usually universalise the particular and presume that those in the developing world are, deep down, just like them.

The instability of compassion

But, as compassion tends towards generalisation, it inevitably suffers from miscalculation. Compassion can be an unreliable guide for action. It needs to be informed by insights that ensure it does not become a fixation or an obsession that says more about the compassionate than the objects of their compassion. Unhealthily for those feeling compassion, if the feeling is not shared by others, it can take the form of moral indignation and eventually emotional rage. Expression of passion becomes the objective rather than addressing the suffering of the person for whom compassion was originally felt. Like love, the more compassion is commanded the more elusive it becomes. Compassion cannot be turned on or off as circumstances allow or convenience demands. If it can, it is not compassion. Consequently, there is uncertainty about the action that compassion requires. What one person considers to be a compassionate response another person might consider too much, because it is paternalism, or too little, because it is little more than tokenism. Given compassion involves a cluster of feelings and no two people feel the same way about the same things, there will be different levels of reaction and response, and no clear way to determine whether one is more apt in the circumstances than the other if the twin evils of paternalism and tokenism are to be avoided.

Modern use of the word compassion infers something that is very near to a sentiment. It is certainly more than a feeling. Compassion involves an element of empathy and sympathy: understanding and concern. Unless compassion guides judgements and prompts action, it is no more than self-indulgence. Genuine compassion drives a desire to alleviate the suffering of others when neither the compassionate nor the suffering are complicit in the cause or continuation of pain. When there is complicity, the reaction and the response ought to described in other terms, perhaps charity. True compassion does not, then, imply any sense of censoriousness or judgmentalism as if suffering is deserved or justified.

Contemporary accounts of compassion tend to be highly personalised. Most writers focus on individuals because, it is implied, only individuals can feel compassion. Compassion is prompted by, or relies upon, emotions that can only exist within a natural person. Individuals within a group can separately feel compassionate and decide to act compassionately but the group cannot be compassionate without the constituent individuals feeling compassion on their own volition. It is not possible to have group compassion if none of its members feel any empathy for the suffering of others. Does this mean that compassion has no place in policy development or political decision-making?

Compassion in the public square

Theologians and ethicists have been considering the place of compassion in religious observance and personal piety since the biblical writers noted that

God was moved by compassion to care for the created order and Jesus reacted with compassion towards the poor, the infirm and the frightened. More than any other system of belief, Christianity has given most shape and substance to western conceptions of compassion and done most to promote its exercise as a personal virtue and institutional value. Those claiming to be disciples of Jesus are called to convey compassion as an expression of solidarity with the sufferer who is another child of God. Compassion is a call to transcend personal self-interest in being open to what others feel.

An axiom of their profession and its teaching that has done much to shape contemporary definitions of compassion, Christians cannot claim a monopoly on the definition of compassion or specifications for its exercise. Nor have Christians made compassion in representative government and political discourse an area of close and continuing interest. In most Western nations over the last century, personal expressions of religious belief have gradually become wholly private matters. It has been left to secular theorists to transition compassion from being an individual obligation to an institutional responsibility. An early non-religious account of compassion by Jean-Jacques Rousseau has been foundational for later work and much related discussion.[10]

In both *Discourse on Inequality* published in 1755 and *Emile* which appeared in 1762, Rousseau observes that feeling compassion (which he refers to as *pitie*, that is, pity) at the sight of a person suffering is a 'natural' response. Sensitivity to suffering is a mark of human maturity; to be indifferent to suffering is a mark of human depravity.[11] There is a sense, however, in which there is a need for an education in compassion so that it takes productive forms, such as identifying with the sufferer and an imperative of 'active beneficence'. To overcome the weak and undiscriminating character of much compassion, Rousseau felt that friendship and gratitude would give compassion the motivation and momentum it needed to overcome 'sterile pity' which was never reflected in action to relieve suffering. Gratitude that one is not suffering will inspire action on behalf of those who are; friendship that one can identify with those who are suffering obliges a response of solidarity.

Rousseau is conscious, too, of a lack of imperative or compulsion. Feeling compassion for someone does not, of itself, impose an obligation to act with compassion. Obligation comes from avoiding the consequences of refusing to show compassion because it is one of the few sentiments able to restrict self-interest and constrain the desire to use power for selfish ends. Without compassion aided by gratitude and friendship, there is no morality, no beneficence and no room for virtue. Its importance comes in promoting the cause of justice, freedom, equality and security. Without compassion, the quest for these common 'goods' would be substantially diminished.

Classical thinking about political life and public administration tends to give priority to the practice of justice and recognition of rights ahead of the imperative to show compassion. The impetus for thinking more about the place of compassion has come from the rise of large and amorphous institutions and the lament that these institutions are heartless and uncaring. They are accused of lacking the emotional capacity needed for expression of empathy. In the transition from the benevolent monarch animated by a love for his or her subjects, there emerged the expectation that representative government would be moved by something else in its dealing with citizens, perhaps compassion. As political parties and public institutions consist of people capable of feeling compassion, their cultures and their outlook are likely to be informed by the values and the virtues that are operative in the expression of compassion. A commitment to human rights and the subsequent evolution of humanitarian law reflects a vision of human solidarity that draws on feelings associated with compassion. Existence of humanitarian law is a reminder of these feelings and a possible source of their individual and collective re-awakening.

Heads and hearts

Admitting compassion into policy development and political decision-making required a dialogue between 'the heart' and 'the head' where one served to inform and perhaps curb the excess of the other. In his inaugural lecture as the new Professor of Economics at Cambridge in 1885, Alfred Marshall announced that his

> most cherished ambition, my highest endeavour, ... to increase the numbers of those, who Cambridge, the great mother of strong men, sends out into the world with cool heads but warm hearts, willing to give at least some of their best powers to grappling with the social suffering around them.[12]

The notion that good policy and sound decision-making was informed by both intellect and emotion – also depicted as an attempt to connect means and ends or material prosperity with emotional wellbeing – has become a dominant theme in public administration. Finding a balance or equilibrium within the dynamic interaction of the heart and the head continues to attract attention.

Addressing the 2006 APEC Symposium on Socio-Economic Disparity held in Seoul, South Korea, the American economist Peter Orszag recalled Marshall's ambition with a modification: 'in the context of substantial increases in income inequality and given the political economy of globalization, warm hearts are necessary for cool heads – there is no "but" needed'.[13] As Paul Krugman, the *New York Times* economics correspondent, noted, it was, however 'too easy to slip from "hard heads, soft hearts" to the reverse'.[14] Writing in the *Australian*, Chris Kenny said Australia needed 'hard heads, fewer soft hearts'.[15] There have been other variations of Marshall's aphorism. Martin Luther King spoke of 'a tough mind and a tender heart'.[16] He called for a balance between reason and compassion in a sermon he delivered on 30 August 1959. He concluded by rejoicing that 'we worship a God who is both tough minded and tender hearted' in that God 'combines in his nature a creative synthesis of love and justice which can lead us through life's dark valley into sun-lit pathways of hope and fulfilment.'

The place and importance of emotion is contentious if not controversial. Consideration of the issues is not helped by the promotion of false dichotomies and binary propositions. For instance, those of liberal or progressive temperaments are sometimes accused of being 'bleeding hearts' whose emotional outpourings are allowed to overwhelm their intellectual instincts and the dictates of reason. For the 'bleeding heart', it is alleged, meaning well is more important than acting sensibly, with short-term reactions prompted by the immediacy of emotion preferred to long-term responses shaped by the needs of considered reflection.

Conversely, those who set aside emotion are sometimes accused of seeking the perfect response when simply settling on a good one is sufficient. Progressives have also argued that taking into account potentially extraneous considerations makes those favouring reason more likely to accept compromise. Fussing over detail can be excused if showing compassion remains an objective; readiness to compromise on matters of principle is a more serious charge. Acting contrary to moral injunctions and ethical precepts and defying the dictates of conscience almost always diminishes individuals and depletes institutions. The need to compromise when devising public policy that is acceptable to both supporters and opponents can cause difficulties and dilemmas for public officials when the policy is prompted by calls for compassion.

False dichotomies and binary propositions can give the impression that a person is either compassionate or heartless – and there is no middle ground. There are, in fact, many possible responses to suffering. There are degrees of compassion and there are often impediments to exercising compassion, such as legislative restraints, and potentially compounding suffering or alleviating one person's suffering at the expense of another's. For public officials, especially those responsible for the management of immigration, there will always be tough choices and difficult decisions that make exercising compromise difficult. This is not surprising as immigration, like many areas of public policy, exist at the intersection of ethics and politics.

The ethics of compromise

Public officials, whether elected or appointed, are involved in politics. Although many definitions of politics are preoccupied with the distribution and application of power, I see politics as a contest of ideas and their implementation. This contest is sometimes reduced to determining the lesser of two evils. Such situations are tragic because the aim is objectionable and the outcome is unpalatable – deciding which option is the least egregious. A moral personal deplores evil irrespective of the amount and regardless of the intention. The defence: 'I did not intend to cause harm and things could have been worse', usually sounds unconvincing or contrived. To avoid such situations, officials are left with no choice but to compromise.

By its nature, a compromise is often a temporary decision; it is not intended to be permanent. Compromise is a creature of circumstance. When circumstances change, the need for compromise no longer exists. A compromise is also often a temporary solution. It is a form of conciliation. Compromise reflects a hope that sentiments or situations will change and principled action again becomes possible. The aim in compromise is to avoid a situation where there are only bad choices. In essence, officials are confronted with the need to pursue the least unpalatable possibility. To compromise is usually to delay. It is sometimes a tactic designed to give time or create space for conviction to carry the day. The tension between principle and practice is not removed but evil might be avoided until the issue is no longer pressing or conflict can be resolved. If the compromise persists, it eventually becomes a form of permission. Connivance appears to observers to be identical with consent and soon becomes a form of consent.

Once an alternative is abandoned, the comprise ends in the worst possible way. There is effectively a surrender to one of the two evils. It prevails by default and without a struggle. The neutrality which was the essence of the compromise is forsaken without the conscience making a moral decision between the competing claims to the least evil. It is not clear whether the compromise results in the lesser or the greater evil. If anything, it is mostly likely to be on the side of *status quo ante*. Compromises are usually made in the direction of inertia. The way things were headed is the likely direction in which they will continue to head when a compromise is involved. A bad practice is allowed to continue although it is bad because the feared alternative will usually be considered worse. The result is a loss of moral integrity and a greater likelihood of justifying what was. Ultimately, compromise may be worse than a direct conflict between the competing evils. And, in any event, some evil has been done that might not be redeemable.

Compromise also places principle against pragmatism. Both have their place. But in the realm of politics, compromise with principle always looks like weakness or selfishness – a refusal to accept criticism or conflict. It is easier to flee than to fight. Sometimes compromise seems to be the only option but this might represent a failure of imagination; an inability to see the issue or the problem with a vision or a vantage point that doesn't lead invariably to moral compromise. Put simply, compromises are often complex and complicated. They are more nuanced than political commentators often recognise. They are rarely easy if the competing evils are sincerely contemplated and conscientiously evaluated.

Rights, wrongs and politics

But are there some principles so important and so compelling that they can never be violated whatever the circumstances? Are there principles considered foundational to social wellbeing that no expediency or exception can be admitted? In essence, are there some principles which, if defied, would be considered either inherently wrong or never justified by the consequences? Or are some things, said to be inherently wrong, only deemed to be so by their consequences? In effect, are some principles unsurpassed in their importance (however defined) so that they have first call on our commitment and conduct?

The issue is whether some principles have either priority or ultimacy? As an example of primacy it may be asked: is it ever right to torture? As an illustration of ultimacy might be to ask: is it ever right to take life? If the answer to either question is 'no', then no other consideration has weight, and no compromise is possible without individuals and societies committing a moral evil. In such instances, mitigation is of no consequence. If a principle has priority or ultimacy it is always, and everywhere, wrong either to ignore it or to balance it with another principle. Are there principles of which it can be said: there are no conceivable circumstances in which their breach even in small measure can be contemplated? In the context of the prevailing moral relativism, are there many things that can be described as absolutely right or absolutely wrong? What kinds of things are 'wrong in themselves' and how many of them are involved in the management of immigration policy?

In reality, there are usually two claims or two potential evils. Aristotle suggested in such circumstances that we chose the higher claim and opt for the least evil. This is not a case of the ends justifying the means. In the case of competing evils, the defining element is the unavoidability of choosing between them. The connection of ends and means, there is no compulsion to act and there is no impediment to choosing a good means. In the case of political choices, the electorate wants the politician to protect the public interest ahead of preserving an electoral advantage. It becomes complex when the public interest is protected in a manner that also preserves electoral advantage. The public interest might be served but *in a manner* that suits the political player.

In matters of compromise, there will usually be a set of empirical judgments and practical analyses that have been considered alongside principles and values that order a society and convey its identity. It is not easy to evaluate principles and practicalities alongside one another. They are not measured with the same tools nor do they sit along a single continuum of analysis. Principles are evaluated with other principles; practicalities are assessed in terms of their social, political, economic and cultural consequences. Practicalities must be assessed in light of uncertainties, possibilities and probabilities. There may even be an element of guesswork if the past is not a reliable guide to the future.

In thinking about principles, negative precepts usually take precedence over positive ones. In sum: principles that prohibit action ('thou shalt not') are favoured over principles that encourage action ('thou shalt'). Warnings against doing something are usually more definite and empathetic. They are clear, concise and are intended to be compelling. The case against stealing is more forceful than the case in favour of honesty. In moral terms, doing some bad is considered much worse than failing to do something good. But individuals will never thrive and society will never advance if the custom is only to restrain vice and never to implore virtue. Telling someone to avoid corruption will not ensure they have integrity. Promoting positive behaviour is more likely to reduce negative behaviour than the issue of warnings or the application of penalties. But when it comes to governments, what are the inducements for them to do the right thing when they are only held to account for doing the wrong thing? Does the electorate reward governments for doing good or only punish when they do wrong? If the latter, governments will strive only to avoid wrong. There is little to be gained electorally from doing imaginative and creative things in pursuit of a good that might end badly.

Much has been written and said about truthfulness in politics. In recent times, the notion of fake news has drawn attention to the premium placed upon truth by politicians and journalists, especially when the latter appear to lack impartiality or practice partisanship of some kind. Much less is said about compassion. As a concept, compassion is more complex because it involves emotions, as I have explained. It is not readily or easily objectified or codified. There are degrees of compassion that are felt more or less deeply by a compassionate individual. What place, then, does a notion like compassion have in political discussion and in political action?

The context of compassion

Most modern political philosophers, ranging from liberals and conservatives to communitarians and postmodernists, have acknowledged that compassion has a place in public life. But when and towards whom? I have already explained that what moves one person to feel compassion might leave another unmoved. Western societies are generally more compassionate towards the young than the elderly; towards those who are like us, not different to us. What makes the sufferings of one group of people more pressing and deserving of compassion than another? Or are the sufferings of one known person to be given priority over the sufferings of an unknown group? The 'CNN factor' – our concern for other peoples is shaped by what attracts the attention of global news networks – can make expression of compassion random, inconsistent and prone to partiality if not favouritism. Selective concern about suffering and pain can make compassion look contrived and capricious. Much can be made of a handful of deaths in a western country while the perishing of a population can be entirely overlooked.

Much of the nightly news features misery and oppression, pain and suffering to which, presumably, the presenter hopes the response will be indignation and compassion. Yet the viewer is unable to do anything about their feelings. They might feel themselves an upright and moral person because they feel concern rather than indifference to the plight of those they see on television. The viewer may not be able to contribute in any tangible way to alleviation of distress. One outcome could be a community of people who feel a stronger sense that they ought to care but the companion emotion might be one of resignation: the causes are too complex and too intractable to be addressed by lone individuals or a group of individuals feeling they care from a distance. Compassion becomes an abstract commodity. It is what people feel. It might shape attitudes but it will not shape actions. This leads to what has been called 'virtue signaling'. Compassion is a mood or a mindset: I am compassionate. It is not a set of visible actions; it may lead to but does not demand a practical response. Compassion has been referred to as an unstable emotion that needs to be translated into action lest it have the effect of dulling genuine conviction. It then becomes either a self-indulgence – I am more caring than my neighbours – or the source of cynicism and the basis of apathy – the world is a bad place and cannot be changed.

The philosopher, Susan Sontag, suggests the issue is the imaginary proximity of suffering people afforded by television and the near inevitability of all but the callous feeling sympathy. She thinks television suggests

> a link between the faraway sufferers—seen close-up on the television screen—and the privileged viewer that is simply untrue, that is yet one more mystification of our real relations to power. So far as we feel sympathy, we feel we are not accomplices to what caused the suffering. Our sympathy proclaims our innocence as well as our impotence. To that extent, it can be (for all our good intentions) an impertinent—if not an inappropriate—response. To set aside the sympathy we extend to others beset by war and murderous politics for a reflection on how our privileges are located on the same map as their suffering, and may—in ways we might prefer not to imagine—be linked to their suffering, as the wealth of some may imply the destitution of others, is a task for which the painful, stirring images supply only an initial spark.[17]

As an illustration, most Australians are disconnected from the experience of geographically displaced people. Televised images of boat people and refugee camps are a cause to think but not necessarily to act.

In the digital age, we are connected with the plight of suffering people previously unknown in far off places. We can read about them, hear their words and see their sufferings via Youtube. No-one is able to say: 'I did not know'. The truth is that, very often, we did not look and we averted out eyes. And because the sufferings of many people compete for compassion, it is better to avoid them all than to ignore one. Thus, the so-called 'CNN factor' may have the effect of de-sensitising television 'viewers' to the need to become 'doers'. As those deserving pity are endless, we have become accustomed to 'compassion fatigue'. Our capacity for compassion is either exhausted or overcome by a sense that the problems are too great and beyond rectification. Seeing too much suffering might dissipate its impact and lead otherwise well-meaning people to regard the deaths of nameless people in unknown places as just another statistic.

There is also the temptation to show compassion for unknown distant persons while being without care for one's nearer neighbours. Or to claim compassion for an idea – that of the asylum seeker – yet disdaining the individual who is fleeing oppression but whose beliefs are extreme and values exclusive. Novelists have noted this phenomenon. The character 'Mrs Jellyby' in *Bleak House* by Charles Dickens was concerned with the wellbeing of a little known African tribe, the Borrioboola-Gha, while remaining indifferent to the needs of her family and friends.[18] In Dostoevsky's occasionally despairing novel, *The Brothers Karamazov*, the story of a certain doctor reveals a similar mindset.

> The more I love humanity in general the less I love man in particular. In my dreams, I often make plans for the service of humanity, and perhaps I might actually face crucifixion if it were suddenly necessary. Yet I am incapable of living in the same room with anyone for two days together. I know from experience. As soon as anyone is near me, his personality disturbs me and restricts my freedom. In twenty-four hours I begin to hate the best of men: one because he's too long over his dinner, another because he has a cold and keeps on blowing his nose. I become hostile to people the moment they come close to me. But it has always happened that the more I hate men individually the more I love humanity.[19]

The same perspective can arise in reverse. Orwin muses: 'nearby sufferings foster compassion in those educated to respond to them; far-off ones provide the insensitive with an alibi for failing to act to relieve those nearby'. The aphorism, charity begins at home, is not foremost an excuse for inactivity but an incitement to respond to the needy people nearby. But if societies with a capacity for benevolence waited until they had addressed and rectified every social problem, there would be no action on problems abroad. As ever, it is a question of priorities.

Hence, the rise of 'conspicuous compassion' which has both positive and negative dimensions. In being marked by the grand statement and the symbolic gesture, it is a general exhortation to care for those in distress and an encouragement to consider those whose needs might not be immediately apparent. In observing the attitudes and actions of the compassionate, we are urged to emulate them – especially if those doing the urging are rich and famous. But compassion is a means, it is not an end in itself. Displays of conspicuous compassion sometimes say more about those asserting compassion and less about those who are purportedly its focus. Charges of tokenism or even insincerity are met with outrage and offence. This is unfair when the empathy is real and the concern is heartfelt. But if neither make any material difference to the bereft and unfortunate, they are little more than self-indulgent expressions of moral superiority. Essentially, it is another form of virtue signalling. A Facebook post is not an *act* of compassion.

In some modes of political debate it is almost more important that someone demonstrates that they care deeply rather than that they have a creative response to alleviating human need. Compassion is not policy objective. It might be the motivation for a policy or be the key consideration in a process but compassion needs a practical means of expression. Simply saying one cares does not change things. Achievements not motivations are what those deserving of compassion will applaud. Displays of emotion in the face of human need, especially by public figures, are usually exercises in attention seeking. It is often about how they want to be seen by others, the reputation they want to generate, the regard in which they want to be held. It is often a projection of a person's better self.

Conspicuous compassion fuels what has been called 'compassion politics' and the 'compassion industry' – policy development and decision-making based on prioritising individual needs over collective wants. These are relatively recent phenomena and reflect a desire to give emotion a more prominent place in public affairs. It has been suggested by conservatives that compassion is the means by which Western political progressives seek to discharge their guilt at not having made the world a better place by virtue of their political activism. In essence, compassion is a form of absolution – the world has not changed but at least an effort has been made to address suffering and alleviate pain. A commitment to exercising compassion is, therefore, a sign of personal conviction that the world ought to change. The existence of this guilt, a sentiment perhaps better termed remorse, is manifest in accepting blame without complicity and responsibility without retribution. If we blame ourselves we can determine the blame that we accept. Many in the West do not like what they, and the society they inhabit, has become.

Embrace of compassion politics is a means of creating distance between one's own identity and the popular image of the affluent, selfish Westerner. It constitutes a simple plea. 'I am not like everyone else: I have a conscience, convictions and commitments. I don't like what the world has become but I am striving to change it.'

This project is also essentially egocentric in focussing on advocates and their activism. The presumption is that it was possible to address suffering and alleviate pain but nothing was done or too little was done too late. This is a more palatable explanation than concluding that the root causes of suffering and pain lie either in the tragedy of the human condition itself or the evil that resides in the human heart. Both conclusions are impervious to the best efforts of the affluent and the privileged. Lasting solutions to intractable problems are not easy to fashion, let alone implement. But concluding that nothing can be done, that there will be always be pain and suffering, is the one outcome some people and groups cannot accept. There are no obvious answers, no adequate process and no easy outcomes.

Discharging this kind of guilt – it might be likened to what bystanders or survivors feel: 'why was I spared when I am no more worthy?' – is even more difficult when compassion is thought to reflect an unequal relationship between the compassionate and those for whom they feel compassionate. The compassionate at least have a choice; they can feel compassionate. Those who are suffering have no choices and no alternative to their suffering. They have to live with unrelieved pain. Pursuing this line of reasoning a little further, compassion itself can be indicted for obscuring and overlooking the root causes of this inequality and for neglecting the systemic factors that demand the application of justice rather than an exercise of compassion.

Compassion and public policy

Advocates for a range of causes intentionally 'play' the compassion card. It resonates. If a public official can't be compassionate, the argument goes, they have probably lost their humanity. Acknowledging compassion's powerful resonances, there have been attempts to redefine or reinvent the word so that it obliges specific action when all it does is compel or propel a response – whatever that might be. As I have suggested, a person can feel compassion but it is one among a range of competing emotions and rival values that need to be considered when settling on a course of action.

For political parties, promotion of compassion is deeply problematic. If a party asserts the need for compassion in one area of public policy it risks being accused of hard-heartedness or inconsistency if it doesn't extend that sentiment to all areas of public policy where people endure suffering and experience pain. The unintended consequences of a party basing its outlook on compassion rather than justice or equity, for instance, means they are unlikely to embrace a policy of 'universal compassion' to obviate the need for anguish when a compassionate response is required. Such a policy commits a party to extending compassion whenever people suffer regardless of the circumstances or the extent and the expense of the most appropriate response. This German philosopher, Arthur Schopenhauer, argued for universal compassion. He believed the foundation of morality was the ability to feel empathy and be moved by the plight of those who were beyond kinship groups.

> Boundless compassion for all living beings is the surest and most certain guarantee of pure moral conduct, and needs no casuistry. Whoever is filled with it will assuredly injure no one, do harm to no one, encroach on no man's rights; he will rather have regard for every one, forgive every one, help every one as far as he can, and all his actions will bear the stamp of justice and loving-kindness. … In former times the English plays used to finish with a petition for the King. The old Indian dramas close with these words: 'May all living beings be delivered from pain.' Tastes differ; but in my opinion there is no more beautiful prayer than this.[20]

While universal compassion might be a noble pursuit for individuals, there is always difficulty in turning any personal prescription into public policy. Much is lost in translation. What looks like a compassionate response to one person might seem callous to another. We think people ought to be charitable but Western societies are increasingly dismissive of charity. The insistence is on the priority of justice and not the provision of charity. I can approach a situation with compassion but how and when is it right to cease showing compassion? Some might say the answer is never, if another person continues to suffer and experience pain. In effect, compassion cannot reasonably be withheld once it has been shown. But how do governments bound by legislation and constrained by procedures show compassion when governmental action is sometimes incapable of nuance or subtlety?

Compassion does not dictate a set of policy prescriptions or procedural responses. And it is also possible that legislators might be motivated by compassion which is lost when their intentions are managed by bureaucrats committed only to compliance. I might feel compassion as a private individual but I might be constrained from acting on that compassion by virtue of my public position. I could feel compassion for my family or friends but I am unable to provide a compassionate response if I am a municipal representative wanting to avoid the charge of nepotism or favouritism, for instance. Policy and practice are always intertwined and the best of both are usually integrated. This is not an argument for overlooking pain or a justification for doing nothing about suffering. It is an appeal for reason and judgment. There are always limits to what government can and should do. Government is not all-powerful nor would citizens of a democracy want it to be. Knowing when and where governments ought to act and where governmental action can give expression to compassion distinguishes irresponsible wishful thinking from responsible political action.

Other than in response to natural disasters, such as earthquakes and tsunamis, and humanitarian catastrophes, such as ethnic cleansing and genocide, calls for a compassionate response from government often fall on deaf ears. There are many situations that invite the exercise of compassion ranging from those suffering from incurable conditions and life-threatening illnesses to the pain endured by domestic and farm animals as a consequence of neglect or cruelty. This compassion might take the form of extended funding for services and facilities, greater or lesser regulation and oversight, the tightening or loosening of restrictions or policies, and creation of programs designed to broaden awareness and increase empathy. But there are always philosophical and practical limits on what government can do and should do. There are circumstances in which non-government organisations and private individuals are better placed to deliver a response to suffering and pain that is prompted by compassion.

Ultimately, compassion is an unsatisfactory basis for public policy based on at least three observations. First, compassion is controversial because it appeals to an individual trait but expects (or assumes) a collective response that relies on consensus that may not exist. Second, compassion is problematic because it can be manipulated and exploited; it is difficult to apply consistently or in equal measures; it can create dependency and undermine self-reliance; and, it is near impossible for governments to be held accountable for its exercise. Love can turn to hate when there is deceit and betrayal. In the same way, compassion can turn into indifference or callousness when it is exploited or abused. Third, compassion has been tainted as a motivation for action by its use as a partisan weapon with one side claiming greater empathy for personal struggles and a stronger commitment to relief of suffering. Compassion is a volatile and unstable commodity in political discourse.

Endnotes

1   See Christopher Janaway (ed.), *Cambridge Companion to Schopenhauer*, Cambridge Univerrsity Press, London, 1999 and also https://philosophynow.org/issues/29/Nietzsche_and_Schopenhauer_On_Compassion

2   Diana Tietjens Meyers, 'Moral Reflection: Beyond Impartial Reason', *Hypatia*, vol. 8, no. 3, Summer, 1993, pp. 21–47.

3   https://www.brookings.edu/articles/compassion-is-good-but-justice-is-better/

4   https://www.clarion-journal.com/clarion_journal_of_spirit/2014/11/the-love-of-god-and-affliction-by-simone-weil-trans-brad-jersak.html

5   Lynn White, 'The Future of Compassion', *Ecumenical Review*, April 1978, p. 99. See https://onlinelibrary.wiley.com/doi/abs/10.1111/j.1758–6623.1978.tb03508.x

6   Charles Birch, *Regaining Compassion for Humanity and Nature*, UNSW Press, Sydney, 1993, pp. 24–25.

7   See the Works of Joseph Butler. He also thought that 'benevolence, considered not as a passion, but as a practical principle of action will strengthen' when someone becomes more acquainted with the 'various miseries of life'.

8   For a consideration of suffering and negative emotions of this kind see https://scholarcommons.scu.edu/cgi/viewcontent.cgi?article=1153&context=psych

9   Clifford Orwin, 'Compassion', p. 325.

10   For an insight into Rousseau's views on compassion, see Jonathan Marks, 'Rousseau's discriminating defense of compassion', *American Political Science Review*, vol. 101, no. 4, November 2007, pp. 727–39.

11   https://www.the-philosophy.com/discourse-inequality-rousseau-summary

12   Alfred Marshall, 'The Present Position of Economics: An Inaugural Lecture Given in the Senate House at Cambridge, 24 February, 1885', Macmillan, London, 1885, 57 pages.

13   Peter R Orszag, 'Warn Hearts and Cool Heads: Promoting growth and Opportunity in a Globalizing Economy', 29 June 2006; Peter Orszag, 'Cool-headed, Warm-hearted Economics', 3 December 2006.

14   Paul Krugman, 'The Conscience of a Liberal', *New York Times*, 21 November 2013.

15   Chris Kenny, *Australian*, 'Coalition needs more hard heads, fewer soft hearts', 4 March 2017.

16   The Martin Luther King, Jr. Papers Project, Draft of Chapter I, 'A Tough Mind and a Tender Heart', July 1962-March 1963.

17   https://wordrustler.wordpress.com/2010/08/03/from-sontags-regarding-the-pain-of-others-3/

18   https://incommunion.org/2006/02/19/mrs-jellyby-and-the-domination-of-causes/

19   For a discussion of this text see https://www.patheos.com/blogs/goodandtruth/2011/08/wisdom-from-father-zosima/

20   A modern exposition of this well known text is offered by Nathan J Robinson at https://www.currentaffairs.org/2017/03/compassion-and-politics

CHAPTER 5

Policy and compassion

Australians take a pragmatic view of government. Unlike Americans who regard the state and its instrumentalities as a necessary evil against whose pretensions and intrusions individual citizens need to be vigilant, Australians generally have a more positive view of civic authority. Governments exist to do things individuals cannot do alone and unaided. Infrastructure development and national defence, for instance, involve careful planning and substantial investment that need to be coordinated to ensure efficiency and effectiveness. This does not to imply that governments are without flaws or failings. Human beings make mistakes – individually and collectively. But the increasing reliance of Australians on the agency of government to serve the common good and promote the public interest is troubling because there is rarely a corresponding discussion about the competence of government and the limits of public administration.

There is an assumption among Australians that governments can and should address pressing issues ranging from preserving peace and increasing prosperity, from securing national borders to preventing drug smuggling, from regulating business to superintending education. There are, in fact, few problems that are not delegated to government by a people seldom concerned with the ever-increasing intrusion of state instrumentalities and public officials into their lives. In areas of government activity that frequently arouse passions and attract controversy, such as immigration and countering religious extremism, institutions and agencies are often expected to display attitudes and to demonstrate aptitudes that are usually the domain of individuals. Few people seem to ask whether government is even capable of the conduct it is criticised for neglecting.

This chapter begins with Australian democracy, works its way towards political processes, and finishes with the place of compassion in one area of public policy – immigration. I want to answer the question: is it reasonable, or even desirable, for democratically elected governments in pluralist societies to devise policies and make decisions that are based on compassion? If the answer is 'no', a few supplementary questions arise: is much of the criticism levelled at the Howard Government, and Philip Ruddock in particular, justified or misplaced? As the responsible minister, was Ruddock deserving of censure given he was the only Immigration official empowered to make personal judgments on applications for refugee protection?

This chapter draws on an observation made in the previous chapter: it is not self-evident that state instrumentalities can be compassionate when compassion draws on emotions and responses found only in individuals. Although the humanitarian component of Australia's immigration program is prompted by concern and propelled by empathy, its management is guided by policies and procedures that were developed within a legal framework that was designed to ensure consistency in approach rather than compassion in action. In answering these questions it could be that some Australians might be wanting governments to be what they cannot be, and to do things they cannot do, because they lack both the capacity and the competence.

Democracy and politics

Australia is a parliamentary democracy based on British customs and conventions that have been modified for local conditions over a number of decades. The procedures and practices guiding and regulating the conduct of the national government have evolved to become, first and foremost, an expression of the public interest. In Canberra, the prime minister, ministers, parliamentary secretaries, members of the Australian Public Service and the Australian Defence Force, are all bound to act in the public interest and, when it touches on Commonwealth affairs, the national interest. Oversight bodies and compliance organisations exist to work against the national interest being subverted by misconduct in public office or abuse of process. But who defines the national interest and how is it determined? Although the public interest is cited in defence of controversial policies and appears throughout many pieces of legislation as an objective test of proper conduct, these two questions have never been adequately answered and continue to be the subject of debate.[1]

Most commentators conclude that the national interest is what the ruling political party determines the national interest to be. This conclusion is no more than an extension of logic. The national government is comprised of the nation's representatives who are bound to act in the national interest which will usually be an amalgam of individual and institutional interests that reflect private wants and public needs. If the national government misunderstands or misconstrues the national interest, the people are entitled to replace their representatives with those who correctly interpret what the public believes serves its interests. Can the public be wrong about its interests and how they are best served? Of course. The public can be misguided and misinformed. Ignorance and fear play an important part in the construction of public opinion.

That being so, governments sometimes want the electorate to remain uninformed about either the origins or outcomes of a policy. Sometimes oppositions mount scare campaigns to instil fears in the public mind about the unintended consequences of a policy. Sometimes the public does not care that short-term, self-serving decisions have long-term and dire consequences. On other occasions the public accepts a level of personal pain in the expectation of sharing a collective gain. Changing the government through the conduct of elections is an imperfect test of whether the national interest has been served but, in contemporary Australia, the voters ultimately decide who will govern the country and what they expect their representatives to do on their behalf. The national interest is, therefore, being constantly negotiated. It is never fixed or immutable. Policies and decisions that are in the national interest one year might be deleterious to the nation's life the next.

To clarify the national interest and to avoid disappointing the electorate, political parties produce policy platforms that they publicise during election campaigns. They contain commitments about what a party will or will not do when in office. Political parties will, for instance, give undertakings to show greater compassion towards people whose sufferings have been neglected or declare a commitment to pursuing unlawful conduct with great vigour. When elected, the victorious party will claim a mandate to implement its policies and expect the opposition parties (and any independents) to 'uphold' or 'respect' the majority will. As the government, the party elected to office acquires the legal authority to pursue its policies, subject to the checks and balances (or the hurdles and hindrances) that are implicit in Australia's system of government. These checks and balances prevent the rise of absolutism and the descent into tyranny but also frustrate the government's entitlement to fulfil the promises and pledges that it made to the voters during an election campaign.

For example, the party that forms government in the House of Representatives usually does not have a majority in the Senate. Australians are not always consistent in their voting habits. In such situations the passage of government legislation involves negotiation which often requires compromise. This negotiation can help and hinder the development of good policy. It is rarely the case of always the one and never the other. The Opposition and minor parties also have an interest in good policy while wanting to accommodate the opinions of those who did not vote for the government. An adversarial political system such as Australia's can actually broaden the base of support for a policy. Amendments to legislation can be good and bad, positive and negative. The need for compromise and concession constrains what would otherwise be unrestrained government and, if their voting habits are any guide, Australians appear to appreciate limits on executive power. No government is ever free of restraint nor does it get everything it wants.

As national governments have very wide responsibilities, oversight of policy and decision-making in the major areas of public administration will be divided among ministers who will devise policy, draft legislation and make decisions within their portfolios that advance the national interest. The minister is responsible to cabinet, the party room and the party member-ship for their performance. They are also answerable to the parliament. The press and, eventually, the people may have something to say as well. In some instances, the minister will personally determine the government's position. This usually occurs when a decision is better made by an individual and not a committee; when a representative makes a determination rather than a matter being settled by consensus.

In Australia we expect that ministerial determinations and decisions uphold natural justice and procedural fairness while reflecting the highest standards of integrity and probity. If the national interest is legally circumscribed, the minister must make decisions mindful of the Constitution, Federal and state law and the nation's obligations as a signatory to international protocols and conventions. The government might find that the action it proposes to take is inconsistent with, or contrary to, laws that previous parliaments have passed. In these situations, the government will need to repeal legislation or draft new bills. It may also need to deal with legislative problems identified by the courts, its parliamentary opponents, academics and activists. The government may need to deal with dissension in its own ranks – among both parliamentarians and the party membership – or counter personal and professional reactions to the policy within the public sector and external service providers. The views of those implementing policy or interpreting legislation are critical to the government's intentions being fulfilled, especially if policies or laws make room for individual discretion. If the government misreads the electorate's mood and does not provide a compelling account of why a program or action is necessary to promote or protect the national interest, it may suffer at the next poll.

Given that so much government activity is tightly regulated and around 80 per cent of the government's annual expenditure on goods and services is fixed, is too much expected of every cohort of parliamentarians when they face an imposing array of forces and factors that resist change and restrain creativity? Does the electorate appreciate the limits within which their representatives work? Even with the best will in the world, do voters realise that the bureaucratic inertia and organisational complexity that characterise Australia's system of government prevents, and sometimes precludes, conscientious legislators from acting in the national interest? In some instances, this inertia and these complexities might compel legislators to countenance actions that may be contrary to their personal convictions and inconsistent with whatever voters think are Australian values.

There is perennial debate about government policy without the necessary realisation that viable options might be few in number if and when the law renders some unavailable, the economy makes others unsustainable and prevailing public opinion makes the rest untenable. In a pluralist, multicultural, liberal democracy with a very large and educated middle class, a competing array of claims and convictions about what constitutes the national interest and how it is best served will be fostered within the community itself. Think tanks and advocacy organisations broaden and, occasionally, deepen the contest of ideas. Because there are a plethora of views, governments hoping to gain the confidence of the people need to confirm their position, show strength, demonstrate resolve, accept opposition and remain committed. The people judge government policies *and* their implementation. Whatever the merits of a policy, weakness and uncertainty will always weigh heavily against a government when it seeks re-election.

Like any democracy, Australia's is far from perfect. It is a work-in-progress. Because the country's democracy is evolving, the people place faith in public institutions and declare confidence in the practices intended to prevent chaos and disorder. Despite religious distinctions and cultural differences, and the persistence of social and economic disadvantage, the Australian people have achieved more together than the vast majority could have achieved alone. Australian society has not disintegrated in the face of disagreements over government policy. Conversations about the authority of the state and the limits of government have not prompted either descent into civil war or the rise of separatist movements. The people have continued to interact with one another in a manner consistent with their view of individual obligations and community responsibilities. Private wealth has been redistributed through taxes, levies and charges to ensure the needs of the poor, disadvantaged and disabled are met and the dignity of the destitute is restored. Australian democracy is, in practical terms, a highly successful experiment in the ordering of human society.

There is, however, widespread discontent with the conduct of political debate and disappointment at the quality of political leadership. Politics is not a public relations exercise but it cannot be conducted in a manner that alienates the people or excludes them from decision-making. Politics is casting a vision of the future and allowing the people to decide if the vision is clear, the common good is served and the national interest is furthered. This is no more challenging than in the management of immigration and the handling of asylum seekers.

Immigration and politics
Until recently the Australian people have been largely content with the way successive governments have conducted the nation's immigration program.

In the 1950s and 1960s, a small number of cases involving the hardships faced by individuals and families occasionally made headlines. But there was general acceptance that welcoming migrants to Australia was very much in the national interest. Migrants contributed to the nation's prosperity and Australian society was enriched by their presence. Without migrants, the Australian economy would have stagnated and Australian culture would have atrophied.

The mood changed with the arrival by boat of the first wave of Vietnamese asylum seekers in November 1977. They came just before a Federal election that the Australia Labor Party (ALP) would lose. The President of the Australian Council of Trade Unions (ACTU) and concurrently the Federal ALP President, Bob Hawke, argued that the Fraser Government should not allow the Vietnamese to remain in Australia because they did not meet the usual immigration entry standards. At a public rally, the man who would become the next prime minister declared that Australia should not take refugees who 'simply landed on our doorstep' because unemployment was too high and the government was being coerced into acting contrary to the national interest. These people were unauthorised and, therefore, unwanted. Hawke was adamant that 'any sovereign country has the right to determine how it will exercise its compassion and how it will increase its population.'[2] The Leader of the Opposition, Gough Whitlam, shared these views and did not dissociate himself from them. Michael MacKellar, the Minister for Immigration, explained that

> no country can afford the impression that any group of people who arrive on its shores will be allowed to enter and remain ... we have to combine humanity and compassion with prudent control of unauthorised entry or be prepared to tear up the *Migration Act* and its basic policies.[3]

From that moment, convincing the electorate that the national interest was being served by an immigration program that included the acceptance of asylum seekers was a pressing challenge.

By 1980, immigration was a serious political issue because its relationship to the national interest was disputed. Several people and parties agitated for an immediate end to immigration because they claimed it was materially inconsistent with the national interest. Their concerns ranged from the possibility of racial tension – that is, the community cannot absorb any new arrivals without social harmony being imperiled – to the likelihood of environmental degradation – the continent cannot sustain a steadily growing population without suffering irreparable damage. Both positions reflected fears about the consequences for Australia's long-term future of persisting with high levels of immigration. These positions tended to coalesce around the political Right and Left. Notably, across the political spectrum there remained concern about the unanswered question of what constituted Australia's optimum population. There has never been political consensus or policy consistency on how many people the economy, the community and the continent can and should support.

The two major parties, the ALP and the Liberal Party of Australia, have traditionally supported a tightly managed immigration program. Both parties have endorsed the national government's entitlement to choose the people it wants as new citizens. When in government, Labor and the Liberals have made discriminating choices about the characteristics of the preferred migrant and the skills the nation requires. The annual migrant intake reflects a number of factors, principally the strength of the economy and the buoyancy of the labour market. Notwithstanding political rhetoric, neither major party has been responsible for consistently high or low annual intakes. The number fell dramatically during the Whitlam years (1972–75) and rose considerably during the latter Howard years (1996–2007). The state of the economy has been the single most important factor influencing immigration and maximising Australia's self-interest. Altruism plays no part in the management of economic migration: Australia wants able and affluent people as new settlers. They bring their money and their skills, both of which have undergirded sustained economic growth.

Managing refugees reflects entirely different concerns although, in time, both economic migrants and asylum seekers become residents and then citizens. The humanitarian program is, by way of contrast, entirely altruistic. That is its point and purpose. There is an expectation, and experience shows it is a reasonable expectation, that refugees will eventually make a positive contribution to the nation although several studies suggest the net cost of refugees may not be as large as estimated over the longer term.[4] Australia accepts people in need of protection from their governments or from their nearer neighbours because they are innocent victims of oppression and cruelty. As a peaceful and prosperous nation with a desire and a capacity to help those in need, Labor and Liberal governments have been willing to fund refugee resettlement because they assume the Australian people have been persuaded that some of the nation's wealth ought to be shared with the world's most vulnerable – being assured that those being resettled are in greatest need. There are Australians who think the nation ought to contribute more of its wealth to alleviating suffering around the world because the nation is so affluent. Conversely, there are Australians who oppose any such expenditure while there are Australian citizens living in poverty and enduring ill-health. These are substantial differences of opinion that are not readily reconciled. Neither view admits any common ground which is why debate over refugee policy becomes acrimonious and governments prefer to avoid it.

The Commonwealth Government also makes arrangements for managing people who attempt to enter Australia without valid travel documents. If those arriving in Australia without a visa apply for asylum, their claim must be assessed under the United Nations Refugee Convention. If the claim is rejected, those arriving without authorisation do not have a legal right to remain. They must be deported unless there are extenuating circumstances. The hazards, torments and dangers associated with their journey to Australia do not contribute in any way to their application for protection. Their story may be sad, tragic even, but their claim for asylum can only be assessed in terms of the Convention and its provisions. The key consideration is the treatment they endured or might have endured had they not fled from their homes. There are many legal considerations involved in assessing applications for protection. An exercise of compassion is not required. Claims are assessed on the basis of facts: principally, the individual's personal circumstances and why they could not remain in their country of origin. Applicants are deemed to be refugees according to the Refugee Convention or they are not. How these people are treated by Immigration officials when they arrive in Australia is, however, an ethical question. As human beings they should be treated humanely. Given the stresses associated with uncertainty, their claims should be dealt with fairly and expeditiously, rather than prejudicially and slowly. These are administrative imperatives which require efficiency not compassion. Treating people decently should not require the exercise of compassion. Recognition of their human dignity is the basis of their entitlement to a civilised response.

While individual asylum seekers are entitled to respect, they are essentially 'processed' as representatives of a larger cohort of people who are collectively facing oppression and persecution. The reason individuals are lost in the system is not difficult to fathom: public administration, including the handling of asylum claims, is conducted on an industrial scale. It is sometimes blunt in its approach and bleak in its outlook. And, from time to time, the processing of individuals might violate whatever are considered contemporary Australian values. Given the number of complex cases processed annually by the Department of Immigration, and they run into the thousands, a comprehensive system is needed to ensure people are also dealt with efficiently and consistently. A stable immigration policy that includes a humanitarian program must be guided by general principles and standard practices. It is utterly impractical for the government to allow immigration policy to be determined by individual cases and particular circumstances. As the Humanitarian Program comes at a substantial cost to the taxpayer (and the precise cost is difficult to determine because expenditures are spread across a range of government programs), there are limits to the number of people Australia can resettle. Given the number of refugees in the world exceeds 20 million (with millions more displaced) and, accepting that Australia cannot possibly absorb so many people, the Government is required to discriminate. There are difficult decisions to be made about those it can and should accept. Some people must and will receive priority, others will not. Compassion has a place in such a calculation. But who is expected to exercise compassion and in what circumstances?

Compassion and conviction

Governments consist of elected and appointed officials. Those who are elected make policy and supervise its implementation. Appointed officials – those employed under the *Public Service Act* – are obliged to fulfil the lawful directions of the government consistent with the legislation that regulates the field of public administration for which they have particular responsibility. Politicians generally adhere to the policy of their party and public servants fulfil the desires of government. Privately, both may disagree with the details of a policy and the manner of its implementation. In the development and administration of policy, there is an expectation that politicians will uphold what are variously described as Australian values, and there will always be some argument about what these are, and that public servants will embody the corporate values of the Australian Public Service (APS) and be 'impartial, committed to service, accountable, respectful and ethical.'[5]

The oaths of office taken by Federal parliamentarians, judges and officials do not mention compassion. There is no creed or charter binding any public official to act with compassion toward anyone and there is nothing formally in place resembling the Catholic Charities' 'Oath of Compassionate Service' modelled on the Hippocratic Oath signed by medical practitioners that was proposed by Robert Lupton in his book, *Toxic Charity*.[6] The nearest thing to a statutory requirement to show compassion is contained in the *Queensland Police Service Administration Regulation 2016* which requires the Police Commissioner to deal with subordinates 'justly, fairly and with compassion.'[7] The Australian Constitution does not mention compassion or impose on any government or any official a duty to act compassionately.[8]

The *Australian Values Statement*, a document that must be signed by everyone seeking Australian citizenship, is a rarity in mentioning compassion.

> Australian society values respect for the freedom and dignity of the individual, freedom of religion, commitment to the rule of law, Parliamentary democracy, equality of men and women and a spirit of egalitarianism that embraces mutual respect, tolerance, fair play and *compassion* for those in need and pursuit of the public good [emphasis added].[9]

Notwithstanding the absence of a requirement for public officials to act compassionately, a number of Federal and state laws include provisions that allow for or encourage the exercise of compassion.

Compassion and immigration

Compassion has had a place in Australian immigration law since 1981 when mention was first made of 'compassionate grounds' as the basis for granting visas. Nearly a decade later the newly established Joint Standing Committee on Migration, with Philip Ruddock as its deputy chair, produced its initial report bearing a title that disclosed the nature of the emerging policy challenge: *Illegal Entrants in Australia: Balancing Control and Compassion*.[10] In addition to outlining procedural and political challenges, the report depicted the handling of unauthorised arrivals in terms of stark choices. The government needed to exercise control over the borders to ensure their integrity was maintained while those who arrived without travel documents were treated with compassion. Compassion could only be extended by half-measures because it needed to be *balanced* by control – which apparently tempered the exercise of compassion. Compassion and control were not usually considered polar opposites nor were they mutually exclusive.

The report suggested that limiting one would make room for the other and that the impulse of one could be reconciled with the intention of the other. It was a curious way to describe an emerging tension in immigration policy and procedure with neither the committee members nor commentators drawing attention to the problems associated with juxtaposing compassion and control. A sceptic might have asked: if the government wants to exercise control, does it lose the capacity to extend genuine compassion? Is the declared intention of being tough on border security incompatible with offering a warm reception to those in need of protection? Surely, an impartial observer might have asked, the committee is communicating mixed if not incompatible messages? It might also be conveying the impression that control denotes strength and resolve whereas compassion invokes weakness and sentimentality.

The committee might have asked whether compassion was the best, or even the right word, to use in attempting to identify the counterbalancing consideration to control. The report assumed consensus on the meaning of the word and its application. This assumption was mistaken with compassion having a more highly contested place in political dialogue where understandings and expectations of elected officials were evolving as compassion was co-opted by political parties as a defining virtue and differentiating commitment. Accounts of compassion had evolved slowly over the preceding few centuries. The emphasis on the need for compassion in inter-personal relations gave way to rapid reinterpretation to encompass an expectation of compassion in social relations. By 1990, compassion had become a political term that could be appropriated by parties of all persuasions in conversations that often overlooked or ignored the complexities of immigration policy. But the absence of agreement on what compassion involved and the responses that it demanded did not prevent compassion from remaining a feature of public policy.

In December 1990, when the Australian Migration Regulations were amended, those who entered the country illegally and were related to an Australian citizen or permanent resident could stay if

> there is any other *compassionate* ground for the grant of an entry permit to the effect that refusal to grant the entry permit would cause extreme hardship or irreparable prejudice to an Australian citizen or Australian permanent resident [emphasis added].[11]

What constituted a compassionate ground? How was compassion to be understood in determining which applications were deserving of compassion and which were not? Could the objectivity of such a determination be described and defended if made subject to an appeal? A judgment that an application is deserving of compassion is not a private adjudication drawing on personal opinions when made by a public official with administrative obligations.

Arthur Glass, a philosopher in law, argues that such a judgement is informed by a number of criteria.[12] He suggests the first source of criteria are linguistic meanings drawn from dictionaries and philosophical works which might convey a sense of the usual meanings or the common uses of compassion. The second source was the intention of the legislation itself – to further the interests of the applicants and their relatives. The third source are departmental guidelines or directions although these might be arbitrary and purely assertion, that is, they offer no help in analysing an application. The fourth source was evolving case law. A fifth and final source were the applications themselves and their handling by public officials.

Glass notes that in determining compassion, 'far less weight has been given to the argument that the illegal entrant provides child care or financial assistance than the claim they provide nursing care or other forms of medical support'. The consideration goes beyond relevance of any situation to an assessment of its gravity. For instance, a case is more deserving of compassion when a person is not only separated from a loved one but when they are made anxious by the return of that loved one to a place where their safety is not assured.

Glass also points to the 'larger cultural inheritance' of literature and art as the source of lessons about compassion which he thinks can applied to administrative decision-making. Unwilling to expect 'a science of deliberation', he thinks there are certain consistent elements in 'the process of discerning the particulars', that is, the ways in which universal sentiments might be applied to specific cases.[13] He finds the notion of a public sense – *sensis communis* – in the work of Immanuel Kant to be a helpful concept. The public sense, a form of collective reason, provides the principles that can be used to make judgments about particular situations that reflect something more than informed consensus. Kant also counsels decision-makers to expand their horizons and embrace the standpoint of others, freeing themselves from private idiosyncrasies. Nevertheless, deliberation will 'always involve subjectivity. After all, the decision is made by a particular person'. Whether they are suitably compassionate to make a reasoned and reasonable judgement, he concedes, 'is to a large extent a matter of chance'.[14] This is a function of life's circumstances. But, he insists, they can be educated to understand better the nature and exercise of compassion – when and where it is appropriate.

Consistent with other Commonwealth legislation dealing with situations not directly covered by regulations or which involve circumstances that might not have been considered or which have been overlooked, the *Migration Regulations 1994* refer to 'compassionate and compelling circumstances' as grounds for the possible issue of a visa in special circumstances. The minister is not required to react or respond with compassion. Although the circumstances are said to be 'compassionate', which is an odd grammatical construction in itself, the implication is that these circumstances might elicit the compassion of an observer – in this case, the minister. There is no description of compassion and no explanation of why it has elevated status as a consideration. The minister is not given any legislative guidance as to what might constitute a compassionate circumstance nor how or why such a circumstance might be sufficient in deciding to grant a visa to an applicant. This vague burden of office is placed entirely on the minister who is left to decide arbitrarily that they were or were not moved to feel and then exercise compassion. If a particular minister is not an empathetic person and is rarely roused to compassion, presumably he or she will not be moved by the circumstances of the application referred to them for deliberation. The wording of this provision is minimal, one might say inadequate, and places both the minister and the applicant in an unfair position.

There were several attempts in the 1980s and 1990s to codify discretionary 'compassionate circumstances' but the insertion of more words and additional phrases reduced the meaning of compassion to little more than sympathy and the exceptional character of these circumstances was lost. The range and character of compassionate circumstances were tested in the courts and produced inconsistent outcomes. This was unsurprising given the nature of compassion. There was also recognition that laws requiring compassion were problematic. It was easier to deal with people whose circumstances had been clarified and whose status had been settled because laws and conventions imposed clear obligations on government. Nonetheless, compassion is still easier to define than it is to appraise when considering some of the questions that arise in the treatment of asylum seekers and the resettlement of refugees.

In terms of the Humanitarian Program and the funds available for its management, how does a national government determine who is the most worthy of protection? Is it a choice between those who are so desperate that they engage a people smuggler and arrive unauthorised or those awaiting resettlement in a refugee camp, often for decades? Or does a hybrid model work more effectively with a quota of planned arrivals and an estimate of unplanned arrivals? Are those who arrive without travel documents more worthy of Australia's protection because they are plainly more desperate given their willingness to embark on a costly and perilous journey? Does this group impose a greater humanitarian obligation on the government? What happens, if and when, the number of unauthorised arrivals increases exponentially and exhausts or perhaps exceeds the annual intake? Moved to compassion by a crisis that appears to be worsening, does the government increase the number of humanitarian places to absorb an enlarged number of arrivals?

The first question is how many asylum seekers can and should Australia accept each year and on what basis is the size of the annual intake settled? A supplementary question would concern itself with the place of compassion in this calculation and whether any limits should be placed on the exercise of compassion. These questions cannot be considered in isolation from the national interest and, because they involve competing ideals and contested ideas, the practice of politics.

Over the past few decades Australia, *per capita*, has been one of the world's largest refugee resettlement countries. Emphasis on the number of refugees that have been resettled expressed as a proportion of the national population has allowed Australia to claim it has taken a 'fair share' of the world's refugees. Although a nation with a larger population may take a greater number, comparisons are invidious especially when the relative economic wealth of different nations is taken into account. Further, the basis for deciding that a certain number of refugees equals a 'fair' share is problematic and unavoidably controversial. The imputation is that showing compassion to refugees is a rationed responsibility and that an international standard of best practice exists. To see compassion in this way is to damage the word's usual and accepted meaning. And, of course, no international standard exists.

Any increase in the number of refugees Australia accepted each year imposes an additional burden on the national budget.[15] Presently, the costs associated with resettlement determines the annual quota that is approved by Cabinet, not the Minister for Immigration. It is an arbitrary figure reflecting the amount the Australian Government is prepared to expend on resettlement through the life of the forward budget estimates. If the existing limits were removed on the basis that compassion should not be constrained, and if Australia's borders were opened to all comers to show solidarity with the suffering, it would be difficult to contain the cost. A number of other practical problems would also need to be addressed. How would the inevitable influx of people be managed in terms of identification checks, health and national security vetting, and the provision of education and housing? Would Australian citizens already on long waiting lists for public housing and elective surgery be made to wait longer to accommodate the needs of recently arrived refugees? What of the need for compassion towards existing residents? Could public support for the Humanitarian Program be maintained if the financial burden on taxpayers were to increase substantially?

Emotion will always play a part in these kinds of deliberations. There is fear among those who are fleeing oppression and fear among those to whom they flee. It is difficult to measure fear against an objective standard or a steady scale. What incites fear in one person may not have the same effect on another, especially if it is fear of the unknown or unknowable. Fear usually distorts moral decision-making. Compassion works in a similar way.

There is more compassion when the causes of another person's suffering and pain pose a real and pressing threat to ourselves. Most Australians do not know what it is like to face political oppression or endure physical intimidation from their government and its agents. Australians do not struggle against systematic persecution nor are they terrified by the spectre of torture. It is difficult for the majority of Australians to enter into the experiences of asylum seekers and to feel compassion for them because the cause of their suffering and pain is alien, if not unknown. Australians may not be moved by personal stories because they do not resonate with their own experiences or they suspect, rightly or wrongly, that these stories are fabricated, at worst, exaggerated, at best, in order to secure resettlement in Australia. Individual Australians are fickle when it comes to showing concern for asylum seekers perhaps because they have equal or more sympathy for native-born Australians enduring acute poverty and material deprivation and think them no less worthy of another chance in life.

It is for these reasons that the Australian public does not participate in managing the Humanitarian Program other than to fund its administration. We usually associate compassion with individuals, but the task of dealing with asylum seekers is entrusted to the government. What, then, are reasonable expectations of government?

Reasonable expectations

Nations are crucial to the conduct of human affairs. They are political, cultural, social and economic achievements. Every person on earth has a nationality. It defines their place in the world. Most nations require and receive the loyalty and allegiance of their citizens who, in turn, have pride in their nation and want to see its potential realised. Governments are expected to defend the national interest against external agents and forces. The citizens of most nations believe the governments they elect are entitled to determine the size and composition of the population. Governments may choose to welcome people from other countries for self-interested reasons. They might decide to accept refugees in a spirit of altruism or from a sense of compassion. Nations are not, however, required to be compassionate. Governments are not expected to be altruistic. That some choose to be compassionate and altruistic reflects values that may not be held by all people or every nation. There is no international law compelling any nation to be concerned about the welfare of any other. Although a number of international conventions oblige certain actions, the absence of an international parliament or a global court with the ability to coerce compliance means these obligations are sometimes resisted or abrogated.

In a democracy like Australia, citizens are entitled to be self-interested and even selfish if they choose. They are not forced to set aside their self-interest other than when its expression has an adverse effect on others and is prohibited by law. People are commended when they resolve to act contrary to their self-interest and decide to help others. But the purpose of government is not to act contrary to the will of the people or in a manner contrary to their self-interest other than when the people themselves indicate their readiness to be altruistic and selfless, which is difficult to determine. When governments decide to be generous to non-citizens, they are expending the taxpayers' money and need to maintain their goodwill in doing so. This goodwill is imperilled when, rightly or wrongly, sections of the electorate are castigated for selfishness or criticised for a lack of selflessness by political elites whose motivation can be characterised (and then dismissed) as little more than intellectual pretension and moral superiority.

Of the qualities sought in a good government, compassion rarely rates a mention among the foremost favourable attributes because it is not obviously consistent with the pursuit of national interest. Compassion has its place in public life but, I will argue, it cannot be the basis for stable public policy. A government without any interest in showing compassion would soon become unpopular. A government whose policies were shaped entirely by compassion would be considered weak and liable to exploitation. Compassion has a role in Australian political dialogue but its place is not obvious. Well, not obvious to me. Describing its place is difficult because there are very different visions in contemporary thinking of what government is and what it exists to do.

No government is without the capacity or the ability to show compassion. Every Australian government has shown compassion through provision of social welfare, the availability of health care based on need rather than the ability to pay, and in preservation of a regressive taxation system. Australia contributes to international humanitarian assistance and disaster relief in addition to its annual foreign aid budget. A lot of money is directed towards people in need with some of these decisions motivated purely by compassion. And yet Australian governments have also been criticised for not showing enough compassion or being tardy in responding to situations that ought to provoke a compassionate response. Those calling for greater compassion often confuse compassion for empathy and sympathy. As a concept compassion is poorly understood and as a conviction it is badly handled. In political debates about the national interest and how it is promoted, compassion is too amorphous to serve as a stable basis for consistent and comprehensive political action. As a conviction, it is too fragile to overcome the force and effect of individual and institutional self-interest. And because it relies on emotion, the exercise of compassion is sometimes undisciplined and may ultimately undermine the development of effective and efficient policy providing durable, sustainable solutions.

Compassion is, I have argued, more than an emotion. It is a sentiment distinguished by its capacity to prompt action. It is neither abstract nor artificial; it is activated when individuals sense suffering and pain. In some settings, we expect to see compassion. If a vulnerable person is being hurt and harmed, we would be appalled if bystanders said and did nothing. Something happens, however, when we make the shift from what we expect of our fellow citizens to what we expect of governments and those they employ. We expect public officials to be dispassionate; to be tempered and cool-headed, not swayed by emotion nor distracted by special pleading. We want consistency and even-handedness in the development of public policy and in the conduct of public administration. But when officials are expected to show compassion, what invariably follows is a corporatised, bureaucratised and depersonalised version of compassion. There is the potential for people needing compassion to receive something other than a compassionate response. Those who are the focus of government 'compassion' often become clients, they become people with rights, if not entitlements, and they are the recipients of professional services and not expressions of heartfelt care. Those who work in government and its agencies may well be genuine but they offer something other than the compassionate response that would flow from a compassionate individual. [It might be termed a 'duty of care' although I am not persuaded that caring is a duty. A burden of responsibility might be a more accurate description.] Where compassion is summonsed, its imperative is changed and its character is altered.

In essence, compassion is disfigured and its expression distorted when it is co-opted for political purposes. In such settings, words are often emptied of their intrinsic meaning. Words are given new inflections that are inconsistent with their conventional use. In political jargon, we now call this 'spin' but it is far from novel practice. Lewis Carroll noted the manipulation of language in his 1865 novel *Alice in Wonderland.*

> 'When I use a word', Humpty Dumpty said, in rather a scornful tone, 'it means just what I choose it to mean—neither more nor less'. 'The question is', said Alice, 'whether you can make words mean so many different things'. 'The question is', said Humpty Dumpty, 'which is to be master—that's all'.

When uttered in political debate, the word compassion has the force of a 'point of order'. It is non-negotiable. It halts proceedings. Because compassion is such a powerful word and is often appropriated for polemical ends, its place in political debate is contested and sometimes controversial.

Refugee advocates such as Ala Sirriyeh argue that a 'notion of compassion based on proximity and solidarity rather than distance and pity is more conducive to the realisation of social justice'.[16] She abhors compassion for asylum seekers being depicted 'within a relationship of power disparity, control and subjugation'. Sirriyeh wants to harvest the emotions that compassion elicits and to mobilise its resonance in everyday conversation while effectively changing the word's common use. Language is, of course, a public possession. Although language evolves, individuals are not entitled to change the meaning of words for their own purposes. The meaning of words can change only through consensus and there is no such consensus in relation to compassion. The previous chapter showed that compassion is commonly concerned with relief of suffering and pain. It is not motivated by a political objective although a political outcome might ultimately be part of a compassionate response.

The problem for Sirriyeh and the likeminded is the existence of people in rich and powerful nations being implored to show some benevolence towards people living in poor and weak countries. This is better termed charity. The problem for Sirriyeh is that she disdains charity and, therefore, dislikes traditional compassion. Her ultimate objective is overcoming global inequality. This is a worthy project but compassion, even with her definition of what it entails, is not the place to start. It will not carry the weight required of a new pivot in international relations. If she wants the existing system of nation-state sovereignty replaced with another way of organising human affairs, a way that has more to do with the redistribution of economic and political power than addressing individual suffering and personal pain, she needs to find a word or a theme other than compassion as the motivation and the means.

The modern world consists of nation-states and a system of international law that is imperfect but necessary in bringing order and stability to the lives of the majority of people. There are losers and victims. That is undeniable and always regrettable. There is disadvantage and inequity in every attempt to regulate human affairs within and across national borders. The current system is the least worst. People born in poor countries with unstable, incompetent and oppressive governments will seek relief from their travail by finding another place to live. Some of these people can and should be assisted to resettle elsewhere. But these efforts to assist will always be located within the kind of unequal relationship that troubles Sirriyeh. The answer is not dismantling the current system of nation-states but addressing the factors that make it impossible for people to remain at home. There is no easy or unproblematic way of addressing, either politically or practically, the disparities that exist between nations. Power and money are never readily surrendered or forgone. Hence, the place and importance of compassion in motivating personal action and moving governments to reconsider their stance on economic matters.

As governments are often slow to act and limited in what they can do, organisations that exist to support and sustain asylum seekers have bypassed public officials and invited private citizens to consider their personal and political attitude to those in need of protection. As compassion is associated with individuals rather than institutions, presenting the plight of the oppressed and inviting compassion is a legitimate way of changing attitudes and prompting action. Private citizens who exercise control over their personal means can be persuaded to move from compassionate reactions to compassionate responses. It is unreasonable for individuals to decline compelling personal action prompted by compassion on the basis that it is always a government activity. This is an abrogation of individual responsibility. In the face of government inactivity, individuals have an even stronger motivation for responding to suffering and pain. These responses can take many forms including political advocacy focussed on increasing the annual humanitarian intake.

The size and cost of Australia's refugee program has rarely been discussed in terms of the public interest although the annual intake and the cost burden are the subject of annual review and maintained at roughly the same level from year to year. Those who point out that Australia takes a very small proportion of the world's asylum seekers imply that the number should be greater. But they do not say why – other than asserting that Australia has the capacity to do so – and they usually do not say how many. The allegation often levelled at resistance to an increase is a lack of compassion. If Australia as a nation *really* felt compassion and was *really* committed to caring, the nation would accept more people and extend a more generous welcome. The inference is that Australia, by which is meant the Commonwealth Government, is reluctantly accepting 12,000–15,000 people each year and is miserly in the assistance it affords. But in the same way that the sincerity and extent of the compassion shown by private citizens cannot be judged in any consistent way, there is no objective guide and no accepted standard against which Australian 'compassion', reflected in the size and cost of the Humanitarian Program, can be reasonably measured or reliably assessed.

Not much is gained from comparing Australia to Canada or New Zealand or the United States because the circumstances of each nation are so different. Rather, the comparisons are more likely to be used by public officials to excuse parsimony than to encourage generosity. There is nothing morally compelling Australia to take more refugees. There is no document dictating how many refugees Australia could and should resettle. The Commonwealth Government settles on an annual figure and advises the UNHCR. The number varies slightly each year. In the last few years there has been a modest rise. At some point, however, there must be acknowledgement that there are limits to the number of refugees Australia can take. There is no point looking to Australia's neighbours for guidance or even an approximation because most do not participate in the UNHCR program. There is no consensus on what the number should be. The two major parties seem to agree it should be between 12,000–15,000 annually. There is certainly no consensus on how the figure ought to be determined other than arbitrarily by the government. This is, and always has been, a political matter.

★★★★

The global movement of people and the plight of minorities forced to flee persecution were two of the most difficult issues confronting the Howard Government when it came to office in March 1996. These were not new challenges. In fact, they existed throughout the period that the previous Labor government held power. In response to a 'wave' of unauthorised boats arriving from Cambodia after November 1989, Prime Minister Bob Hawke told a national television audience on 6 June 1990 that 'we're not going to allow people just to jump that queue by saying we'll jump into a boat, here we are, bugger the people who've been around the world'.[17] The Cambodians would be sent 'back to where they came from'. The new arrivals would be detained while their claims were assessed. This was the first time asylum seekers had been referred to as 'queue jumpers'. The Labor Government's firm stand was intended to deter others from coming.

Labor's policy did not change when Paul Keating replaced Bob Hawke as prime minister in December 1991. In fact, it became more rigorous on 1 September 1994 when the Keating Government instituted a system of mandatory detention for anyone arriving in Australia without valid travel documents under the provisions of the *Migration Reform Act 1992*. Intended as an interim measure, the Immigration Minister, Gerry Hand, told the House of Representatives: 'The Government is determined that a clear signal be sent that migration to Australia may not be achieved by simply arriving in this country and expecting to be allowed into the community'.[18] The legislation removed the existing 273-day limit on detention, removed judicial review and made the person being detained liable for the costs of their detention. Anyone arriving in Australia by boat would be ineligible for a bridging visa. They would be detained until they were released into the community or deported.

The management of the Immigration program had changed substantially. The debate in 1988 that later contributed to John Howard's demise as

Opposition leader was short and sharp. It reflected differences of opinion but did not greatly influence matters of practice. By 1995, immigration had become an issue that resonated with different parts of the electorate but for very different reasons. There was the perennial lament, based largely on economic factors, that the annual intake of migrants was too large and that the program's administration was inefficient. The new lament, based mainly on moral considerations, was concerned with the treatment of asylum seekers and the intentionally harsh processing regime introduced by the Keating Government. These laments were rapidly converging at the beginning of 1996 to make managing immigration more complex than ever before. The international and domestic challenges confronting the Minister for Immigration were escalating and without much progress being made on the place of compassion in the development and delivery of government policy.

Endnotes

1   See Tom Frame (ed.), *Who Defines the Public Interest?*, Connor Court, Brisbane, 2019 for a detailed assessment of the complexities associated with public interest claims.

2   https://insidestory.org.au/queue-jumpers-and-the-perils-of-crossing-sydney-harbour-on-a-manly-ferry/

3   MacKellar's remarks are quoted in https://quadrant.org.au/magazine/2015/03/boat-people-1977-election/

4   For a summary of these studies see https://www.kaldorcentre.unsw.edu.au/publication/cost-australias-asylum-policy

5   https://www.apsc.gov.au/aps-values-1

6   Lupton, Robert, *Toxic Charity: How Churches and Charities Hurt Those They Help*, Harper Collins, New York, 2011.

7   https://www.legislation.qld.gov.au/view/pdf/inforce/2017–07–01/sl-2016–0044

8   https://www.aph.gov.au/About_Parliament/Senate/Powers_practice_n_procedures/Constitution.aspx

9   https://immi.homeaffairs.gov.au/help-support/meeting-our-requirements/australian-values

10 Joint Standing Committee on Migration (JSCM), *Illegal Entrants in Australia: Balancing Control and Compassion*, Parliament of Australia, Canberra, 1990.

11 Australian Migration Regulations 131 A(1)(d)(v)

12   Arthur Glass, 'The compassionate decision-maker', *Law Text Culture*, no. 3, 1997, pp. 162–175.

13   Glass, 'The compassionate decision-maker', pp. 168–69.

14   Glass, 'The compassionate decision-maker', p. 172.

15   A recent report commissioned by Oxfam Australia claims that increasing the size of the Humanitarian Program to 44,000 annually would enhance economic growth, increase private consumption and boost the jobs market. See https://www2.deloitte.com/au/en/pages/economics/articles/economic-social-impact-increasing-australias-humanitarian-intake.html

16   Ala Sirriyeh, *The Politics of Compassion*, p. 166.

17   https://pmtranscripts.pmc.gov.au/release/transcript-8028

18   The speech is quoted in https://www.aph.gov.au/About_Parliament/Parliamentary_Departments/Parliamentary_Library/pubs/BN/2012–2013/Detention

CHAPTER 6

Immigration and ideology   1996–1999

W hen Prime Minister Paul Keating announced that the Australian people would go to the polls on 2 March 1996, few commentators gave his Government much chance of being re-elected. After 13 years of Labor rule, the people appeared to want a change. All polls predicted a comfortable victory for the Coalition led again by John Howard. It seemed after so many humiliations, setbacks and defeats, the man who had dubbed himself 'Lazarus with a triple by-pass' would actually become the nation's leader. Howard told the public he had learned the lessons and overcome the problems which had beset his leadership of the Liberal Party during the 1980s. He was a changed man.

Leaving the past behind

To dissipate any lingering controversy from the launch of 'One Australia' in August 1988, Howard touched briefly on immigration in a series of 'Headland Speeches' articulating the Liberal Party's philosophy and vision ahead of the 1996 election. In addressing 'National Identity' on 13 December 1995 he observed that

> Immigration has played, and will continue to play, a vital nation-building role in Australia's development. The strength of a culturally diverse community, united by an overriding and unifying commitment to Australia, is one of Australia's unique and enduring achievements and one of our great national assets.[1]

The Coalition's immigration policy rested on four pillars. First, the immigration program would not discriminate on the basis of race, religion, gender, nationality or country of origin. Second, noting the potential for immigration issues to inflame public opinion and divide the community, the program needed to enjoy the confidence of the Australian people. Third, the program would serve the national interest and be maintained 'around' existing levels. Fourth, the program would be balanced to include international, environmental, economic and social considerations. Each migrant application would be considered against clear and stringent legal criteria that would not be subject to ministerial discretion. The respective quotas and targets within the program would be strictly administered to ensure the program was viable in all respects. The policy's main critics were not from the Labor Party. Two Right-wing fringe groups, Australians Against Further Immigration and Reclaim Australia: Reduce Immigration, decided to field candidates against both major parties but attracted little media attention or much popular support. They were shunned by the press and ignored by the voters.

The Coalition won a resounding victory, improving its vote in all states. It was an impressive result reflecting the electorate's frustration with the Labor Government and handing the Coalition the second largest majority in the House of Representatives in Australian political history. Paul Keating announced he would resign the leadership of the Labor Party and leave parliament. In Berowra, the re-election of Philip Ruddock was universally expected. He had a substantial margin going into the campaign and most observers expected it would only get bigger. Ruddock increased the Liberal's primary vote in Berowra by 3.38 percent to achieve an overall swing on a two-party preferred basis of 6.2 percent. Ruddock would be included in the first Howard Ministry, the only question being which portfolio. The Departments of Social Security and Immigration both thought Ruddock might become their minister, the former because he had been the shadow minister for the past three years, the latter because of his experience in this area of public administration. No promises had been made prior to the election although it was no secret that John Howard intended to keep most of his shadow ministers in their portfolios. Senator Jim Short fully expected to be appointed the Minister for Immigration after three years of effective service as shadow spokesman. Distributing portfolios was about to become a complicated exercise.

Howard decided that Senator Jocelyn Newman was not his preferred choice as the Minister for Defence although she desperately wanted the portfolio and had been the shadow minister for the previous few years. Her husband Kevin, a former Fraser Government minister and her son, Campbell, a future premier of Queensland, had both been Army officers. Howard decided to appoint the straight-talking former president of the National Farmers Federation, Ian McLachlan, to Defence instead. The new prime minister had wanted to bring McLachlan back onto the front bench for some time after he resigned in March 1995 as shadow environment spokesman over the Hindmarsh Island Bridge controversy. Howard then offered Newman the Social Security portfolio. This was a sufficiently senior post to give her a seat in cabinet. Howard, who pledged to reduce the cabinet to 14 members on winning office, then had to identify a suitable post for Ruddock who had been a member of the shadow cabinet. He also had to balance state representation and the number of senators in his cabinet and ministry.

As the media were reporting that Howard was telephoning his new ministers, Ruddock was attending a community event at the local Pacific Hills Christian School. Journalist Michelle Grattan rang the Ruddock home, expressing surprise that the ministerial hopeful could not be contacted. When Heather Ruddock asked about the latest gossip regarding portfolio allocation, Grattan reported that her husband was to be offered Immigration and Multicultural Affairs. This was Ruddock's personal preference whether it came with a seat in cabinet or not. Soon afterwards he was formally offered the post and accepted without hesitation. Senator Jim Short, a former Treasury officer from Victoria, became Assistant Treasurer to Peter Costello, another Victorian. Short was entitled to feel disappointed. He had been an effective shadow immigration spokesman and there was no hint prior to the election that he would not retain the portfolio in government. In the absence of any explanation, he was left to ponder the possibility that Ruddock had been working against him. This was untrue but it looked to the Victorian members of the newly elected government that their colleagues from New South Wales, the prime minister's home state, had done well. Howard had intentionally appointed more ministers from New South Wales because the Liberals had done much better there electorally. Short accepted the Assistant Treasurer role as a loyal party member but his disappointment remained, later remarking that he had 'derived the greatest personal satisfaction' from his time as shadow Immigration spokesman.

Short could at least console himself with the knowledge that Ruddock had been actively involved in immigration matters for many years and had not worked against him. The other notable aspect of Ruddock's appointment to Immigration was that it did not come with a seat in cabinet. Senator Nick Bolkus had been a member of the Keating Cabinet as had his predecessors, Gerry Hand and Robert Ray. While there was criticism of the incoming government for downgrading the importance of Immigration by locating the portfolio within the outer ministry, Howard was adamant that he would limit the size of cabinet. It was later expanded, however, to include the Attorney General (from 6 October 1997 after a portfolio reshuffle) and the Minister for Immigration (from 21 October 1998 following the 1998 election).

New beginnings

On 11 March 1996, Heather and Philip Ruddock were driven through the gates of Government House in Canberra for the swearing-in of the first Howard Ministry. It was the day before the new minister's 53rd birthday. After 23 years of diligent service, he was given the chance to manage affairs of state in a field of government activity that meant much to him. The only regret was the absence of his parents. Max had died 20 years earlier; his mother had passed away in May 1994.

Although the appointment might, in the eyes of some, have been designed to make John Howard look magnanimous after the divisive immigration debate in August 1988, Ruddock was professionally equipped and personally committed. He had shown interest in immigration and multiculturalism at a time when many of his colleagues were diffident or even hostile. None of his more ambitious colleagues had expressed an interest in the portfolio and most were quietly relieved he accepted. Immigration was not quite a political graveyard but the work consisted of managing conflicts and avoiding controversies. In any event, commentators noted that Ruddock had always been his own man and would stand firm against Howard on matters of principle. He knew more about the portfolio than almost all of his colleagues with the exception of Jim Short and had a clear agenda for reform. This was a helpful attribute given what was about to happen in the Department of Immigration. Community stakeholders, such as ethnic affairs councils, welcomed Ruddock's appointment. They regarded him as a friend and ally.

Shortly after the election, the Howard Government announced that six departmental secretaries would not be reappointed. Having decided to reduce the number of departments, the Government needed two less secretaries but did not comment on why the other four were not reappointed. There was naturally a great deal of speculation about the reasons, most notably in the case of Michael Costello who had served as a Labor political staffer. The Coalition was, not surprisingly, criticised for politicising the public service and engaging in a form of ideological warfare by imposing on departments individuals whose views were more in line with its thinking. The critics failed to notice they were replaced with other serving, or former serving, senior members of the Australian Public Service.

The removal of Chris Conybeare who headed Immigration was harder to understand. He had been the Secretary of the Department of Immigration since the peremptory sacking of his predecessor, Ron Brown, in the ministerial *interregnum* between Robert Ray and Gerry Hand in 1990. Hawke opposed Brown's approach to codifying regulations and ministerial discretion and wanted him gone. Conybeare was now gone too. No public statement was ever issued explaining the reasons. When I asked a number of Coalition ministers including John Howard, Philip Ruddock and Jim Short, and a number of senior public servants including Max Moore-Wilton, Michael L'Estrange, Peter Shergold, Allan Hawke and Bill Farmer for their understanding of why Conybeare was removed, none could bring to mind a compelling reason – or any reason for that matter. The matter remains unexplained, at least publicly. Ruddock was not consulted and played no part in either the removal of Conybeare or the appointment of his successor.

The new head was Helen Williams, the former Secretary of the Department of Tourism. In 1985, she was the first woman to become the secretary of an Australian Commonwealth department and transferred to the Department of Immigration and Multicultural Affairs in March 1996. Williams, who had not previously worked in the portfolio, recognised Ruddock's familiarity with the department and acquaintance with its processes. The two Deputy Secretaries were considered outstanding public servants. Mark Sullivan later headed the Departments of Family and Community Services and then Veterans Affairs' before becoming the chief executive of the ACTEW Corporation. Dennis Richardson later headed ASIO and the departments of Foreign Affairs and Trade, and then Defence, and was also Australian Ambassador to the United States.

The shadow minister was Duncan Kerr, a lawyer from Tasmania, who had been Minister for Justice in the Keating Government. Kerr had no particular experience or expertise relating to either immigration or multiculturalism although he was an authority on legal affairs in Papua New Guinea and had considerable involvement in Indigenous affairs prior to entering the Keating Ministry. He held the post for just over 12 months in an Opposition party room that had been substantially reduced in size after Labor's heavy election loss.

Economic imperatives and impediments

Ruddock believed his initial and most pressing task was different from that facing his predecessors when they entered office: he needed to restore public confidence in immigration procedures which, he contended, were subject to well-documented abuses and highly-publicised rorts. He was also obliged to strengthen the public's willingness to accept the core purposes of the program. He first had to deal with the legacies of the previous administration. The Keating Government's Immigration policy had promoted increased family reunion, greater cultural diversity and wider use of ministerial discretion. Labor's policy lacked clear goals related specifically to the national interest and the promotion of immigration had steadily become more politicised. Katharine Betts, a sociologist specialising in population growth, noted that '70 percent of the public thought the number of migrants coming into the country was too high'. There were also high levels of concern about access to, and use of, welfare benefits among new migrants.[2] The program was bulging because the size and the composition made little sense in terms of advancing the national interest. Public attitudes would only change if government action brought an end to scams and frauds, special pleading and convenient deals. Ruddock was determined to reform policy and practice. He was required to consider a series of complex questions that transcended the day-to-day management of people moving in and out of Australia.

The most fundamental questions concerned population.[3] Opinions held by scholars and politicians varied considerably. The Whitlam Government had heard in 1975 from the National Population Inquiry (the 'Borrie Report') which concluded that a zero population growth strategy was an unrealistic policy option.[4] Professor Wilfred 'Mick' Borrie, a demographer and sociologist, thought the continent could handle of population of 50–60 million. The Hawke Government commissioned the National Population Council to produce a report that proposed an optimal population policy rather than recommending an optimum number. Both had emphasised the importance of population policy to national development and the need for active government consideration. Population growth should not be left unregulated. Neither provided sufficient impetus for a national population policy although a parliamentary committee examining long-term growth strategies chaired by Labor's Barry Jones noted the link between population and ecologically sustainable growth and heard from Jonathan Stone, Professor of Anatomy at Sydney University, who contended Australia's population should be stabilised at 23 million by 2040.[5]

Did Australia want to pursue a population exceeding 40 million people or engineer a steadily declining population? To what extent did (or should) responsible ecology limit Australia's population growth? Was economic growth sufficient to accommodate increasing population and at what rate? Did Australia have the necessary infrastructure, either present or planned, to sustain a continually growing population? What strategies existed to prevent the continued rapid expansion of Sydney and Melbourne?

During his first year as the Minister for Immigration, Ruddock advised his cabinet colleagues against adopting a comprehensive population policy despite the insistence of his predecessor, Senator Jim Short, that immigration could only be managed within an agreement on the ideal or optimum population.[6] He argued there was no evidence the country was approaching its population limit and, given Australia's relatively low fertility rate, it did not need a formal population policy beyond the annual alteration of immigration settings. He argued: 'A formal population policy would reduce the government's flexibility to respond to humanitarian crises, fluctuations in compositions of demand driven components of the migration intake and the needs of an Australian economy for key skills that may be in short supply'. He did, however, recognise the pressing need to deal with overcrowding in the capital cities.

New research nominated the existence of family ties as the primary factor determining an immigrant's choice of settlement location. He told Cabinet:

'I am concerned about the extent to which new arrivals settle in Sydney and Melbourne rather than regional Australia and the lesser populated states and territories ... I am also concerned about the skill shortages that are evident in some regions'. His answer was giving families from regional areas additional rights to sponsor relatives who wanted to settle in Australia. The Department of Finance did not think the proposal was practically workable or economically viable. Another approach was needed.

The Minister might not have been able to dictate where new arrivals lived but he could address the skills shortage by changing the overall emphasis of the immigration program. Ruddock immediately wound back applications for entry into Australia based on family reunion, a policy which extended beyond marriage partners and children to extended family members including aged parents, aunts, uncles, nephews, nieces and other cousins. With almost one quarter of the Australian population born overseas, family reunion was dominating the overall numbers and change was urgently needed. Caps were immediately placed on every family reunion category with some unhappiness in relation to the restricted sponsorship of parents.

Marriage partners, de facto partners and same-sex partners were not able to be capped given their close personal relationship with sponsors. There was evidence, however, that this category of family reunion was the subject of abuse. Integrity measures needed to be introduced. These included requiring the sponsor and the sponsored to meet before applying; applicants for family reunion would be interviewed separately where sponsored parties came from countries deemed as high risk source countries; sponsored parties were prevented from using the Australian legal system to dissolve the relationship in order to sponsor another relationship partner (often a previous partner in the country of origin); sponsored partners were given temporary residency for two years unless the sponsor partner died, children were born or the sponsored party was victim of domestic violence; and, sponsors were restricted to a maximum of two sponsorships with a two year gap between each sponsorship. In one notorious case, an Australian citizen had sponsored nine marriage partners with the Government eventually deciding the man's real intention was rorting the family reunion regulations. Introduction of these integrity measures led to a dramatic reduction of approved partner sponsorships with the number of approvals halved. The clear implication was that a significant loophole had been closed. The task of recalibrating a smaller program in favour of skilled migration then became much easier to implement.

Recalibration and change

On 3 July 1996, the Government announced that the annual immigration intake for 1996–97 would be reduced. Some 8500 places would be cut from family reunion, producing a short-term budget saving. This reduction continued a trend that had started during the term of the previous government when the number of new arrivals was slowly lowered from the peak of 145,000 in 1988–89 to 95,000 in 1995–96. The planning figure for 1996–97 was 83,000. Space was also needed for resettlement of more than 8000 refugees who had fled civil unrest in Kuwait, Iraq, Lebanon, Sri Lanka and China before 1993. Ruddock explained: 'These people have been in Australia for many years. All entered Australia legally and have remained in Australia on humanitarian grounds, approved by the former Government.'[7] This was one of only a handful of occasions that Ruddock successfully advocated for an increase in the Humanitarian Program. Curiously, the Howard Government abolished the Office of Multicultural Affairs and the Bureau of Immigration, Multicultural and Population Research in 1996 at the very moment the latter's outputs would have brought clarity to an emotive public debate that was being steadily overcome with ignorance.

As expected, the Coalition was criticised by ethnic groups, business leaders and academics for previously saying that immigration levels would be maintained were it to win office. Since the 1993 election campaign, the Coalition had linked the annual migrant intake to the prevailing economic conditions. This was a sensible policy and a reasonable position. Unlike the Keating Government, the Howard Government had a clear view of what it wanted to do and why, expressed in terms of the national interest. As the economy was still languishing and sustained growth would not be delivered until 1999, a reduction in the intake could be justified as being close to the average of the previous four years.

The Government publicly attributed high unemployment for the need to reduce the intake but was inevitably condemned for pandering to those calling for cuts to the immigration program on non-economic grounds. Ruddock was accused of lacking compassion by targeting family reunion and over-looking the anguish caused to new arrivals by separation from their loved ones. The government was steadfast; Ruddock was unmoved. The overall aim was reconfiguring the annual intake to reflect the government's vision of the national interest and to reduce costs by excluding all new migrants, other than those in the Humanitarian Program, from access to Austudy and welfare benefits for a period of two years. He would, of course, have preferred no reduction in the 1996–97 intake to avoid criticism that the Coalition remained anti-immigration. The decision to reduce the intake was based purely on economic analysis. The overall size of the Immigration program (around 85,000) was maintained over the next four years to be followed by a series of steep increases after 2000 when the anticipated economic growth materialised.

Contrary to the claims of critics and some of his party room colleagues, Ruddock could show that skilled migration was revenue positive and a key element in nation-building. This was a logical observation given that skilled workers would be expected to fill labour market shortages and pay taxes. Conversely, family reunion was relatively revenue neutral with any skilled entries being counter-balanced by those who were more likely to be welfare dependent or not working. Refugee and humanitarian resettlement, although an important part of the program, was revenue negative. The overall cost of the Immigration program was an important consideration in the development of policy given the incoming government needed to find considerable reductions in expenditure to address a substantial budget deficit – the $8 billion 'black hole' – inherited from Labor in addition to repaying $96 billion of accumulated government debt. Although there would be no 'new' money until the budget had been 'repaired', Ruddock had demonstrated that Immigration was a vitally important economic ministry and not just a social affairs portfolio. Immigration would help to address the problems of an aging workforce and a national skills deficit.

With the annual intake temporarily reduced, recalibrating the 'mix' of migrants became even more time critical. A second complementary measure involved implementing the 'Temporary Business (Long Stay) (Subclass 457) visa' program that had been proposed by a committee established in 1995 by Paul Keating and headed by Neville Roach to inquire into the 'Temporary

Entry of Business People and Highly Skilled Specialists.'[8] The 'Roach Report' sought to smooth administration of 'intra-company transfers', simplifying the process for international corporations bringing senior executives and technical specialists into Australia. This category of visa was designed to fill the shortage of highly skilled workers (generally in larger companies) following deregulation of the finance sector, the start of the resources and construction boom and the continuing information technology revolution. Detailed vetting standards were applied to visa sponsors to ensure the program's integrity. [The use of 457 visas was never intended for a wider range of labour market entrants and, after becoming the target of harsh criticism, was abolished by the Turnbull Government in 2018.][9]

In terms of the Humanitarian Program, the Coalition announced an immediate change. Successful onshore applications for asylum and protection would be counted against the annual refugee quota which was set at 12,000 places. Further, the next of kin of those granted refugee status and resettlement would also be counted in the Humanitarian Program rather than as family unions. The Government's clear preference was to fill the refugee quote from people overseas selected on the basis of need. This created a tension: the Government was required to resettle successful onshore applicants and could not determine either the number or whether those granted refugee status were in most serious need of protection.

The Government contended that under Labor the program had been undermined by too many people trying to subvert or corrupt the system with false claims, forged documents and dubious practices. During Refugee Week in June 1996, Ruddock, spoke about 'those who seek to pass themselves off as refugees, but have other agendas', and the difficulties the department faced with those who gave such people 'legal advice'.[10] The focus would be on assessing evidence of persecution and claims of discrimination. The Coalition claimed a majority of voters wanted an end to unauthorised arrivals by sea to preserve the integrity of the Humanitarian Program. A series of surveys demonstrated public unease over the arrival of people who transited through poor countries where they were safe in order to access richer countries where they could settle; had the means to pay people smugglers to circumvent the usual legal processes for seeking and securing asylum; and, used international conventions and Australian regulations to 'play the system'. The public were not convinced that these were the people in greatest need. While most Australians believed the nation ought to accept refugees and be prepared to invest in their resettlement, they did not appreciate being told they were prejudiced when they had firm views about who should be accepted or mean-spirited when their taxes were used to fund the refugee and humanitarian program. The Opposition would attempt to portray the Coalition's policy as contrary to the Refugee Convention in principle and lacking in humanity in practice. The Government would be criticised for encouraging racism and damaging the nation's international standing.

A population policy in small parts

Having begun the shift in the mix of migrants, an Australia-wide community consultation was undertaken to generate broader acceptance of the Immigration program. These meetings comprised representatives from diverse advocacy groups, interested citizens and those who proposed smaller immigration programs, often for environmental reasons. Ruddock travelled throughout the country addressing community organisations in regional towns and suburban centres accompanied by departmental officers and ministerial staff. To explain the changes in both the size and mix of the program, demographic modelling covered expected population growth over the ensuing half century with the annual intake reduced to around 85,000 and the prevailing birth-rate maintained. The modelling suggested that Australia's population would grow until around 2025 and then experience net decline. As earlier modelling had tracked economic growth and immigration growth and showed them to be causally connected, the community consultations explained that the Australian economy was likely to stagnate without higher immigration. The economic benefits of an immigration program that emphasised skilled entry and demonstrated procedural integrity served to alleviate a good deal of community concern that migrants were taking Australian jobs and exacerbating unemployment or increasing dependency on the social welfare budget. Proving to be effective, Ruddock made these community consultations an annual commitment for the seven and a half years he held the Immigration portfolio. The only statistics that changed were the latest intake numbers and the local birth-rate. These initiatives reflected heartfelt concern for migrants who were targets of discrimination and ill-will from their locally born neighbours.

Ruddock combined a willingness to consider innovations in policy and procedure alongside an unwillingness to bend or break rules and regulations. One of the first submissions considered by the Howard Cabinet concerned dual citizenship. On 9 April 1996, Ruddock told Cabinet that it was 'anachronistic and inconsistent' for a country built on migration to deny its people dual citizenship. He explained:

> The existing restrictive law impacts most heavily on Australian-born adult Australian citizens. These people cannot apply for and acquire another nationality without losing their Australian citizenship (except in certain unusual circumstances). By contrast, it is estimated that there may already be as many as 4 to 5 million dual national Australian citizens. This is because migrants becoming Australians can, subject to the laws of their existing nationality, retain their first nationality, and children with migrant backgrounds often acquire two or occasionally more citizenships.[11]

He did not think that 'those Australians who currently possess dual citizenship are disloyal or lack a commitment to Australia'. That being so, 'it is timely to allow all Australians to acquire another citizenship should they wish ... This would be a positive move which I believe would be well received by most sections of the Australian community'. Cabinet did not agree until 2002. This would not be the first time Ruddock had to bide his time to secure reforms he thought the people would welcome.

He did not need Cabinet approval to introduce the Electronic Travel Authority (ETA). This revolutionary system was designed by a senior departmental officer (and future deputy secretary), Ed Killesteyn. It applied initially to tourist visas and soon included business entry. The ETA saved considerable money and staff time that could be used elsewhere in the department. It enabled people from countries whose citizens did not usually over-stay their visas to apply online for permission to enter Australia as individuals or automatically through airlines, travel agents and Australian border agencies. The new system prompted occasional complaints from 'high risk' countries that were unhappy with the rigor of the process that applied to their citizens. Although Britain was often singled out for the large number of its citizens who were over-stayers, the relative over-stay rate was actually very low. But

the Minister insisted that those who over-stayed their visa had no legal entitlement to remain in Australia and would be removed, irrespective of their
country of origin. The tabloid media soon reported the case of a mature age
English couple who had overstayed their visitor visas for 19 years. They had
settled permanently in Australia and were operating a pet shop in southern
Sydney. Although thoroughly enmeshed in the local community, Ruddock
determined that an over-stayer was an over-stayer and the length of their
over-stay was irrelevant if the Immigration regulations were to be applied
fairly and firmly. The couple was deported and the Minister demonstrated
his resolve.

Tolerance and populism – the Hanson 'phenomena'

Alongside restoring public confidence in the Immigration program, Ruddock
sponsored an initiative to promote racial tolerance throughout the Australian
community. A community awareness campaign was promised in the 1996
election campaign and introduced in August 1998.[12] In launching 'Living in
Harmony', the Minister referred to Australia's innate sense of justice and the
custom of giving others a 'fair go' having helped to create a modern, diverse
and accepting community that esteemed shared values and respected differences. Ruddock claimed that Australia's acceptance of new arrivals was no
accident and was the result of hard work by everyone. If Australia were to
maintain its record as one of the world's most successful multicultural societies,
Australians needed to make clear that there was no place for racism in their
country. Partnership arrangements and community grants accompanied the
program with Harmony Day marked throughout the nation annually on 21
March. Although the White Australia Policy had been abandoned decades
earlier and a quarter of the population were born overseas, it was still possible
for a populist politician to inflame the prejudice that apparently persisted in
parts of the Australian community.

As the Coalition sought to make its mark on immigration policy and
practice, the Government was obliged to deal with complication and controversy that few predicted – the rise of Pauline Hanson. After she gained
pre-selection as the Liberal candidate for the Queensland seat of Oxley,
Hanson was quickly dis-endorsed for her views on Indigenous welfare and
criminality.[13] She ran as an Independent although her name appeared on the
ballot paper as the Liberal candidate. Hanson managed to win the previously

safe Labor seat with a primary vote of 48.61 percent. Her views on immigration were then unknown. Indeed, Howard later wrote: 'she did not strike me as a person who was about to have a major impact on Australian politics'.[14] By way of contrast, the views of Graeme Campbell, the Independent member for Kalgoorlie, were well-known.[15]

Campbell, who previously represented the electorate on behalf of the Labor Party, encouraged voters to support candidates fielded by Australians Against Further Immigration (AAFI) in two by-elections conducted during 1994. The following year he spoke at a national seminar hosted by the Australian League of Rights and at an AAFI meeting where he criticised Labor's immigration policy. He was formally expelled from the ALP in November 1995 and sat for the duration of his parliamentary term as an Independent publishing, with Mark Uhlmann, a manifesto entitled *Australia Betrayed*.[16] Campbell was re-elected in March 1996 securing 35.13 percent of the primary vote. Campbell had been an agitator against immigration for some time but attracted nothing like the attention focussed on Hanson's condemnation of what she considered preferential Indigenous welfare.

In her maiden speech to Parliament delivered on 10 September 1996, Hanson made plain her position on immigration. Her views were unambiguous and she was unapologetic. In a speech that received international media coverage, she stated:

> Immigration and multiculturalism are issues that this government is trying to address, but for far too long ordinary Australians have been kept out of any debate by the major parties. I and most Australians want our immigration policy radically reviewed and that of multiculturalism abolished. I believe we are in danger of being swamped by Asians. Between 1984 and 1995, 40 percent of all migrants coming into this country were of Asian origin. They have their own culture and religion, form ghettos and do not assimilate. Of course, I will be called racist but, if I can invite whom I want into my home, then I should have the right to have a say in who comes into my country. A truly multicultural country can never be strong or united.[17]

Although Hanson was commenting on matters that were clearly within his portfolio, Ruddock's initial response was conveyed by a spokesman: 'She was saying Australia should abolish multi-culturalism: well, Australia is a multi-cultural society and has been for a long time. The Government has made clear its continued support for multi-cultural policies'. John Howard persisted with what one commentator called a 'conspicuous silence'.[18]

The Immigration Minister chose to respond to Hanson's speech in an interview with Laurie Oakes on Channel Nine's *Sunday* program.[19] In typically restrained tone, Ruddock said her comments were unfortunate 'because they reflect a degree of xenophobia that we think is very unhelpful ... We are a very successful country in settling large numbers of people from all over the world'. When asked why the Howard Government had not immediately condemned the speech, Ruddock said: 'We don't wish to particularly build up the comments by Pauline Hanson into a major issue'. And why was the prime minister silent? 'I think that the Prime Minister would expect that comments that ought to be made on this should come from me. And I have made them'. Although the Minister did not think racism was on the rise in Australia 'and in comparison to the problems that exist in other parts of the world they are infinitesimal in Australia', he left open possible changes to the *Racial Hatred Act* which the Keating Government introduced in October 1995. The Coalition was critical of the Act during its time in opposition because it allowed civil penalties against people who incited racial hatred. Nonetheless, the Howard Government was committed to combatting racism through a $5 million education campaign that had been announced in the budget. He also explained that when 20 government parliamentarians congratulated Hanson after her speech it did not mean they endorsed her sentiments. They were simply observing protocol and the usual parliamentary courtesies. The Coalition certainly had no wish to reopen the controversies of 1988.

Hanson's views were reported throughout the Asia-Pacific region. John Howard thought ignoring her was the best response. He did not want to draw further attention to a maiden speech he thought was 'deranged'. Ten days later, Howard told a meeting of the Queensland Liberal Party's state council that since the Coalition's victory in March 1996, Australians had been released from the grip of government sponsored political correctness and were able to 'speak a little more freely and a little more openly about what they feel'.[20] He was not referring to Hanson, whom he still wanted to ignore, but specifically to a cartoon in the *Age* newspaper that had appeared several years earlier concerning native title. Some commentators, the *Australian*'s Paul Kelly foremost among them, nonetheless inferred that he was giving her views some kind of green light. Howard's response to Hanson was widely criticised for its indifference to the offence her views had caused and because it was, in any event, ineffective as her media profile continued to grow. Her strident views alarmed Australia's nearer neighbours and had the potential, according to the Deputy Prime Minister, Tim Fischer, to jeopardise imports and local jobs.

Hanson's most vocal parliamentary critic on the Government benches was not the Minister for Immigration but the newly elected Liberal member for Bradfield and future Leader of the Opposition, Dr Brendan Nelson, who had worked as a medical practitioner in remote Aboriginal communities. On 6 October 1996, Nelson proposed a bipartisan motion condemning Hanson for 'appealing to a primeval instinct'. The prime minister was willing to support Nelson's motion after expressing reservations about a similar motion drafted by Opposition Leader Kim Beazley. A motion opposing racism and affirming a non-discriminatory immigration policy was debated in the House of Representatives on 30 October 1996. The prime minister praised the contribution of 'Asian communities' to the promotion of the liberal values he held dear and restated his rejection of discrimination 'based on ethnic background, nationality, race, colour of skin, religious or political conviction'.[21] The resolution did seem too little, too late. By early November, public protests against 'Hansonism' were escalating, with an estimated 10,000 people marching in Melbourne against the rise of racism, as the Australian League of Rights pledged its support for Hanson and her anti-Asian immigration campaign.[22]

Ruddock was personally appalled by her views and worked with the Department to gather facts and collect statistics that refuted each of Hanson's claims. But she had unleased a wave of anti-immigration sentiment that was not easily placated or readily quelled. The need for an anti-racism campaign long after the demise of the White Australia Policy had taken many parliamentarians by surprise. The complicating factor was the elevation of support for immigration to the status of a virtue. For many commentators, merely questioning the need for overseas immigration and simply criticising the program's composition was a form of xenophobia, if not racism. It seemed like these were taboo subjects because any discussion would elicit unacceptable sentiments and encourage intolerance. It seemed like free speech was being curtailed in an area of government activity deemed 'out of bounds' for community conversation. Hanson seemed to thrive on controversy and was undeterred by vehement reactions to her views. On 13 December she announced plans to establish a new political party to contest the next election. It would be called 'One Nation'.

Ruddock's response to Hanson reflected his temperament. It was not his way to shout or become agitated. He would present the facts and commend the exercise of reason. Migrants were not a drain on public sector finances, they did not adversely affect the current account deficit nor drag down the average weekly income. Migrants did not generally create ethnic ghettoes or broaden the range of people forming an economically stressed underclass. They were aspirational, if not ambitious, grateful for opportunities unavailable in the countries from which they had come. There was no evidence that social cohesion was declining or that the national identity was fragmenting. Nor was there any evidence (because there was no research) into how Australians with no special interest and no particular insight into immigration came to their conclusions about the optimal size of the immigration program and the Humanitarian Program. The Government did not have reliable data on the numbers the public would accept. It looked to outsiders like guess work based on rough perceptions of community attitudes. Lack of evidence did not serve as a brake on the expression of prejudice and ill-will.

There was, however, one element of Coalition policy that appeared to have originated with One Nation. It suggested that refugees should be given temporary rather than permanent protection in the event that circumstances in their country of origin improved to the extent they could return home.[23] Ruddock was vehemently opposed to the idea.

> Can you imagine what temporary entry would mean for them? It would mean that people would never know whether they were able to remain here. There would be uncertainty, particularly in terms of the attention given to learning English, and in addressing the torture and trauma so they are healed from some of the tremendous physical and psychological wounds they have suffered. So, I regard One Nation's

approach as being highly unconscionable in a way that most thinking people would clearly reject.[24]

But 12 months later the Howard Government introduced Temporary Protection Visas (TPVs) for asylum seekers who had arrived without travel documents. The ground had shifted after the UNHCR advised the Australian Government that it could offer temporary protection and was not obliged to offer permanent protection. Although the Minister had made the decision after taking departmental advice, One Nation seemed to have been the source of a substantial policy shift.

'Australian' multiculturalism

The Government's attitude to ethnic affairs – what happened among migrants once they entered Australia – was also different. Observers noted that Howard was less emphatic when it came to defending multiculturalism. In fact, he disliked the term and did not use it in his speeches and when he did, he referred to 'Australian multiculturalism'. Howard's critics repeated Hawke's line of August 1988: if Howard is not a racist, he is definitely an opportunist. Political historian, Judith Brett, thought equating Howard's personal unease with muted racism was mistaken. She believes

> [it] is the result of his views about the role of secondary associations in the lives of individuals and of governments in the lives of nations. Liberalism is wary of supporting particularist institutions that might impose group-based obligations on individuals which constrain their freedom of choice and action. So Howard rejects policies that 'simply ensnare individuals in ethnic communities'.[25]

Brett contends that Howard's target was 'Paul Keating and the association of his prime ministership with controversial interpretations of the future direction of Australian nationalism'. Howard was opposed to 'Labor's view of the state as an agent of cultural change, and multiculturalism as an official ideology imposed from above'.[26]

Howard promoted the existence and importance of an Australian ethos in the face of claims that Australia was a 'federation of cultures'. He was concerned about cultural fragmentation but stressed his conviction that individuals come before the state and that any ideology imposed by elites or, worse, by the state, is an offence against the primacy of the individual and likely to fail. There is a sense in which the supreme authority of the state within the international global order was the corollary of the primacy afforded the individual and his or her flourishing domestically. While the world moves towards various forms of collaborative multi-lateralism, the Australia promoted by the Howard Government stood against the entitlement of non-elected bodies and institutional officials to dictate policy to national governments.

Ruddock broadly shared these views. The Australian Government was responsible to the Australian people for the management of immigration, including the handling of the Humanitarian Program. The Government inherited laws and procedures from the Keating Government which it would retain or reform. International organisations were welcome to comment on Australia's administrative arrangements but they could not dictate the manner in which the Commonwealth pursued its policies and conducted its affairs. This resolve would be tested in relation to the management of refugees. Drawing on two decades of personal experience, Ruddock had very firm views on the best way to assist refugees. His views on dealing with claims for asylum and the dogged commitment he showed to acting consistently within the law and refusing easy avenues for compromise, were destined to make him one of the most respected but also one of the most reviled politicians in Australia's recent history.

Revealing a revised refugee processing regime
When elected in March 1996 the Coalition had no intention of dismantling the mandatory detention system established by the outgoing Keating Government. Ruddock was aware this system was the subject of strong criticism on grounds of both principle and practice. Although a long-standing member of Amnesty International, he accepted the need for those who arrived in Australia without valid travel documents to be detained while their claims for asylum were considered. Throughout his first year as Minister, Ruddock sought counsel and took advice on viable options for handling unauthorised arrivals. In September 1997, he addressed the parliament.

> I do not intend to leave the system flawed. I intend to ensure that the system is run with integrity. I intend to ensure that the former

government's measures to contain abuse of our judicial system are given effect. I want to assure the House that I am intent on ensuring that those people who are genuine are accommodated and at the end of the day there is a safety net; and that safety net is me, as minister.[27]

He believed that, at the review stage, too many people were having their claims accepted that had previously been denied. Further, as asylum seekers were not required to pay for legal proceedings, many appeals were made that had no chance of success. Persistence did not pay any dividend for the applicants other than to extend their time in detention, albeit in Australia. Opportunities of legal redress made the Immigration process more expensive, the period of review protracted and the courts much busier. In October 1997, he approved release of a departmental discussion paper entitled, *Refugee and humanitarian issues: Australia's response.* In a brief introduction, he stressed his 'long standing personal commitment to assisting refugees fleeing persecution' and reminded readers that 'both prior to being minister and as minister, I have visited a number of refugee camps around the world'.[28] He reported that 'the intake of refugees has been maintained at 4,000 per year' within a Humanitarian Program set at 12,000 places, and noted that 'this Government has allocated an additional $20 million over a four-year period ... [for] a range of post-arrival services to resettled refugees, including for victims of torture and trauma'. He explained that the Humanitarian Program needed 'broad community support' based on the integrity of the selection processes.

Although the humanitarian component of the Immigration program was never more than five percent of places, it was Australia handling of claims for asylum that accounted for most media interest. The commentary changed little over the ensuing five years. Refugee advocates did not accept Ruddock's insistence that Australia should only accept refugees when they used official processes. They accused the Minister of perpetuating a system that was contrary to international conventions and which inflicted harm on already damaged people. They contended that Australia should have taken a good many more refugees than it did and asserted that the Coalition exploited community fears of asylum seekers for domestic political advantage.

The most damning criticism was highly personal: Ruddock was chastised for lacking compassion in his approach to refugees. This was a very serious charge to level against a person who had devoted much of his parliamentary service to helping vulnerable people. Ruddock had either faked his concern or descended into hypocrisy. If this were true, he was certainly guilty of staging an elaborate deception. He had been visiting refugees camps throughout his parliamentary career and had been an advocate for refugees when most of the country was indifferent to their plight. Ruddock was aware of the difficult decisions he needed to make in managing the Humanitarian Program from his first day in ministerial office. He knew controversy was not far away. The stage was well set for conflict.

People smuggling

Early in the 1990s people smugglers, known as 'snakeheads', were starting to exploit trafficking opportunities from resettled people who had previously fled Vietnam and been given asylum in China. The last Immigration Minister in the Keating Government, Senator Nick Bolkus, had sponsored legislation to ensure that those who been granted asylum in China could not make similar claims if they arrived unlawfully in Australia by boat. The newly elected Howard Government was left with the task of repatriating these people to China. The situation was further complicated by the commencement of people smuggling to Australia, Canada and the United States. Ruddock also wanted to clarify the continuing status of the 5,500 People's Republic of China nationals who entered or remained in Australia after the 1989 Tiananmen Square massacre. In 1992 Ruddock condemned the Hawke Government for saying that no Chinese student living in Australia at the time of the massacre would be obliged to return to the Peoples' Republic. Given that 40 percent of these students had over-stayed their visas and were illegal immigrants in June 1989, Ruddock remarked:

> these matters should have been dealt with on the basis of individual people and not determined on class grounds ... this severely compromised Australia's immigration program because every other group of people who might want to make claims for refugee status believes that it is entitled to the same sort of concessional arrangement because of that decision.[29]

Ruddock made a number of trips to China to discuss how irregular movements could be resolved in favour of an orderly Chinese visitor program. Four years later, Australia became the first Western country to implement an Approved Destination Status with the Chinese Government creating a major tourist market for Australian operators. The Chinese student visa program was also restored.

In his second year as minister, Ruddock visited Croatia, Bosnia and Serbia to gain a first-hand sense of break-up of the former Yugoslavia and its impact on displaced people. The former Communist dictator, Marshal (Josip Broz) Tito, had encouraged intermarriage between Croats, Serbs and Bosnians as part of his vision for a united Yugoslavia. Such people had effectively become homeless as they were unable to resettle in any one of the newly created independent countries. These couples were accorded priority as candidates for resettlement. Another concern was the displacement of around 200,000 Serbs during the ethnic cleansing of an area of Croatia known as Krajina by the Croatian Army during *Operation Storm* in 1995. The area was the historical borderland and military frontier of the Austro-Hungarian Empire until the nineteenth century. When being driven through the region, Ruddock was shown many burnt out farmhouses devoid of inhabitants.

By then, Serbia had around 600,000 displaced people to manage within its borders. Political tension was building around the leadership of President Slobodan Milosovic and boiled over in the Kosovo War of 1998–99 displacing even more people. The number of displaced Kosovars was so large that the former Yugoslav republic of Macedonia and neighbouring Albania threatened to close their borders. Developed countries established temporary settlement arrangements to relieve the pressure; Australia agreeing to take some 4000 Kosovar refugees under *Operation Safe Haven* at a cost of $100 million – five times the nation's annual contribution to the UNHCR. Temporary accommodation was provided throughout the country including Army Reserve barracks in Singleton, Albury-Wodonga and Brighton (Tasmania).[30] The Kosovars would definitely return home when it was safe for them to do so. The UNHCR suggested that would be in April 2002 although it did nothing to facilitate their return.

A visit to South Africa, Rwanda, Kenya and Egypt in January 1999 gave Ruddock a sense of that continent's dire refugee situation and its scale. South Africa, having signed up to the United Nations Refugee Convention, was rapidly becoming a destination country for a large number of asylum seekers (estimated to be around one million) from elsewhere in Africa. Rwanda was recovering from genocide in 1994 and also accommodating a huge influx of refugees from the Democratic Republic of the Congo which was also gripped by civil strife. A visit to the Kakuma Refugee Camp on 17 January 1999 was a defining personal and professional moment in Ruddock's life.

Kakuma camp: an enduring conviction

Kakuma was a large UNHCR Refugee Camp situated in the semi-arid part of northern Kenya, some two hours by plane from Nairobi.[31] Accompanied by the Kenyan Minister for Home Affairs, Ruddock and his party landed on the camp's dusty dirt airstrip to a huge crowd of welcomers including dancers, singers, musicians, Girl Guides and the local Turkana people. It is something of a tradition in Africa for visitors to be greeted by large groups of people. The warmth of the welcome was overshadowed by the enormity of the Kakuma Refugee Camp. It was then a place of refuge for 80,000 people accommodated in four distinct (and separate) precincts: South Sudanese, Somalis, Ethiopians and Great Lakes peoples. The precincts had been created to avoid internal conflicts within the camp and made visitors feel like they were seeing four countries rather than four camps. The tour included visits to a feeding centre, kindergarten, hospital, disability centre, a refugee home and, finally, a meeting with refugee elders.

In the midst of the heat and the dirt stood a very tall Southern Sudanese woman with an imposing presence, impeccable English and wearing an immaculate cream and black dress. She was an Economics Graduate from the American University in Cairo. She explained with great eloquence that women and children were always the victims of armed conflict. Nations like Australia, she implored the visitors, should bear that in mind when resettling refugees. Her articulate plea and the scale of the refugee situation in Kakuma profoundly affected Ruddock and impressed on him the need to protect Australia's offshore refugee resettlement program which he considered was at potential risk from the growing number of onshore applications. He was to mention this single encounter and this one woman many times in his political life. Her influence on him was profound and enduring.

As critics railed against Australia's asylum seeker policy, the plight of the 80,000 people in Kakuma and the pleading of that articulate South Sudanese woman remained pressing considerations. Ruddock was more determined than ever to ensure that the Australian Government, working with UNHCR, would determine those most in need of Australia's protection. In the latter years of the Howard Government an orderly resettlement of many African refugees was arranged, many coming from the Kakuma Camp. Among them were Southern Sudanese women and children who were victims of bitter internal conflict in a nation that would eventually be divided into two. Burundian refugees from Tanzania as well as other displaced Africans from Liberia and Sierra Leone were also included in Australia's resettlement programs.

As the global movement of people continued to gain momentum and magnitude, Ruddock supported a whole-of-government approach to immigration, especially in handling unauthorised boat arrivals which required the combined efforts of the departments of Immigration, Defence and the Attorney-General. On advice that people smugglers would expand their activities and intelligence suggesting that the number of people who might attempt to enter Australia without authorisation was increasing rapidly, Ruddock was determined to close legislative loopholes and to block devious exploitation of legal processes. He relied on the advice of the highly respected Des Storer, the First Assistant Secretary heading the Department's Parliamentary and Legal Division. The Minister directed that a running list of proposed amendments for parliamentary consideration be maintained to ensure the continuing integrity of the *Migration Act*. Instead of bending rules or simply ignoring them, Ruddock was committed to making running repairs to the Department's systems and procedures through legislation and regulation.

Separating politics and administration

Ruddock tried to avoid the twin evils of politicising the Department and being its captive. When he went perilously close to exceeding his authority, both Helen Williams and her successor as departmental secretary, Bill Farmer, provided timely reminders of what the *Migration Act* and the conventions of ministerial office permitted him to do but also prohibited him from doing. His comprehensive agenda, which foregrounded immigration as a tool of nation-building and relied on comprehensive systems to manage the program, did not prevent him from being guided by departmental officials to whom he was always courteous and polite. They provided advice, often without it being sought, and he asked questions and floated ideas. In Immigration, the

Minister and the Department were of like mind and a harmonious working relationship developed despite the newly elected Howard Government's initially mixed views of the public service and its performance. There were no internal factions and no revolts in Immigration. Some public servants were uneasy about aspects of Coalition policy but they also recognised the entitlement of the elected government to pursue its policies without their being sabotaged by independently minded officials.

Despite the rise of Pauline Hanson, Immigration was not considered a looming election issue in 1997 or early 1998. During its first two years in power the Coalition had reduced the annual migrant intake by nearly 20 percent with the planning figure of 85,000 for 1996–97 being further reduced to 77,000 for 1997–98 in May 1997. Ethnic organisations and advocacy groups were naturally not happy. They were also perplexed by the Minister's explanations for the phased reductions if they were not actually prompted by Hanson's campaign – something he strenuously denied.

In May 1997, Ruddock attributed the reductions to 'continuing unacceptable levels of unemployment' although he had consistently and cogently argued that migrants did not cause unemployment nor damage the jobs market.[32] The previous year he explained that 'with the demand they create for goods and services on arrival, migrants create at least as many jobs as they take. This is particularly the case for business and other skilled migrants'. He was now suggesting there was a 'relationship' but not a 'correlation' between unemployment and immigration. While playing down Cabinet's emphasis on skilled migration ahead of family reunion, he conveyed another mixed message when he mentioned the Victorian Premier, Jeff Kennett, had argued for an increase of 20,000 skilled migration places. It looked to a passive observer that Hanson's views were having an impact.

Immigration was still an election strength for the Coalition. Despite its Minister being accused of undermining long-standing bipartisanship on immigration and promoting prejudice in his handling of asylum seekers, the Coalition's re-election policy was given the confident title, 'Immigration: Building on Integrity and Compassion'. The unifying theme had not changed since 1996. The Government would operate 'a compassionate immigration program managed with integrity, enjoying the community's confidence, and ensuring that through their commitment, new migrants contribute to a stronger Australia'. The program would reflect the national interest, include the continuing mandatory detention of illegal arrivals, the restriction of access to the courts for review of decisions of the Refugee Review Tribunal 'in all but exceptional circumstances' and maintaining the Humanitarian Program at 12,000 places.

The Coalition claimed that it had reshaped the program to make skilled migration, constituting 52 percent, the main focus within two years yielding a substantial benefit to all Australian taxpayers in reduced welfare assistance and greater economic activity, especially in the jobs market. Family reunion still accounted for 45 percent of the intake. The most notable element of the policy was the penultimate two sentences: 'The Coalition will not tolerate blatant queue-jumping. This practice unfairly benefits a minority at the expense of the majority with equal or superior claims to entry'. Notably, Labor continued to support mandatory detention of unauthorised arrivals but claimed its approach was more humane. It was difficult to see the difference.

In any event, the 1998 election was dominated by taxation and not immigration. This was the issue on which both major parties were content to pitch their case to the voters. The Coalition went to the electorate pledging a new system that would include a 10 percent broad based consumption tax, known as the Goods and Services Tax (GST). Pauline Hanson naturally attracted considerable media attention as she contested the seat of Blair as a One Nation candidate after the boundaries of her seat of Oxley were changed in a manner that spilt her supporter base following a redistribution in 1997. One Nation called for zero net migration and claimed the Coalition's policy 'will irreversibly alter the natural and urban environments, economic viability as well as undermining the maintenance and further development of a unique and valuable Australian identity and culture'.[33] Despite her controversial views, immigration barely rated a mention in an election that served as a plebiscite on the proposed consumption tax. After commentators ridiculed Hanson's proposed two percent 'Easytax' on all financial transactions as incoherent and unworkable, she nonetheless attracted 36 percent of the primary vote. It was not enough to win the seat. Distribution of her preferences did, however, help to elect the Liberal candidate.

The Liberal Party expected there to be swings away from the Government even in safe seats after the very substantial swings towards the Coalition in the 1996 poll. The pledge to implement a GST was clearly a vote loser across the country but the extent of the electorate's concern about the new tax was not apparent until election night. The Government's 45 seat majority was cut to 13. Labor won more votes than the Coalition on a two-party preferred basis. Had some of the Labor vote been distributed slightly differently, the Government may have lost office in the biggest one term turn-around in Australian electoral history. In Berowra, Ruddock suffered a 4.24 percent swing against him although he still received 54.36 percent of the primary vote. There was no need to consider preferences. The Labor candidate improved her party's vote with a swing of 5.84 percent. The One Nation candidate polled 6.03 percent of the primary vote. It was a good result for the Coalition in Berowra because it could have been much worse.

As he had been in the portfolio for only 30 months and had become immersed in initiatives and reforms, there was never any suggestion that Ruddock would be moved from Immigration to another portfolio in late 1998. There had been too many Immigration ministers during Labor's years in office. There had been five in the period between March 1983 and March 1990, and seven in all. They had served, on average, for less than two years. The frequent turnover of ministers had been partly blamed for policy confusion and legislative incoherence. Ruddock would stay in Immigration. He was also made 'Minister Assisting the Prime Minister for Reconciliation' drawing on his earlier work in Aboriginal affairs. Ruddock would have oversight of the Government's continuing response to the 1997 report on the relocation of Aboriginal children and fallout from Howard's decision not to accept the report's recommendation of a national apology. His ministerial duties would be further expanded in January 2001 to include Aboriginal and Torres Strait Islander Affairs. His elevation to Cabinet reflected the enlarged importance of immigration in national affairs and the place of immigration in managing a series of regional conflicts from Bougainville to East Timor.

The East Timor challenge

As the twentieth century drew to a close it became impossible for Australia not to play a greater role in the affairs of East Timor. After Indonesia's invasion, occupation and annexation of the former Portuguese colony in 1975, successive Australian governments had been concerned with treatment of the local population, especially those who actively opposed Indonesia's presence.

By 1998, as the quest for Timorese independence gained momentum, the Indonesian Government offered a phased autonomy plan. The Australian Government advocated a new approach: an independence referendum within a decade. Surprising the Howard Cabinet, Indonesia and Portugal announced in May 1999 that a plebiscite would be held. The East Timorese people could choose between the autonomy plan or independence. The vote, to be supervised by the United Nations, was scheduled for August 1999. Within hours of the plebiscite result being announced, violence erupted around the capital, Dili, after an overwhelming majority of eligible voters chose independence. Howard consulted the United Nations Secretary-General, Kofi Annan, and approached the United States President, Bill Clinton, to support an Australia-led international peace-keeping force (INTERFET) to enter East Timor, end violence and restore civil order. The Indonesian Government then announced its withdrawal. INTERFET personnel arrived in Dili on 20 September.

Early in September 1999, East Timor's most prominent resistance leader, Xanana Gusmao, was released from house arrest in Jakarta. He sought refuge in the British embassy for almost two weeks before secretly taking a commercial flight to Darwin where he planned to organise a government-in-exile. Ruddock met Gusmao in Darwin to canvas a number of matters including repatriation of 1400 East Timorese, mostly United Nations workers and their families, who sought refuge from post-plebiscite violence within the United Nations' Dili compound where they had been trapped. RAAF Hercules C-130 transport planes had evacuated this group in September to a tent city in Darwin where they were accommodated for a month before being resettled elsewhere under a second safe haven arrangement.

Ruddock was insistent that provision of safe havens in acute refugee situations was dependent upon orderly refugee resettlement including a temporary resettlement program accompanied by public confidence in its integrity. Vietnamese boat arrivals from the mid 1970s were relatively small in number – 111 in 1976, 868 in 1977, 746 in 1978 and 304 in 1979 – and were quickly addressed through offshore processing, with Australian authorities working closely with international agencies, governments in the region, and resettlement countries. Later boat arrivals, especially from mainland China in the 1990s – 225 in 1991, 220 in 1992, 86 in 1993, 977 in 1994, 242 in 1995 and 661 in 1996, had been carefully managed by government-to-government engagement that identified what were effectively attempts at economic migration assisted by people smugglers. In 1998, the number of recorded boat arrivals was 200. A year later the figure had increased to an unprecedented 3740. The efficacy of this approach was being challenged on many fronts and a new strategy was required of the Minister. The focus on Ruddock's personal values was about to become more intense.

Endnotes

1   https://australianpolitics.com/1995/12/13/national-identity-howard-headland-speech.html

2   Katharine Betts, 'Immigration and public opinion: understanding the shift', *People and Place*, vol. 10, no. 4, pp. 24–37.

3   For an excellent overview of population policy and political decision-making see https://www.aph.gov.au/About_Parliament/Parliamentary_Departments/Parliamentary_Library/pubs/rp/RP9697/97rp17

4   https://www.researchgate.net/publication/271685138_The_Borrie_Report_Issues_of_Population_Policy_in_Australia

5   Report of the House of Representatives Committee for Long Term Strategies, *Australia's Population 'Carrying Capacity': One Nation, Two Ecologies*, Canberra, December 1994.

6   Jim Short, 'Immigration policy: the Liberal contribution', in Ken Aldred, Kevin Andrews and Paul Filing (eds), *The Heart of Liberalism*, Albury Press, Melbourne, 1994, p. 118.

7   The Hon. Philip Ruddock MP, Ministerial Press Release, 13 June 1997.

8   'Business Temporary Entry: Future Directions, Committee of inquiry into the temporary entry of business people and highly skilled specialists' (Roach Report), Parliament of Australia, Canberra, 1994

9   The evolution of the 457 visa category and its longer term consequences are detailed in https://www.industry.gov.au/sites/default/files/2019–06/characteristics-and-performance-of-457-migrant-visa_sponsoring-businesses.pdf

10   Quoted in https://www.eurekastreet.com.au/article/why-i-quit-the-department

11   https://www.smh.com.au/politics/federal/john-howard-s-government-opens-way-to-dual-citizenship-and-foreshadows-a-crisis-20181219-p50n5o.html

12   The first two years of the program are assessed in http://www.multiculturalaustralia.edu.au/doc/immdept_4.pdf

13   The full text of her offending letter to the *Queensland Times* dated 6 January 1996 is reproduced in Helen J Dodd, *Pauline: the Hanson phenomena*, Boolarong Press, Brisbane, 1998, p. 39.

14   John Howard, *Lazarus Rising: a personal and political autobiography*, Harper Collins, Sydney, 2010, p. 256.

15 Graeme Campbell, *Immigration and Consensus: A Discussion Paper*, privately published pamphlet, 1991, 11 pages.

16 See also Graeme Campbell and Mark Uhlmann, *Australia Betrayed*, Foundation Press, Perth, 1995.

17 https://www.smh.com.au/politics/federal/pauline-hansons-1996-maiden-speech-to-parliament-full-transcript-20160915-grgjv3.html

18 See Jeff Archer, 'Hanson, Howard and the Importance of Symbolic Politics', in Bligh Grant (ed.), *Paul Hanson: One Nation and Australian Politics*, University of New England Press, Armidale, 1997, chapter 5.

19 Ruddock's interview with Oakes was widely reported. The fullest account was offered by Tony Wright, 'Ruddock Takes Cool Line on Hanson', *Sydney Morning Herald*, 16 September 1996

20 https://pmtranscripts.pmc.gov.au/release/transcript-10114

21 https://parlinfo.aph.gov.au/parlInfo/search/display/display.w3p;db=CHAMBER;id =chamber%2Fhansardr%2F1996-10–30%2F0072;query=Id%3A%22chamber%2Fha nsardr%2F1996-10–30%2F0071%22

22 https://marxistleftreview.org/articles/how-we-stopped-pauline-hanson-last-time/

23 Pauline Hanson's One Nation, 'Immigration, Population and Social Cohesion Policy', Brisbane, 1998, p. 14.

24 https://www.researchgate.net/publication/242211533_temporary_protection_of_ refugees_australian_policy_and_international_comparisons

25 Judith Brett, *Australian Liberals and the Moral Middle Class*, Cambridge University Press, Melbourne, 2003, p. 195

26 Brett, *Australian Liberals and the Moral Middle Class*, p. 196.

27 Philip Ruddock, CPD (Reps), 24 September 1997, p. 8304.

28 https://parlinfo.aph.gov.au/parlInfo/search/display/display.w3p;query=Id%3A%22 media%2Fpressrel%2FLRW46%22;src1=sm1

29 https://parlinfo.aph.gov.au/parlInfo/search/display/display.w3p;db=CHAMBER;id =chamber%2Fhansardr%2F1992-05–05%2F0019;query=Id%3A%22chamber%2Fha nsardr%2F1992-05–05%2F0031%22

30 https://www1.health.gov.au/internet/main/publishing.nsf/ Content/cda-pubs-cdi-2000-cdi2402-cdi2402a.htm and for a local experience see https://www.singletonargus.com.au/story/1681338/ operation-safe-haven-our-refugee-experience/

31 https://www.unhcr.org/ke/kakuma-refugee-camp and for a recent commentary see https://www3.bostonglobe.com/news/bigpicture/2018/07/07/kakuma-refugee-camp/WA4vybjw2gpDMns0bn5VpN/story.html?arc404=true. Ruddock also mentioned this visit in his 2016 valedictory speech in Federal parliament.

32 *Australian Financial Review*, 22 May 1997, p. 4. See also: https://www.pc.gov.au/ about/governance/annual-reports/annualreport9798/annualreport9798.pdf and Alison Preston, *The Structure and Determinants of Wage Relativity: Evidence from Australia*, Routledge, London, 2001.

33 The full text of One Nation's Immigration policy statement is accessible at: athttps://australianpolitics.com/1998/07/01/one-nation-immigration-policy.html

CHAPTER 7

Border protection   1999–2001

Beyond the electoral division of Berowra in Sydney few Australians knew much about Philip Ruddock before he became the Minister for Immigration in March 1996. He had briefly attracted national attention in 1988 by crossing the floor and voting against his own party on immigration policy. For the greatest part, however, he quietly and diligently went about his parliamentary duties. He was neither flamboyant nor controversial. Journalists considered him a 'grey man', yet another 'suburban solicitor', who worked assiduously to maintain the Liberals' firm grasp on a safe seat.

By 1999, Ruddock was one of the most talked about and readily recognisable faces in Australian politics. He never hid from journalists and gave frequent press conferences at which reporters were able to ask their questions and then question his answers. Ruddock spoke clearly although not always concisely. He provided highly detailed information to journalists and avoided the temptation to offer mere 'sound bites'. Some of Ruddock's colleagues thought he interpreted policies and explained decisions when he might have 'promoted' the former and 'sold' the latter. Although he was also responsible for Indigenous and ethnic affairs, most media attention focussed on just one part of his steadily growing portfolio: the Humanitarian Program within the Department of Immigration. He was routinely asked about specific cases involving family tragedy and personal hardship, and how the government was intending to respond. The immediacy of human suffering often overshadowed the fraught interactions that existed between global agencies, the Commonwealth government and the Australian legal system. Much public reporting certainly overlooked the international conventions which obliged certain actions on the part of the Australian Government, including actions with unintended consequences, that the Minister for Immigration argued were contrary to Australia's national interest and which required a tailored local response.

Conventional conflicts

Australia's humanitarian program was shaped principally by the United Nations (UN) Convention Relating to the Status of Refugees.[1] The Convention was drafted in the shadow of the descending 'Iron Curtain' of Soviet-backed political oppression that separated Eastern Europe from the rest of the world after 1945. The Convention defined a refugee as someone outside their own country who is unable or unwilling to return home because of a 'well-founded fear of persecution' on grounds that include race, religion and political affiliation. Those fleeing persecution can seek protection by applying for refugee recognition at a United Nations' High Commission for Refugees (UNHCR) office or camp while they wait for resettlement selection. Fearing harm at home is not, in itself, sufficient for a person to be deemed a refugee. A person who applies for refugee status is an asylum seeker. On the fiftieth anniversary of the Convention, there were 12 million refugees and some 50 million people displaced from their homes with many living in formally recognised camps.[2] Less than 0.1 percent of UNHCR-recognised refugees are settled in developed countries each year. This meant that many people seeking protection tried to gain entry to a Western country by their own means. The majority had little choice but to pay a 'people smuggler' and take their chances in travelling to a safer place. Under the Refugee Convention it is not illegal to seek protection without either travel documents or formal authorisation. Further, signatories to the Convention must protect refugees and cannot return them to their homes if the threat of persecution remains.

As a signatory to the Convention, Australia is a major contributor to the UNHCR's work. In 2001, it was one of only ten UN member states to offer offshore refugee resettlement. Notably, Australia had not been the preferred destination of refugees until the 1970s. An island at the bottom of the world surrounded by a large body of water was among the least likely and least accessible places for people fleeing persecution. When civil wars in Vietnam and Cambodia produced political outcomes, however unstable, those who feared repression looked to Australia as a staunchly anti-communist state for protection. Later, as a society that protested against military dictatorships and sectarian strife, a society that was both democratic and secular was an

attractive destination for those seeking political liberty and religious tolera-
tion. As a stalwart of the (British) Commonwealth of Nations, Australia had
a certain appeal and presumably some sympathy for those who fortunes took
a decided turn for the worst when the last vestiges of colonialism ended in
Rhodesia and South Africa, Sri Lanka and Hong Kong.

But Australia was less interested in dealing with global or regional instability
and the casualties of power politics; the immigration program was designed
principally to build the Australian economy and undergird the prosperity
of the people and nation. There was recognition that Australia had specific
responsibilities under international law but, for the greatest part, they could
be discharged in a manner that did not disrupt domestic priorities. Where
Australia differed from other nations was its vigorous assertion of the absolute
right of sovereign states to determine the movement of people across its
borders. This assertion has been interpreted in various ways by commentators
with distinct agendas and scholars from different disciplines. But international
humanitarian law discounts national sovereignty and requires nations like
Australia to admit refugees. Hence, the desire to find other mechanisms and
to promote an alternative discourse that allowed Australia to regain and then
retain sole authority for the movement of people across its borders.

The policy of the Keating and Howard governments was clear and consistent: to deter unauthorised entry of people seeking asylum through a range
of legal and practical measures that made it difficult to reach Australia,
principally by boat. Offshore islands were excised from the migration zone
to prevent people from arriving at remote territories, like Christmas Island,
and then applying for an Australian visa, preventing boats carrying asylum
seekers from reaching the offshore islands or the mainland, and detaining
unauthorised arrivals in secure facilities until their claims were assessed. In
the decade after the Coalition came to power in 1996, Australia resettled an
average of 12,000 people under refugee and humanitarian schemes each year.
As mentioned in the previous chapter, the Howard Government decided
early in 1999 to accept 4000 Kosovars who were targeted for violence in the
civil wars that devastated the Balkan states following the implosion of the
Yugoslav Federation between 1990 and 1992. When civil strife ended and the
threat of harm receded, the Kosovars returned home.[3] The universal goodwill
extended to these people was withheld from those who arrived off Australia

by boat in the second half of 1999. A rapid rise in the number of such arrivals caused concern within government departments and increasingly within the country, with fears that an 'invasion' was underway.

The Howard Government believed Australia was becoming too attractive a destination for asylum seekers on two grounds. First, applications for asylum were more likely to be successful if the applicant reached Australia and gained access to the Australian legal system which would, at the very least, delay their removal from Australia. Second, people found to be refugees were assured of welfare, work rights and eventually citizenship. Political oppression *pushed* vulnerable people out of their home countries; overly generous support for those accepted for resettlement was *pulling* people towards Australia. Between June 1999 and July 2001, 8316 asylum seekers landed on Australia's shores. An average of 39 boats were reaching Australia each year. This was not a large number when compared to the human tide that was moving across eastern Africa and Europe but it was substantial enough for Ruddock to warn that 'whole [Middle Eastern] villages are packing up ... If it was a national emergency several weeks ago, it's gone up something like 10 points'.[4] In support of the claim that onshore applications were dealt with more generously, he 'observed' that 84 percent of asylum seekers who came by boat had their claims accepted but only 14 percent of those from the same countries were found to be refugees when processed by the UNHCR office in Indonesia. Of the 5936 people placed in detention between 1 November 1999 and 31 May 2001, 85 percent were found to be refugees and granted temporary protection visas (rather than citizenship and permanent residence). [Notably, 640 places were not allocated in the 1998–99 program and more than 2040 places were not allocated in the 1999–2000 program.] Hence, the Government's preference for offshore processing.

There were other changes to weaken the pull factors. In October 1999, Ruddock introduced legislation which prevented those on Temporary Protection Visas (TPVs) from sponsoring spouses and children while those who left Australia to visit relatives were now unable to re-enter the country. Additionally, those on protection visas were not granted the usual social security and resettlement assistance. There were other changes to the law that made it even more difficult for those who were not part of the formal UNHCR resettlement program to enter Australia. These changes seemed prudent to some commentators but punitive to others. Was the aim to reduce rorts or to discourage new arrivals? The answer was both.

The Howard Government's policy

Ruddock's visit to Africa early in 1999 and his previous visits to other refugee centres set the tone for the Howard Government's policy on what became known as 'border protection'. Boat people, organised by smugglers, continued to arrive from Indonesia on Australian territories like Ashmore Reef, as well as Christmas Island and, to a lesser extent, Cocos Island. As the number of boat arrivals increased so did the management challenges. Many of those seeking to enter Australia had destroyed their travel documents making the process of identity and security checks more cumbersome, especially in relation to the latter as countries of origin needed to supply information. Immigration officers became aware that interview tapes were being sold on the black market in Islamabad, Pakistan. Under Australia's *Freedom of Information* legislation, departmental officials were required to provide a record of interview to applicants for protection. When interview questions were changed, some interviewees complained that these were not the same questions that had been asked on the tapes. Immigration officers were also being requested by name, presumably because they were deemed to be more amendable to granting refugee claims. Some applicants came with considerable amounts of cash, mainly American currency, while others asked for particular kinds of toiletries, such as brand name shampoos, to be provided in the detention centres.

These were signs of a well organised trafficking program. There appeared to be a good deal of information sharing among applicants and money was changing hands, potentially provided by family members already in Australia. Ruddock continued to think of those wallowing in overcrowded refugee camps like Kakuma. He wanted the department to prioritise them as part of a finite refugee and humanitarian resettlement program that would not be expanded to include an infinite number of unauthorised arrivals. The Minister was unable to forget the South Sudanese woman dressed in cream and black. Her pleas would not be ignored by his department. The question: 'who is in greatest *need* of Australia's protection' was becoming a complex and vexed question. When overcrowded, poorly provisioned boats operated by people smugglers sank at sea between Indonesia and Australia, and the number of drownings increased, relatives of the victims and community leaders accused the Howard Government of having 'blood on its hands'. This was the beginning of another new chapter in Australia's immigration policy.

By the late 1990s, people smuggling operations from Iran, Iraq and Afghanistan started to focus on accessing Australia through Malaysia and Indonesia, both of which had visa waivers for travellers from some Islamic countries. These groups came from source countries where a well-founded fear of persecution could be readily established while some were committed to family reunion and economic migration. Ruddock's immediate concern was the potential for people smugglers to increase dramatically the number of unauthorised boat arrivals who would eventually consume the entire resettlement program. In 1999 alone, 2356 (63.4 percent) unauthorised boat arrivals were given TPVs. Arrangements for mandatory detention were also failing because of the inability to accommodate the increasing number of people in existing centres on the mainland at Port Hedland and offshore on Christmas and Cocos Islands. New facilities were urgently needed. Disused accommodation at Curtin Air Force Base was re-opened.

At Woomera there was a former Australian Defence Force (ADF) training facility that could be renovated to host new boat arrivals. While the accommodation was basic, medical and other facilities could be fast tracked with the erection of demountable buildings. Steps were later taken to open negotiations with the Port Augusta City Council for construction of a purpose-built facility which would become the Baxter detention centre. Family groups were a special focus as the Howard Government looked for ways of removing women and children from detention facilities and relocating them in the community. Alternative family housing was relatively easy to provide where the Commonwealth owned houses, such as in Woomera township. In other places, community settlement required negotiations with local government authorities, such as in Port Augusta, and took longer to finalise. With asylum seekers more mobile and increasingly aware of international conventions, the world's refugee challenge was rapidly changing and Australia needed to be proactive in pursuing its own national response. Those who believed this response was inefficient and lacking in compassion were growing in number and in the strength of their convictions.

Criticisms and condemnations

Immigration policy had never really functioned either as a vote winner or vote loser for the major parties. The Howard Government's immigration policy, however, generated considerable and continuing public controversy that could have fuelled a protracted 'race debate' in which Pauline Hanson would have been the only winner. By 1999, Philip Ruddock was the political face of the Government's policies. Although he enjoyed the Cabinet's complete confidence, Ruddock was usually alone in publicly defending the Government's policy and the practices it mandated. He never hid from the controversy associated with these policies and practices, appearing on television programs, such as the ABC's *Q & A*, where he was always assured of a hostile reception. In making announcements that he knew would attract strident criticism and provoke moral condemnation, he accepted that opposition and unpopularity were inevitable. Notably, Ruddock did not revel in notoriety nor did he ever seek sympathy. When community criticism frequently bordered on personal abuse, he invariably remained calm and courteous. At times, it looked like the weight of enlightened opinion from four separate quarters was arrayed against him.

The first category consisted of the Coalition's Federal parliamentary opponents: the Labor Party and, initially, the Australian Democrats who shared the balance of power in the Senate from 1999 to 2004. [The Democrats would be replaced after 2007 by the Australian Greens as the 'third party' most likely to secure the balance of power.] They were committed as opposition parties to identifying bad policy and highlighting poor administration in the cause of better government and improving their fortunes at the next election. The Labor Party had, of course, provided the foundations upon which the Coalition's immigration policy was built. There were influential members of the caucus and shadow ministry always opposed to mandatory detention and offshore processing who pressed for their abolition after the defeat of the Keating Government. Labor was politically vulnerable in this area of policy and found difficulty speaking with a consistent voice. Divisions within the Labor caucus over these issues became acute in 2001.

The second category of critics were a small cohort of Liberal party backbenchers opposed on humanitarian grounds to their own party's policy. Petro Georgiou and Russell Broadbent from Victoria, Judy Moylan and Mal

Washer from Western Australia, and Bruce Baird from New South Wales would have been included among the Liberal 'wets' in the 1980s. Referred to as the 'small "l" liberals' or the 'Moderates', they thought the Coalition's immigration policy was regressive and callous, lacked compassion and was contrary to genuine liberal sentiments. Their aim was to 'soften' the detention regime while offering more generous support to asylum seekers. They were considered disloyal by some in the Liberal Party.

The third category were human rights lawyers, such as Julian Burnside in Victoria and George Newhouse in New South Wales, who thought the Government's treatment of asylum seekers was essentially unlawful and entirely unhelpful to the promotion and protection of human rights within Australia and internationally. They sought to frustrate the Coalition's attempts to exclude the courts from the administration of the Immigration program on the grounds that it placed government decision-making beyond judicial review – something they felt was contrary to the rule of law and procedural fairness.

The fourth category were refugee advocates, ranging from socialist radicals like Ian Rintoul, community activists such as Trish Highfield and church workers led by Father Frank Brennan, who believed the Government's treatment of asylum seekers was wrong in principle and possibly criminal in conduct. This category also consisted of individuals and organisations claiming to speak for those silenced and rendered anonymous by Coalition policies. Some went beyond public and political advocacy with activities that included participating in demonstrations and protests, providing material support to refugees and their families, and funding legal action against the Department of Immigration.

The nation's legal officers might have been considered a fifth category of opponent. Although they were only able to deal with cases brought to them for decision or review and were lacking the power and the prerogative to be proactive, the nation's judges and tribunal members asserted a place for themselves in the oversight of Australia's immigration policy. Legal officers frequently made decisions and determinations that curtailed the exercise of executive power or asserted the authority of the courts to intervene in the administration of policy. On several notable occasions, the courts were critical of the Minister for Immigration and, contrary to custom and protocol, the Minister for Immigration was critical of individual judges and the court system generally. In August 2000, the Family Court of Australia found in *B and B v the Minister for Immigration and Multicultural Affairs* that the continuing detention of children violated Australia's international human rights obligations.[5] In response, Ruddock was critical of what he considered yet another instance of the courts acting 'in excess of their power'. He argued that 'arrangements that the parliament intended should operate [were] being unwound by judicial actions'.[6] On another occasion he chastised the Federal Court's intervention in an immigration matter as an instance of 'unelected and unresponsible officials' thwarting the will of the people's representatives.[7]

Their function, he contended, was interpreting and applying the law and not resisting and opposing government policy and decision-making. Ruddock argued the nation's legal officers were occasionally given to bouts of judicial activism which had the effect of frustrating the democratic entitlement of the responsible government to administer the nation's affairs.[8] The issue often placed before the courts was discerning the limits of ministerial authority. For the Minister for Immigration, the issue was limiting legal restraint on the use of mandatory detention and onshore processing. While it may have looked like Ruddock was personally committed to making his office the final arbiter on every matter related to the Humanitarian Program, he was temperamentally opposed to the arbitrary application of executive power. He believed, however, that the court system was being manipulated, if not abused, by those who sought to impede the Government's policies which, he reminded critics, were backed by a democratic mandate. Because the courts could not act on their own initiative and were entitled and expected to deliberate on matters referred to them, they cannot be considered a fifth category of 'opponent' notwithstanding their criticisms.

The Government's opponents were united in their criticism of Ruddock for implementing harsher policies than those pursued by other Western nations and for finding, as they saw it, more draconian ways to deter the travel of asylum seekers to Australia. The unintended outcome of Ruddock's approach – or the entirely intended outcome if his staunchest opponents were correct – was the spread of fear based entirely on misinformation. These fears were exacerbated by the Government's apparent indifference to bigotry. Instead of focussing on the comparatively small number of people who undertook the perilous journey by boat, advocates thought Ruddock should have concentrated on the much larger number of people who came through the nation's airports with false identities and criminal intent.

Ruddock's actions were indicative, it was asserted, of a wider malaise with the Coalition. The entire Howard Government was chastised for politicising the Humanitarian Program and demonising asylum seekers by referring to them as 'queue jumpers', a term that was first used by Prime Minister Hawke, and as 'Illegals' because they had allegedly violated Australia's immigration laws. The Government was accused of implying that those who came to Australia by boat were less worthy of protection and more likely to threaten national security; of inciting racial prejudice and encouraging xenophobia; shirking the nation's humanitarian obligations and traducing Australia's long-standing reputation for showing generosity towards the vulnerable.[9] Critics thought Ruddock's commentary on asylum seekers had become 'increasingly dismissive and distorted'.[10] The Minister was condemned for lacking humanity in perpetuating a system that was causing further harm to those entitled to compassion and in need of care. Opponents insisted that Australia was not facing an 'invasion' of asylum seekers and talk of a looming 'crisis' was alarmist. Why, then, was the Government responding so vigorously to the increasing number of unauthorised boat arrivals?

There were six motivations for the Howard Government's strong stand. First, it feared that 'favourable' treatment of some would result in the influx of a great many. Australia would lose control of its borders and be swamped by a mass movement of people it would be unable to control. Second, it feared creating precedents through either policy or practice that would make it easier for non-refugees to access the Humanitarian Program. Third, it wanted to limit the capacity of international covenants and the ability of international organisations to compel a democratically elected government to act contrary to what it considered was the national interest. Fourth, it feared the economic cost and the administrative burden of enlarged or, at worst, unrestricted flows of asylum seekers who could access the financial benefits of assisted resettlement. Fifth, it wanted to preserve community goodwill towards the Humanitarian Program given that the costs associated with its conduct were borne by taxpayers. Sixth, and this was its main motivation according to the critics, the Howard Government sought electoral advantage in exploiting the attitude of some Australian voters towards asylum seekers.

The first five motivations can be considered together as they involve risk mitigation and economic management. The final motivation is the most controversial and is naturally rejected by the Coalition (and by Labor when it was in power). But did the Government actually gain any electoral advantage from its stance of asylum seekers? The answer was not complicated according to the critics: yes, the Government sought and secured votes by playing the 'race card'. An 'invasion' of asylum seekers would swamp Australia and render the country unrecognisable to longstanding residents. In sum, the Government manufactured a crisis to give the impression that it had saved Australia from a terrible misfortune. It did this as a means of increasing domestic political support and 'wedging' the Opposition Labor Party whose members were divided on their own policy position. Ruddock was accused of making false and misleading statements that were intended, whether wilfully or not, to harden the attitude of Australians towards asylum seekers and to give the impression, wrongly it was argued, that the Government's strong stance was necessary to stop the system being rorted and Australian generosity exploited.

Two Sydney University academics, Mary Crock and Ben Saul, argued that it was

> meaningless to compare the refugee caseloads in Australia with those in a UNHCR camp. Asylum seekers who make it to Australia by boat or plane have frequently endured hardships that ensure that only those with the most serious claims persevere. The UN camps tend to house women, children and loss-mobile refugees, many of whom cannot meet the strict legal definition of a refugee because they lack a public or political profile. Comparing the caseloads is a false comparison.[11]

They noted that Australia took fewer refugees than countries with much smaller populations (although they did not resettle them) while the number of people who arrived in Australia by air with valid visas and then sought asylum was much greater until 1999–2000. Only 22.7 percent of asylum seekers were successful in having their claims recognised in 1999 compared with 72.5 percent in the United Kingdom and 88.3 percent in the United

States. Those who were unsuccessful were deported. Where, then, was the problem and why the need for such a disproportionate response?

In response to these charges, Ruddock made the point repeatedly that those who came by boat took a place in the Humanitarian Program that *might* have been given to a refugee whose plight *might* have been worse than those who had sufficient funds to pay a people smuggler. The Government was committed to helping the neediest people as places in the program were strictly limited by budgetary constraints. Ruddock was also critical of the UN Refugee Convention which, he claimed, had been manipulated by an overly generous interpretation of its original intentions to include individuals 'seeking relief from domestic problems [or] ... feeling civil wars rather than persecution'. In response, the Federal Parliament passed laws in September 2001 that re-interpreted the Refugee Convention to effectively circumscribe the definitions of 'persecution', 'particular social group' and 'non-political crime'. The Government also expanded the discretion of Immigration officers to reject claims when 'they have reason to believe' an applicant is not telling the truth. Asylum seekers who had passed through 'safe third countries' could also be refused protection because they had not taken 'all possible steps' to find another safe place in which to take refuge. Ruddock remarked:

> For the most part, unauthorised arrivals are not fleeing directly to Australia. Most have lived for extensive periods of time in third countries where documentation supporting their claimed identity and background is often available and have travel patterns into and through the region that would reasonably indicate they possessed formal travel documentation of some sort before arriving in Australia.[12]

According to the UNHCR, Australia was alone in its view that the Convention was being interpreted too generously. Establishing the truthfulness of any claim was nonetheless difficult given the existence of language and cultural barriers and the usual absence of any written material corroborating the asylum seeker's claims. The Howard Government was frequently irritated by, and generally dismissive of, the commentary on Australian policy offered by international officials, particularly those with the United Nations. The Coalition believed the United Nations had been captured by special pleading and vested interests that routinely took the form of critical appraisals of the conduct of developed nations whose governments provided most of the organisation's funding.

Interfering or monitoring compliance?

Ruddock's own attitude towards international agencies was shaped by a particular experience in March 2000. It was then that he attended a meeting in Geneva of the United Nations Committee on the Elimination of Racial Discrimination (CERD) to present a long overdue report on Australian activity. It had been ten years since Australia last reported and the Minister attended in person because the Howard Government suspected Australia would be the subject of strong criticism. After reciting a list of the Coalition's initiatives and achievements, Ruddock conceded that 'one of the greatest blemishes in Australia's history has been the treatment of our indigenous peoples'. The Committee's rapporteur on Australia, the American civil rights lawyer Gay McDougall, then presented a litany of concerns ranging from constitutional issues to the Howard Government's decision not to issue a formal apology to the 'stolen generations'. CERD implored the Howard Government to fulfil its responsibilities under the Refugee Convention whose operation was beyond the Committee's charter.

Ruddock reacted with some indignation, arguing the Committee had not adequately informed itself about Australia's social conditions before criticising the Australian Government and that, by way of contrast, the Minister had considerable experience in his portfolio responsibilities. He appeared indifferent to the Committee's identification of domestic laws that were inconsistent with, or contrary to, international conventions that Australia had signed and ratified. The Committee either did not know or did not care that the Australian minister was unmoved by this line of argument. In Ruddock's view, Australian law had precedence and priority because it had been passed by democratically elected parliaments.

The Australian Government was unimpressed with the grilling its Minister had endured. The Committee's response to Australia's report was, according to Attorney General Daryl Williams, 'an unbalanced and wide-ranging attack that intrudes unreasonably into Australia's domestic affairs'.[13] CERD was too attentive to the opinions of non-government organisations (NGOs) and 'failed to appreciate the nuances of Australia's complex race relations'.

The Government expressed anger that Australia 'which is a model member of the UN, is being criticised in this way for its human rights record'. A few days later, the Minister for Foreign Affairs, Alexander Downer, announced that the Australian Government would conduct a wide-ranging whole-of-government review of Australia's obligations and responsibilities with respect to UN conventions and treaties.[14]

This was a prototype 'Brexit' moment for Australia. In common with other democratically elected governments, the Howard Government did not like being censured by international bodies and being embarrassed politically. Had these bodies praised the Government's performance, and CERD certainly applauded the many actions Australia had taken to fulfil its obligations under the Convention, there would naturally have been a different response from the Immigration and Foreign Affairs ministers. The Committee would have been commended for his insight rather than chastised for its oversight. But the Coalition did not accept that entities of this kind were entitled to comment on what it considered domestic political issues. The Howard Cabinet believed these inquiries encroached on the sovereign rights of the Australian people and the prerogatives of those they elected. John Howard made his own views clear:

> We are not told what to do by anybody. We make our own moral judgements ... Australia's human rights reputation compared with the rest of the world is quite magnificent. We've had our blemishes and we've made our errors. And I'm not saying we're perfect. But I'm not going to cop this country's human rights name being tarnished in the context of any domestic political argument ... Traditionally these matters are the prerogative of states.[15]

Indeed, Australia had a good human rights record and the nation was well regarded around the world but its treatment of asylum seekers had provoked the 'deep concern' of several United Nations committees. The Howard Government was not accused of lacking compassion but failing to fulfil its obligations under conventions to which Australia was a signatory. Many of these obligations concerned the drafting of legislation, the imposition of safeguards and the reporting of progress irrespective of whether their fulfilment actually enriched the lives of disadvantaged Australians or enhanced the opportunities available to them. Despite these 'concerns', Ruddock was pragmatic and consistent in his approach to the portfolio. He never drifted from the message he formulated in 1996: 'the success of the [Immigration] program depends on a question of balance. In a globalised, high-tech, highly competitive world, this balance is more important than ever to ensure that immigration, both short and long term, continues to be a coordinated, integral part of Australia's future development'.[16] The national interest would shape the objectives and order the priorities.

After his dealings with CERD, critics still did not seem to realise that Ruddock could not be embarrassed or shamed, chastised or compelled into changing his stance. His Cabinet colleague, Treasurer Peter Costello, thought his opponents consistently misread his mood.

> As Minister for Immigration his job was to administer a system that had become exceptionally legalistic. As a lawyer he saw it as his responsibility to act in a dispassionate way and not be swayed by public opinion, enthusiasm or passion. This technique worked well when he was being cross-examined in interviews. He would patiently, and at great length, explain the situation and try to cool the temperature. It sometimes gave the impression that he was cold and clinical. But he was under enormous pressure during this period (2001), with demonstrations aimed at his home and family. The demonstrators failed to understand that the more they targeted him, the less likely he was to change his position on any of the issues.[17]

Further, critics failed to observe that the Howard Government consistently resisted the pressure applied by all international organisations and refused to comply with the provisions of any international agreement that it deemed contrary to its vision of the national interest. This reflected a well-developed and deeply-held view of state sovereignty and the accountability of elected governments. The Coalition's stance was an initial marker of the trend in different parts of the world to step back from multilateralism.

The Coalition, and the Coalition alone, would determine Australia's response to the many challenges associated with the global movement of people, especially what it deemed illegal movement. With the number of boat arrivals steadily increasing by the second half of 2001, Royal Australian

Navy ships were deployed to international waters between Indonesia and Christmas Island (an Australian territory) to turn back often unseaworthy boats crowded with asylum seekers but short on lifesaving equipment. The Howard Government devised *Operation Relex* to deter and disrupt the people smuggling networks operating on the southern coast of the Indonesian island of Java. In August 2001, with a Federal election less than three months away, the Operation took a new twist.

MV *Tampa*

The event that heralded a change in the Government's approach to asylum seekers and hardened condemnation of its policies by elements of the media and the academy became known as the 'Tampa controversy'.[18] A group of mainly Hazara Afghani asylum seekers and some Iraqis had paid people smugglers to convey them from Java to Christmas Island, a passage of some 500 kilometres, in a 20-metre wooden Indonesian fishing vessel named the *Palapa 1*. On the morning of 24 August 2001, the vastly overcrowded *Palapa* became stranded some 140 kilometres north of Christmas Island. A distress signal prompted a request from the Rescue Coordination Centre (RCC) Australia for all ships in the area to respond. The nearest vessel was the Norwegian freighter, MV *Tampa*, in transit from Fremantle to Singapore. In accordance with international law, *Tampa* was cleared by Indonesian authorities to convey those recued (433 asylum seekers and the *Palapa*'s five crew) for medical treatment to the closest suitable port with the ability to receive freighters. *Tampa* set course for a short passage of approximately twelve hours to the ferry port of Merak. Notably, Indonesian authorities had accepted responsibility for coordinating the rescue and recovery operation.

Half an hour after *Tampa* altered course for Merak, some representatives of those rescued asked to speak with the ship's master, Captain Arne Rinnan. He later told the *Observer* newspaper: 'A delegation of five men came up to the bridge. They behaved aggressively and told us to go to Australia. They said they had nothing to lose.' Rinnan was concerned that unless *Tampa* turned around and proceeded towards Christmas Island, which was 7 hours nearer in steaming time but did not have the facilities necessary for berthing a large container ship, he and the ship's crew of 27 would be unable to manage the 438 rescued passengers. Fearing violence, *Tampa* altered course by nearly 180 degrees and headed for Christmas Island. When Australian authorities were alerted to the developing situation, they insisted that *Tampa* should proceed as previously authorised to Merak as the rescue had occurred in Indonesia's search and rescue zone. As *Tampa* altered course again for Merak, there was a commotion on the ship's upper deck. Rinnan feared that some of those rescued would jump overboard, threaten the crew or stage a riot. To avoid losing control of his ship, Rinnan decided to head to Christmas Island knowing well he did not have permission to enter Australian waters.

When MV *Tampa* arrived off Christmas Island in August 2001, Ruddock was briefed on the unsuitability of the port facilities to handle the Norwegian vessel and the practical difficulties of disembarking 439 people by barge. Ruddock was especially concerned about the precedent that would be set if *Tampa* were permitted to off-load the asylum seekers. He told journalist Peter Clack as the controversy unfolded:

> I feel that I have to do what is right, and to always make these judgements not only in terms of how individuals are immediately affected, but the way decisions are perceived and acted upon by others. Here we have a situation where a vessel is forced to take people to an island in a huge container vessel that is unable to receive it, and which now puts the lives of Australians who may be involved in any form of assistance mission at risk, as well as some of those who are rescued at sea. I am driven by the view that what is in the national interest is always sufficiently articulated, and at times you have to make a decision.[19]

Ruddock was now at the forefront of global attention and, to some degree, international condemnation when the Australia Government made its position plain: the asylum seekers rescued by *Tampa* would never be allowed onto the Australian mainland. An impasse soon developed as the Norwegian ship anchored off Christmas Island. In answer to an Opposition question in the House of Representatives on 30 August 2001 implying the government was heartless, he went on the offensive.

> The government is acutely aware of the need to meet humanitarian obligations. Why would we put so much effort into ensuring that there are supplies, that the issue of people's safety is dealt with and, as I announced today, that porta-loos are provided. There have been no

offers from those who own the ship to bring humanitarian assistance to bear, and yet they use agents around the world, they ply their trade around the world and gain commercial advantage from that. One could be forgiven for thinking that the matter that is driving those who want to see a resolution of these issues by forcing these survivors on Australia in these circumstances has more to do with commercial profit and getting the vessel back on line than it has to do with the circumstances of the individuals involved. I make the point that obviously vessels will not be sent back to the high seas in circumstances where that would endanger people's lives. Any suggestion that we would do so flies in the face of our record, not only in the case of *Tampa*, but our record generally. Australia has been proud of its humanitarian record, and to bring it into question in this way says more about those who raise these questions in that form than it says about us.[20]

After the impasse persisted for nearly a week – a week that included the '9/11' terrorist attacks on buildings in Washington and New York – those rescued from *Palapa* were conveyed in the heavy lift ship HMAS *Manoora* to Nauru for offshore processing as part of the Howard Government's hastily devised 'Pacific Solution'.

In response to another question on 18 September about the preparations being made to process the ex-*Tampa* contingent of asylum seekers, Ruddock assured Federal Parliament that:

These measures are consistent with our international obligations. These measures have been looked at very carefully in terms of our work with the United Nations High Commissioner for Refugees. We are not walking away from ensuring that people who need protection get it. We are ensuring that those people do not get a better outcome, if they are smuggled into Australia, than they would get in dealing with the organisation best equipped to deal with their claims. Nobody should oppose measures that will effectively address people smuggling. If further measures are required to deal with it, I would hope that we continue to get ongoing cooperation.[21]

The *Tampa* controversy had raised a series of policy issues and practical matters that were bound to be controversial. Indonesian people smugglers were willing to put human lives at serious risk for financial gain. There was a presumption that corrupt Indonesian officials were involved in the people smuggling networks. The Australian Government wanted to see an end to this criminal activity but could not directly involve itself in Indonesia's domestic affairs. The conduct of the asylum seekers was also problematic. Threatening the ship's crew may have constituted an act of piracy. Contrary to international law, *Tampa*'s master was compelled to proceed to Christmas Island instead of Merak. Christmas Island presented its own practical problems. It did not have the necessary infrastructure making the proposed off-loading of those rescued a hazardous operation that imperilled the wellbeing of Australian citizens. There was a serious dispute at home and abroad over the interpretation of international law. The Government claimed it had the legal right to exert control over its borders and to prohibit *Tampa*'s entry into territorial waters, notwithstanding the insistence of asylum seekers that they be landed on Australian soil. The Government further asserted its legal authority to conduct an orderly refugee and humanitarian settlement program. Ruddock claimed that capitulation in these circumstances would have created a dangerous precedent that people smugglers would seek to exploit without hesitation. Every merchant ship steaming through the sea lanes south of Java risked being 'commandeered' by asylum seekers determined to enter Australia.

This entirely unscripted and unparallel episode prompted a new approach to unauthorised boat arrivals. The practical details took some time to finalise because a number of government departments including Foreign Affairs and Trade, Defence, Attorney-Generals and Immigration were involved. The Government also sought bipartisan support from the Labor Opposition which risked being 'wedged' in the lead-up to a Federal election it still expected to win. The electorate strongly supported the Coalition's handling of the 'Tampa controversy' with an ACNeilsen poll putting public support at 77 percent.[22] Other surveys suggested 90 percent of the people approved the Government's decision to deny the Norwegian ship entry into Australian waters. Labor was in real danger of appearing to be weak or indecisive in contrast to Howard and Ruddock who looked strong and resolute. The principles upon which the so-called 'Pacific Solution' was based were soon in place. Ruddock quickly introduced legislation into the House of Representatives to amend the

Migration Act. The much-maligned legislation was eventually passed with Labor's support on 27 September 2001.

The Government's strategy, to deter asylum seekers from making the hazardous journey to Australia by boat, had three parts. The first was excising a number of external territories, such as Ashmore, Cartier, Christmas and Cocos Islands from the migration zone. People who landed on these islands were not deemed to have arrived on Australian territory for the purposes of seeking asylum. Second, naval vessels would patrol the waters between Australia and Indonesia to intercept and turn back any vessel bound for Australia. Third, asylum seekers intercepted in international waters who could not be returned to Indonesia were transported to third countries for processing. Manus Island in Papua New Guinea and the small island nation of Nauru became offshore processing centres. The 'Tampa controversy' prompted a substantial change in the Government's approach to asylum seekers. It marked, according to journalist Mark Davis, the advent of 'the politics of cruelty'. He claimed the Howard Government wanted to avoid anything that would humanise the asylum seekers, all for domestic political advantage.[23] Ruddock was damned by a number of commentators for exploiting misery and harvesting prejudice. The looming election campaign was the critical factor in much of the criticism directed at Ruddock although it is doubtful the Howard Government would have taken a different approach had *Tampa* arrived off Christmas Island the day after the election.

There was yet one more notable incident involving asylum seekers ahead of the 2001 election that would harden the Howard Government's treatment of asylum seekers and deepen political opposition to its policies.

The 'children overboard' affair

Early in the afternoon of Saturday 6 October 2001, HMAS *Adelaide* (commanded by Commander Norman Banks RAN) intercepted Suspected Illegal Entry Vessel (SIEV) 4 in waters 100 nautical miles north of Christmas Island.[24] Pursuing its 'deter and deny' mission as part of *Operation Relex*, the guided missile frigate attempted to turn SIEV 4, an Indonesian fishing boat named *Olong* overloaded with asylum seekers, back to Indonesia. When *Olong* refused to comply with the frigate's direction, *Adelaide* despatched a boarding party with orders to turn the boat round. The passengers became agitated. Some attempted to sabotage the vessel in the hope of being rescued and taken to Christmas Island, believing their claims for asylum had a better chance of success than elsewhere. At dawn on Sunday 7 October, as the situation on *Olong* became more tense, 14 male passengers went over the boat's side into the water.

During an unrecorded radio conversation, the commander of the ADF's Northern Command, Brigadier Mike Silverstone, believed he heard Commander Banks say that 'a child was thrown over the side' of SIEV 4 – a statement Banks later denied making. A report that children were thrown overboard from SIEV 4 was swiftly relayed to members of a high-level government taskforce on people smuggling that had been established in Canberra. It was coordinated by the Department of the Prime Minister and Cabinet and consisted of representatives from several departments including Immigration and Defence. As the Minister for Immigration, Ruddock received a telephone briefing on the incident from the secretary of his department, Bill Farmer. Towards the end of a scheduled mid-morning media conference that mainly dealt with other matters, Ruddock then informed journalists that a boatload of Iraqi asylum seekers had been intercepted en route to Christmas Island. He added: 'disturbingly, a number of children have been thrown overboard, again with the intention of putting us under duress ... I regard this as one of the most disturbing practices I've come across. It was clearly planned and premeditated'.[25]

The political salience of this report was obvious. The children overboard story led national news bulletins and made front page newspaper headlines on 8 October as *Olong*, under tow from *Adelaide*, began to sink. The Navy believed sabotage was the cause. As the boat slowly slid below the waterline, 223 asylum seekers and Indonesian crew were taken on board the Australian frigate. Eleven days after the stricken *Olong* was abandoned, another boat packed with asylum seekers sank off Indonesia with heavy loss of life. Subsequently known as 'SIEV X', news of the tragedy broke on CNN three days later. The *Australian* carried the story of the sinking on its front page with a map indicating its likely location. The death toll was 353 men, women and children. There were only 44 survivors. When the Leader of the Opposition, Kim Beazley, attributed the tragedy to the Howard Government's 'failure of policy', Howard refused to accept any blame on behalf of the government because the vessel had sunk in Indonesian waters. Claims that the Australian Government may have known the boat was leaving Indonesia and could have prevented the tragedy or that ADF surveillance units knew the boat was sinking but did nothing in response, did not gain any traction until well after the election. The sinking of SIEV X made an increasingly tense election campaign even more volatile.

Towards the end of the election campaign, media reports suggested the story of children being thrown overboard was baseless and that John Howard, the Minister for Defence, Peter Reith, and possibly Ruddock, knew the story was false but did nothing to correct the public record. Three days after the election, Howard initiated an inquiry to determine what had occurred on 7 October 2001, why incorrect information was conveyed to ministers in the first instance and whether correct information was later provided but ignored or overlooked.

Ruddock was adamant that nothing contradicting the initial report ever reached him. When asked about speculation the story was false a week after the initial reports, Ruddock said:

> Well, there's no speculation on it ... I don't know why Australian sailors who saw it would want to lie. I don't know why I would put myself in a situation of reporting on something like that if it were untrue. I mean, it'd be highly risky, I think, for me to use those reports if I thought they were untrue and then have people contradicting me.[26]

On the Tuesday after the election, Ruddock's media adviser, Steve Ingram, received a telephone call from the prime minister's office to inform him there were doubts about the initial report. Ruddock's electorate campaign manager, Rick Forbes, recalled:

> Philip queried Ingram plainly and succinctly: 'then it is not as we have been told previously?'. Ingram stated carefully that the advice from the Prime Minister's Office was that the initial reports from the Immigration Department should no longer be relied upon and that the investigation into the matter was continuing. Philip who is usually unflappable and inscrutable was clearly unhappy with the news and indicated that he would wait for the outcome of the completed investigation. It was

clear to me that this was the first time Philip became aware that sufficient doubt existed over the accuracy of the initial reports from his Department that he should no longer rely on them.[27]

Two internal departmental investigations were followed by two inquiries initiated in the Senate by Labor with support from crossbench senators. The majority reports of both Senate inquiries were, as expected, critical of the government, accusing ministers and their staffs of misleading the Australian people and alleging the deception had a bearing on the election result. This was inaccurate. The 'children overboard' affair made no difference to the election result. None. The inquiry reports were also unfair. Ruddock was never privy to information supplied by Defence to Howard and Reith after 8 October and was unaware that uniformed and civilian Defence staff suspected or knew the reports were wrong until advised by Ingram after the election. But Ruddock was nonetheless tainted by the odium that accompanied the incident and the subsequent inquiries.

Despite suspicions that children may never have been thrown from SIEV 4, the Coalition sought a third term in office at the Federal election held on 10 November 2001. After Labor led the polls throughout the first half of 2001, the inevitability of an Opposition victory gradually receded following the Aston by-election in July. After the 'Tampa controversy' in August and the '9/11' terrorist attacks in the United States, the Coalition looked more likely to be returned to office. By election day, only one polling organisation still had Labor in front. As counting began, there was a 1.93 percent swing in the two-party preferred vote towards the Coalition throughout the country. After entering the election with a 13-seat majority, the Coalition gained two additional seats at the expense of Labor. In voting for the House of Representatives, One Nation lost more votes than the Greens attracted. In Berowra, Ruddock managed a 4.1 percent swing to secure 58.57 percent of first preference votes. On a two-party preferred count, he had achieved a 2.28 percent swing which was better than the national average. In Berowra, the Labor and One Nation candidates recorded the biggest negative swings while the Green vote improved but only marginally.

There was no clear trend in the distribution of the minor party vote nationally, discounting the apparent influence of immigration on the result. But critics continued to allege that the Government's recent approach to immigration was calculated to maximise domestic political advantage. The most fulsome condemnation of the Coalition's campaign strategy was Peter Charlton's chapter, '*Tampa*: the triumph of politics', in David Solomon's edited collection, *Howard's Race: Winning the Unwinnable Election*.[28] Charlton accused Howard of seeing in the arrival of MV *Tampa* 'a perfect opportunity to exhibit a clear policy difference between the Coalition and Labor, a difference that a ruthless and wily politician might be able to exploit'. He alleged that Howard used *Tampa* to 'wedge' the Opposition whose members professed a range of views reflecting a vastly different constituency on what was now being called 'border protection'. While the 9/11 terrorist attacks might have overshadowed the arrival of *Tampa*, they amplified the message.

> The reality of the Coalition's political campaign is plain to see. It began with demonising people seeking refugee status in this country. It continued with harsh and oppressive conditions in detention centres. It thrived on media blackouts and selective briefings to friendly journalists.

Charlton contended that the Liberals had appealed to a hard-line, authoritarian, racist element in the community making the 2001 election a very low point in the nation's history. He singled out Ruddock for criticism, alleging he abandoned his previously heartfelt principles to 'implement John Howard's divisive, racially suspect, fear-based campaign against desperate refugees'.[29] The final chapter in Solomon's book, 'Election race or race election?', relied heavily on the views of former Liberal leader, John Hewson. In a newspaper opinion piece published eight days before the election, Hewson wondered whether the result would be a victory of prejudice over policy. Hewson accused Howard of exploiting *Tampa*, playing the race card and lacking a 'genuine passion for policy'.

Solomon quoted the conservative English magazine, *The Economist*, which damned the Coalition for failing to embrace multiculturalism and promoting xenophobia. As a gesture in the direction of political balance, Solomon also quoted Lynton Crosby, the Federal Director of the Liberal Party, who had presented an election post-mortem at the National Press Club.[30] Crosby complained that 'many commentators are falling for the ALP's line that our victory was due only to the MV *Tampa* and the issue of illegal migrants. This is wrong. It denies the Government's position in successive opinion polls prior to the *Tampa*'. Crosby said that *Tampa* had only a reinforcing effect in the minds of voters who had already noted the differences between the two parties. Solomon was unconvinced: *Tampa* was the definitive event of the campaign because it made immigration a key issue upon which voters would need to exercise a choice. He cited polling that showed 10 percent of those who voted for the Coalition did so because of its stand on 'boatpeople'. He thought the Coalition had bought its way out of electoral difficulty with policies that could be characterised as either sensible or opportunistic, depending on whether the observer was a beneficiary.

Labor strategists persisted in claiming the children overboard affair had 'robbed' them of victory. Not only was the story concocted from the start, the truth was deliberately concealed from the electorate. Apart from the inaccuracy of these claims, non-partisan political commentators, such as Paul Kelly, and academic analysts, such as Murray Goot, have both concluded that children overboard had absolutely no bearing on the election outcome.[31] The incident might have influenced the political debate but it did not alter the behaviour of voters at the ballot box. The people voted either for or against the Coalition for other reasons. The people of Berowra certainly did not turn against their local member for his involvement in either *Tampa* or children overboard. He was soon to become the 'Minister for Immigration and Multicultural and Indigenous Affairs' and there was still much to be done.

Endnotes

1   For the full text see https://www.unhcr.org/en-au/1951-refugee-convention.html
2   https://www.unhcr.org/en-au/news/press/2001/7/3b6027264/unhcr-marks-50th-anniversary-un-refugee-convention.html
3   For more details of this initiative and others in the 1990s see https://www.aph.gov.au/About_Parliament/Parliamentary_Departments/Parliamentary_Library/Publications_Archive/online/Refugeess6
4   https://www.smh.com.au/national/credibility-overboard-20011108-gdf9oq.html
5   For a discussion of the case see http://classic.austlii.edu.au/au/journals/FedJSchol/2002/4.pdf
6   Reported in the *Age*, 1 August 2003, https://www.theage.com.au/national/court-decision-flawed-ruddock-20030801-gdw5an.html

7   https://www.smh.com.au/national/ruddock-ambushed-over-refugee-stance-20020423-gdf7yz.html

8   The tussle between Ruddock and the courts is canvassed by Bryan Horrigan, *Adventures in Law & Justice: exploring big legal questions in everyday life*, UNSW Press, Sydney, 2003, chapter 9.

9   See the comments of Margaret Reynolds, president of the UN Association of Australia and former Federal Labor minister, 'Human rights and border protection in the balance', *Weekend Australian Financial Review*, 7–8 December 2002, p. 50.

10   Mary Crock and Ben Saul, *Future Seekers: Refugees and the Law in Australia*, Federation Press, Sydney, 2002, p. 4.

11   Crock & Saul, *Future Seekers*, pp. 124–25.

12   Letter from Ruddock to Fr Frank Brennan, quoted in *Tampering with Asylum*, p. 55.

13   Attorney-General News Release, *CERD report unbalanced*, 26 March 2000.

14   Minister for Foreign Affairs, Media Release, 'Government to Review Treaty Committees', 30 March 2000.

15   See www.pm.gov.au/media/pressrel/2000/AM1802.htm, 18 February 2000.

16   Philip Ruddock, 'Immigration and Australia's population in the 21st century', opening speech at the Centre for Economic Policy Research workshop, Australian National University, May 1996, Discussion Papers, p. 9.

17   Costello, *The Costello Memoirs*, p. 167.

18   For a comprehensive treatment of the controversy see Tom Frame, *Trials and Transformations, the Howard Government, Volume 3, 2001–2004*, UNSW Press, Sydney, 2019.

19   Peter Clack, 'Caught in the eye of an immigration hurricane', *Canberra Sunday Times*, 2 September 2001, p. 19.

20   https://parlinfo.aph.gov.au/parlInfo/search/display/display.w3p;db=CHAMBER;id=chamber/hansardr/2001–08–30/0070;query=Id:%22chamber/hansardr/2001–08–30/0000%22

21   See https://www.aph.gov.au/About_Parliament/Parliamentary_Departments/Parliamentary_Library/Publications_Archive/CIB/cib0102/02CIB05; and Katharine Gelber and Matt McDonald, 'Ethics and Exclusion: Representations of Sovereignty in Australia's Approach to Asylum-Seekers', *Review of International Studies*, vol. 32, no. 2, April, 2006, pp. 269–289.

22   https://www.smh.com.au/national/polls-and-bombs-20010904-gdhuy2.html

23   Mark Davis, *The Land of Plenty: Australia in the 2000s*, Melbourne University Press, Melbourne, 2008, p. 220.

24   See my chapter 'A certain political scandal' in Frame (ed.), *Trials and Transformations*, pp. 119–51.

25   https://www.smh.com.au/national/credibility-overboard-20011108-gdf9oq.html

26   https://www.smh.com.au/national/credibility-overboard-20011108-gdf9oq.html

27   Email from Rick Forbes dated 12 February 2019.

28   Peter Charlton, '*Tampa*: the triumph of politics', in David Solomon (ed.), *Howard's Race: Winning the Unwinnable Election*, Harper Collins, Sydney, 2002.

29   Peter Charlton, '*Tampa* – the triumph of politics', p. 83.

30   https://australianpolitics.com/2001/11/21/lynton-crosby-2001-federal-election-analysis.html

31   Paul Kelly, *The March of Patriots*, Melbourne University Press, Melbourne, 2009, chapter 42 and Murray Goot, 'Turning around the votes – the 2001 election', in Tom Frame (ed.), *Trials and Transformations*, chapter 6.

CHAPTER 8

Ministerial discretion   2003–2004

Public administration is about more than following rules and regulations. The conduct of Australia's Immigration program was certainly subject to detailed legislation with a steady stream of amendments extending the rules, tightening the regulations and dealing with fresh challenges and emerging pressures. As the world changed, the global movement of people headed in new and unexpected directions. The *Migration Act* received sustained attention and required constant review.[1] Both the Labor Party and the Coalition agreed that some discretion to decide difficult and problematic cases ought to remain with the Minister for Immigration. There was an expectation that in certain cases the minister might, and possibly should, exercise discretion on the basis of compassion notwithstanding the problems and pitfalls associated with making compassion a consideration in public policy and giving compassion a place in the exercise of public leadership. It was in the exercise of ministerial discretion that the incumbent's vision and values could be personally expressed. This was something worth preserving and, in some instances, promoting.

The initial wording of the *Migration Act* enacted in 1958 gave the Minister for Immigration discretion in granting visas and entry permits to non-citizens. This discretion could (and was) delegated to officers of the department. The scope for exercising discretion was very wide. It was neither defined nor circumscribed other than by guidelines which were set out in departmental policy instructions. As these guidelines were not part of the legislation, neither the minister nor the minister's delegate was legally bound to follow them. By 1989, the *Migration Act* needed an overhaul. The regulated and unregulated global movement of people was challenging the immigration laws of most countries as the world's population became more mobile. Many of the amendments were recommended by the FitzGerald Report which had been tabled in Parliament the previous year. The report noted the 'indiscriminate conferral of uncontrolled discretionary decision-making powers' in the *Migration Act*. These powers were 'broad and unstructured' and had created 'a great deal of uncertainty' especially when considering 'strong compassionate or humanitarian grounds' for granting visas. The Committee drafted a model bill that included 'identifiable policies and criteria for decision making [which] will be clearly set out in statutory rules'. Ruddock agreed with the Committee's conclusion and concurred with its recommendation.

The Minister for Immigration, Senator Robert Ray, tabled a series of amendments in early-1989. He proposed removing most of the existing avenues for the exercise of ministerial discretion, explaining that:

> The wide discretionary powers conferred by the *Migration Act* have long been a source of public criticism. Decision-making guidelines are perceived to be obscure, arbitrarily changed and applied, and subject to day-to-day political intervention in individual cases.[2]

The Opposition's Immigration spokesman, Alan Cadman, thought the amendments were about 'cutting political patronage out of immigration, cutting any sleazy aspect out of it'.[3] But when the bill amending the *Migration Act* came to the Senate for consideration, the Coalition and the Australian Democrats argued the amendments had gone too far in removing too much ministerial discretion. An amended version was negotiated and passed by the Senate in June 1989. The Minister continued to express his uneasiness.

> I have only one objection to ministerial discretion. It is a remaining objection and one I will probably always have. What I do not like about it is access. Who has access to a Minister? Can a Minister personally decide every immigration case? The answer is always no. Those who tend to get access to a Minister are members of parliament and other prominent people around the country. I worry for those who do not have access and whether they are being treated equally by not having access to a Minister.[4]

Six months later further amendments were introduced in the Senate. Whereas the minister had almost unlimited discretion prior to 1989, the Act now limited discretion to applications that were prescribed by both legislation and regulation. In the context of the tightly codified visa categories that were now a feature of the *Migration Act* (there were 80 classes of visa and 143 sub-categories), the minister had a residual power that could be used in exceptional cases. Ruddock argued that discretion was emblematic of the need for ministerial leadership and a statement of where the power in the portfolio ought to reside.

> Who should determine migration policy in Australia? Should it be government officials, the bureaucracy, or should the government of the day determine, ultimately, who should enter Australia? Some might argue that the government of the day can do that simply by passing legislation as we have here, and then it is up to the Public Service to apply it; others, such as myself and certainly those members on this side of the House, are of the view that in particular circumstances it may be appropriate for the government of the day to be able to make decisions in individual cases.[5]

Significantly, the minister could exercise discretion in considering a visa application where there was a compelling 'compassionate' circumstance not anticipated by the legislation. The minister was not required to exercise discretion and could not be compelled to exercise discretion. Further, the minister had to exercise discretion personally; it could not be delegated. The exercise of discretion was not subject to judicial or tribunal appeal. It was final. The Minister was required, however, to advise the Federal parliament when discretion was exercised but there was no compulsion to provide a detailed statement of the reasons.

The minister could determine that the Act should not apply in a particular instance or he or she could substitute a more favourable decision for one handed down by a merit review tribunal if such a decision was considered to be in the public interest. Ruddock thought this was an important provision, especially when quick decisions were needed in relation to compassionate circumstances involving someone suffering 'severe illness'. He also drew attention to the place of the public interest. It was not limited solely to public issues. Consideration of the public interest could involve ... unusual, unforeseen or other features that are deserving of a favourable response against the background of Australia being a compassionate and humane society.[6]

While the potential for corrupt ministerial conduct remained, a former Commonwealth Ombudsman, John McMillan, defended the existence of ministerial discretion in sections 351 and 417 of the *Migration Act* because it plays

> an important role in permitting or facilitating action that tempers the harsh, unpredictable or unintended effect that can arise occasionally in the administration of a heavily codified system of rules of the kind found in the *Migration Act and Regulations*. In an area such as migration decision-making, where the decisions can markedly affect the living situation not only of those about whom a decision is made, but also their relatives and accomplices in Australia, it is vital that a safety net scheme ... is preserved in some form or another.[7]

The exercise of ministerial discretion was the subject of continuing parliamentary interest after the courts identified a number of definitional problems in the legislation and the regulations when dealing with appeals lodged by unsuccessful visa applicants. Not for the first time, aspects of the legislation and regulations needed further review and, in some instances, amendment.

In 1992, the Joint Standing Committee on Migration Regulations (with Ruddock serving as the deputy chair)[8] tried to differentiate between humanitarian and compassionate grounds for the granting of a visa after Justice French had earlier found in the *Damouni* case that there was little valid legal distinction between compassionate and humanitarian grounds under the *Migration Act* although the distinction was a crucial element of the Government's policy and departmental procedures.[9] The department had developed a comprehensive set of criteria that essentially defined and differentiated them. Senator Ray had explained that the humanitarian category was 'intended to incorporate a wider group than those who fall within the convention definition of a refugee.'[10] A person claiming to be a refugee did not have the option of securing humanitarian status. Following a series of court rulings, applicants were only required to show that in returning them to their country of origin they would face a situation that 'would evoke strong feelings of pity or compassion in an ordinary member of the Australian public'.[11] Most notable is the inference that pity and compassion are similar 'feelings' if not, in reality, the same emotion described using two different words. Nor did the court comment directly on the difficulty of defining compassion only that there was no valid distinction between compassionate and humanitarian grounds in the operation of the Act. Clearly, words and their meaning mattered and the need for clarity had become more pressing.

In wanting to preserve the distinction, the Committee sought definitions that were sufficiently flexible to accommodate those in actual humanitarian need rather than 'those who are simply faced with hard times'. It suggested that humanitarian grounds 'relate to an individual being disadvantaged as a result of membership of some group or class which is being treated differently by the state in an applicant's country of origin or last permanent residence'. Conversely, compassionate grounds related to 'severe misfortune and sufferings which individuals experience in their personal lives as a result of unusual and distressing circumstances personal to them'. Based on these definitions, compassionate grounds were identified with the family reunion elements of the immigration program while humanitarian grounds were linked with the criteria for overseas refugee and humanitarian resettlement programs.

Both the Government and the Opposition were concerned that the number of onshore applications for asylum had risen dramatically from 564 in 1988–89 to 13,954 in 1990–91 and were fearful about the mass movement of refugees. In the absence of completely reliable mechanisms for determining those who were genuine refugees and those who were not, and accepting that many of the decision-making structures then in place were inadequate in dealing with a surge in unauthorised arrivals, the Committee referred to a looming crises and the possible 'avalanche of claims'. Its counselled the Government to 'avoid the extremes of being excessively generous on the one hand and of being excessively restrictive and cold-hearted on the other'. It recommended that the Refugee Review Tribunal (which was established by the Keating Government in 1993 alongside the Migration Review Board) be authorised to refer cases directly to the minister for the possible exercise of discretion on humanitarian grounds. These would be exceptional cases. According to the committee's bipartisan report, 'balance had to be maintained between control and compassion.'

There was an expectation that the minister would exercise discretion but there were few accurate estimates of how many cases might be involved. Ray feared being swamped with hundreds of referrals. During the life of the Keating Government, Ray's successor, Gerry Hand, exercised ministerial discretion on 81 occasions over three years (1990–93) while his successor, Nick Bolkus, exercised discretion on 311 occasions over the same time span (1993–96).[12] In the seven years he was Minister for Immigration, Ruddock exercised his (section 417) discretionary powers 2513 times. On 1046 occasions he used this power (under section 417) to substitute a more favourable decision than the Refugee Review Tribunal, and 516 times he used it (under section 351) to substitute a more favourable decision than the Migration Review Tribunal.[13]

In two notable instances early in the life of the Howard Government, Ruddock had used his ministerial power to deny political activists entry into Australia. The *Migration Act* contains a broad and comprehensive power allowing the Minister to refuse or cancel a visa on the basis that a person is not of 'good character', perhaps because of past criminal conduct, general conduct or association with an organisation involved in criminal conduct. A visa can also be refused or cancelled if the minister thought a person would vilify a segment of the Australian community or incite discord that might endanger a segment of the community. Applications to enter or remain in Australia were considered on their individual merits.

In November 1996, Ruddock refused to grant a visa to the leader of North Ireland's Sinn Fein party, Gerry Adams, on the grounds that he was not a person of 'good character'. Adams had been previously linked to the Irish Republican Army (IRA) and allegations that he had either participated in, or promoted, sectarian violence in Ulster.[14] This was controversial but not unexpected as Adams had been refused permission to enter other countries. After the Good Friday peace accords were concluded in April 1998, Ruddock did not oppose Adams being granted a visa. Ruddock also banned the British historian and 'Holocaust denier', David Irving, on the same grounds in 1996. Irving had been convicted of an offence in Germany, deported from Canada, gaoled in Britain and previously denied entry into Australia.[15]

In July 1997, Lorenzo Ervin, arrived in Australia to conduct a speaking tour. Ervin was an American citizen and a member of the Black Panther Party. He had been convicted of air piracy and kidnapping in 1969 and was sentenced to two life terms in prison. He was later convicted of assaulting a corrections officer and given another ten year sentence. After his visit attracted publicity that had concerned the prime minister, the Acting Minister for Immigration, Senator Amanda Vanstone, cancelled Ervin's visa on 10 July and had him detained in Brisbane.[16] Ervin claimed to have been 'beaten' by immigration officers. Howard then instructed Ruddock to return from an overseas visit and attend personally to the case. Ervin asked the High Court to review his case but the matter was not heard because legal counsel for the Minister proposed that Vanstone's decision be set aside. Ervin was released and given until 25 July to provide evidence of 'good character' and why he should be allowed to remain in Australia. Ervin complained that this was insufficient time for him to obtain evidence and documents from the United States. Ruddock was unmoved and refused to grant any extension of time. Nor did he accept Ervin's claim that he had been granted 'executive clemency' for his convictions. The United States Federal Parole Service confirmed they had no record of him ever being pardoned.

Ervin met members of Melbourne's Indigenous community and then spoke to a packed meeting at Collingwood on July 23 about black activism and the Black Panther movement. He departed Australia on 24 July to avoid another period of detention. He told a reporter: 'I have no desire to leave before the period of my original visa, but the reality is a gun is being put to my head. I will leave, but I'll leave under protest.'[17] In a media release the following day, Ruddock stated:

> My decision to cancel Mr Ervin's visa was based solely on the require-
> ments of the Act and regulations and had nothing to do with the issue
> of free speech, a principle to which the Government is very commit-
> ted. Mr Ervin's views on various issues are freely available in Australia,
> including via the Internet.[18]

While Ruddock dealt with claims the government was restricting political debate, the more pressing issue was the failure of systems that should have alerted the Department of Immigration to Ervin's criminal record. Ruddock issued another media release on 27 July to confirm that remedial action was being taken to prevent any recurrence. In the wake of Ervin's departure, the Minister was accused of violating basic principles of free speech and political association. His ban on Ervin was also deemed an act of 'white supremacy' by Left wing organisations because political far Right groups had first alerted the government to his visit and demanded action.[19]

Ruddock intervened in many cases over the next six years. The increasing exercise of ministerial intervention simply reflected the growing number of requests, increasing from 814 in 1996–97 to 5969 in 2002–03.[20] Ruddock exercised discretion on average between 1-in-10 and 1-in-20 cases referred to him each year. He made favourable decisions in response to 10.8 per cent of requests in 1996–97 compared with 8.1 percent of requests in his final year as Minister for Immigration (2002–03).[21] Mary Crock and Ben Saul claimed in their book, *Future Seekers: Refugees and the Law in Australia*, the substantial increase in the number of section 417 visas being issued was not because Ruddock was necessarily more compassionate than his predecessors. They contended that the Coalition tightened departmental guidelines in 1999 making more cases subject to the application of international conventions and, therefore, ministerial review.[22]

Between 29 May and 26 June 2003, Ruddock was the subject of parliamentary debate on his exercise of ministerial discretion. Laurie Ferguson, Labor's spokesman for Citizenship and Multicultural Affairs, alleged Ruddock had granted visas on at least three occasions between 1998 and 2002 after the applicants made large donations to the Liberal Party. These were serious allegations of misconduct in public office that the media reported under the headlines 'Visagate' and the 'cash-for-visa' scandal. The allegations were exacerbated by the possible involvement of the Department whose officers may have facilitated or been party to misconduct. If any of these allegations were proved or if enough 'political mud' could be made to stick, Ruddock would be obliged to resign and the Howard Government seriously embarrassed.

The first case concerned the Maha Budhi Monastery located in the Berowra electorate which was granted 10 temporary residence permits for religious workers over a three year period. The monastery subsequently donated $100,000 to the Liberal Party. The second case concerned Filipino businessman Dante Tan who was initially granted a business skills visa. After his visa was cancelled due to non-compliance, he made a $10,000 donation to the Liberal Party and his visa was reinstated. Tan was later granted citizenship. When the circumstances of his case were reported by the media, Tan fled Australia. The third case involved a Lebanese man, Bedweny Hbeiche, who was unsuccessful in his appeal for asylum and twice sought to have Ruddock review the case. Four months after a donation of $3000 to the Liberal Party was made on his behalf, Hbeiche was granted a visa because 'new information' had been supplied to warrant reconsideration of his claim. In two of the three cases, those making the allegations noted the involvement of a local travel agent, Karim Kisrwani, who was said to be Ruddock's friend and another generous donor to the Liberal Party.

After the Shadow Minister for Immigration, Julia Gillard, expressed dissatisfaction with Ruddock's answers to parliamentary questions and two Opposition censure motions were defeated on party lines, the Labor dominated Senate agreed on 19 June 2003 to hold an inquiry into the exercise of ministerial discretion in the granting of visas from the time the Coalition won office in March 1996. The Senate Select Committee Inquiry into Ministerial Discretion in Migration Matters would examine:

> the use made by the Minister for Immigration of the discretionary powers available under sections 351 and 417 of the Migration Act 1958 since the provisions were inserted in the legislation; the appropriateness of these discretionary ministerial powers within the broader migration application, decision-making, and review and appeal processes; the operation of these discretionary provisions by ministers, in particular what criteria and other considerations applied where ministers substituted a more favourable decision; and the appropriateness of the ministerial discretionary powers continuing to exist in their current form, and what conditions or criteria should attach to those powers.

Outwardly, Ruddock was unfazed by the whole matter. He dismissed the censure motions as nothing more than political stunts. They were, he said, 'quite malevolent' and part of a 'deliberate attempt to diminish me'.[23] He had previously stated: 'I have never exercised my personal discretion in return for a donation'.[24]

The story quickly gathered momentum in the press.[25] In an article published in Melbourne's *Age* newspaper, Russell Skelton and Meaghan Shaw inferred from data supplied by the Department of Immigration that Ruddock was inclined to show favouritism to certain ethnic groups.

> According to official statistics, Lebanese have made 146 successful appeals for visas on humanitarian and non-humanitarian grounds, and Fijians a record 173 since 1999. Tongans, whose major problems seem to be lifestyle related, also did exceptionally well with 79 being granted non-humanitarian visas. But no Afghans and only 5 Iraqis attracted ministerial sympathy in that period.[26]

Skelton and Shaw concluded that very few people from the Middle East were approved 'because of the way most arrived and the lack of family connections'. Conversely, Lebanon was not among the leading 10 nations from which asylum seekers originated. Critics claimed that Ruddock also applied ministerial discretion in a manner that sought to deter asylum seekers from coming to Australia and punishing those who came by sea.

The *Green Left Weekly* argued the use of ministerial discretion was deeply flawed in principle and in practice.

> Corruption and cronyism is an inherent risk when discretional decisions made by the minister are immune from scrutiny ... For a single person to hold discretionary power over tens of thousands of people's lives is wrong. Such powers should be transferred to the courts. Only this would remove the temptation to hand out favours or use the power as a means of punishment.[27]

The Committee continued working until its report was tabled in the Senate in March 2004. By then, Ruddock had been succeeded as Minister for Immigration by Senator Amanda Vanstone. The inquiry received 43 submissions and 30 supplementary submissions from Commonwealth agencies, lawyers and migration agents, academics and advocates, community organisations and private individuals. It conducted seven public hearings in Canberra and Sydney, hearing from a total of 51 witnesses.

The non-government members of the Committee complained that its requests for information were denied or delayed by the Department of Immigration which appeared to be frustrating the inquiry at the request of the new minister. The information being sought, departmental officials explained, was personal, private or confidential and involved people who were not involved in the inquiry. Further, the information sought was difficult to extract from a large number of unrelated files. Without context, tabulating the information would make no sense. In making blanket requests for vast amounts of material, it looked like the Committee was hoping to stumble across a single document that objectively proved what Ruddock's detractors could only infer. In the face of departmental opposition, the Committee majority report concluded the Minister was unwilling to 'expose the decision-making process to close scrutiny'.[28] Vanstone thought requests for information amounted to 'little more than a fishing expedition'.

The Committee's report comprised three main elements. First, it did not receive any evidence that the minister had issued visas in the hope, or in response, to political donations. Given the minister's office and the department declined to provide the inquiry with all of the information it was seeking, the most that could be said was the allegations were neither proved nor disproved. Former Democrats senator, Andrew Bartlett observed that 'the inquiry didn't unearth any 'smoking gun' regarding the allegations towards Minister Ruddock (or, in my view, even a damp water pistol)'.[29]

Second, the report questioned 'whether there is sufficient transparency and accountability for decision making and whether the volume of cases decided by the minister in person in recent years is problematic'. The Committee warned that:

> In assessing the appropriateness of the ministerial discretion powers, the Committee is concerned that vesting a non-delegable, non-reviewable and non-compellable discretion with the Immigration Minister without an adequate accountability mechanism creates both the possibility and perception of corruption. At a minimum, the Committee wants to see external scrutiny of decision making made an integral part of the ministerial discretion system.[30]

Third, the Committee remained concerned that people at risk of harm could be returned to the places from which they had fled and, while affirming the 'appropriateness' of ministerial discretion, recommended amendments to its exercise to provide increased transparency. The UNHCR took advantage of the inquiry to criticise the Australian refugee status determination system, contending that ministerial discretion should act as a safeguard but was not 'in itself sufficient to secure the obligations of Australia under the 1951 Convention because by its very nature it is non-compellable and non-reviewable'.[31]

Press commentary on the Committee's report was more subdued than its coverage of the original allegations. There was not a great deal to report. The allegations had been neither proved or disproved. Ruddock naturally claimed vindication from the Committee's report:

> decisions made by me as Minister for Immigration were not influenced by inappropriate factors, including donations to the Liberal Party. The Labor Party has made assertions of a link, but following exhaustive efforts has not produced evidence to support their claim. They were left with innuendo and smear, but nothing to back it up.[32]

This was a predictable political response. Had the Committee actually been given and exhaustively examined all the material it sought, his vindication would have been complete rather than conditional. Vanstone and the Department were justified in resisting some of the Committee's requests for information. These requests were speculative and excessive. The Committee sought documents that were properly labelled confidential and were rightly protected by privilege.

The Committee report was notable in several unexpected ways. It revealed the extent to which Ruddock had used ministerial discretion and his willingness to show compassion. When and why he chose to be compassionate is not clear because he was not obliged to record the circumstances nor to declare the convictions that shaped his decision. Ruddock preferred that his exercise of discretion should largely go unnoticed although he was obliged to report to parliament the fact but not the detail of its use. If the press overlooked the frequent exercise of discretion, he was not about to draw their attention to it. He continued to fear that compassion would be mis-interpreted as weakness and misunderstood as establishing a new avenue for ministerial review. Despite being lampooned in the press as cold and heartless, Ruddock was unwilling to counter popular perceptions by publicising the many cases in which he had shown care and compassion. He was usually indifferent to media reporting. He needed public support for the Immigration program; he did not need, and made no effort to elicit, the approval of journalists and the approbation of commentators.

Ruddock was only accused of official misconduct once in his parliamentary career and that was during his time as Minister for Immigration. He had a reputation for honesty and candour. He was never associated with political sleaze or personal attacks. The allegations brought against him by Laurie Ferguson and Julia Gillard were politically motivated and little more than an attempt to smear Ruddock's reputation. No-one in the Liberal Party nor the Department believed he was capable of misconduct let alone corruption. There were certainly flaws in how ministerial discretion could and should be exercised but there were other ways of addressing the issues.

Endnotes

1   https://www.legislation.gov.au/Details/C2018C00337
2   https://www.aph.gov.au/Parliamentary_Business/Committees/Senate/
     Former_Committees/minmig/report/footnotes#F33
3   https://www.aph.gov.au/Parliamentary_Business/Committees/Senate/
     Former_Committees/minmig/report/footnotes#F34
4   https://www.aph.gov.au/Parliamentary_Business/Committees/Senate/
     Former_Committees/minmig/report/footnotes#F35
5   CPD (Reps), 21 December 1989, p. 3458
6   CPD (Reps), 21 December 1989, p. 3460.
7   http://classic.austlii.edu.au/au/journals/AIAdminLawF/2000/11.pdf
8   Joint Standing Committee on Migration Regulations, *Inquiry into conditional migrant entry*, Parliament of Australia, 1992.
9   For a thorough discussion of the case and its consequences see Mary Crock, 'Judicial Review and Part 8 of the *Migration Act*: necessary reform or overkill?', *Sydney Law Review*, vol. 18, 1996, p. 267 http://www.austlii.edu.au/au/journals/SydLawRw/1996/14.pdf
10   Robert Ray, Ministerial Press Statement 15/91, 15 March 1991. In 2000, the Senate Legal and Constitutional References Committee questioned the adequacy of 'non-compellable, non-reviewable Ministerial discretion' to avoid a person being 'forcibly returned to a country where they face torture or death' and sought a new

means of offering protection to people unable to gain refugee status under the Refugee Convention.

11 See Evan Arthur, 'The Impact of Administrative Law on Humanitarian Decision-making', paper presented to the 1991 Administrative Law Forum, Royal Institute of Public Affairs (ACT Division), Canberra, 29–30 April 1991.

12 Senator Chris Ellison, Answer to Question Without Notice (Speech): Immigration, Ministerial Discretion, Senate, *Debates*, 17 June 2003.

13 Tabled Documents, Senate, Ministerial Statements made during 1996–2002 under the *Migration Act* 1958 tabled in the Parliament as at 30 June 2003.

14 https://www.independent.co.uk/news/australia-bans-gerry-adams-over-ira-links-1351393.html

15 Irving was again refused a visa in 2003, see https://www.smh.com.au/national/irving-refused-aussie-visa-again-20030117-gdg4ed.html

16 Media Release from Acting Minister for Immigration and Multicultural Affairs, Senator the Hon. Amanda Vanstone, 8 July 1997.

17 See also a statement made during his detention, https://libcom.org/library/statement-australia-lorenzo-ervin

18 See also *Re: Minister for Immigration and Multicultural Affairs Ex parte Ervin*, 10 July 1997.

19 'Deportation of Ervin an act of white supremacism: Sponsors', ABC online, 9 July 1997.

20 DIMIA Submission to the Select Committee on Ministerial Discretion in Migration Matters, Table 8T, Appendix, August 2003.

21 Percentages calculated from data contained in Table 9T, DIMIA submission, op. cit.

22 Mary Crock and Ben Saul, *Future Seekers: Refugees and the Law in Australia*, Federation Press, 2002, p. 62

23 CPD (Reps), 5 June 2003, p. 16281.

24 CPD (Reps), 29 May 2003, p. 15465.

25 Mark Riley, 'Ruddock's cash-for-visa quagmire deepens', *Sydney Morning Herald*, 18 June 2003 and an editorial 'Visagate raffle ripples widen', *Australian*, 8 July 2003.

26 Russell Skelton and Meaghan Shaw, 'Ruddock may face inquiry on intercention', *Age*, 7 June 2003.

27 Sarah Stephen, 'Cash for visas scandal: Ruddock must go!', *Green Left Weekly*, 25 June 2003.

28 Report – Inquiry into Ministerial Discretion in Migration Matters, Senate, 2004, p. 8.

29 Andrew Bartlett, 'Ministerial Discretion in the Migration Act: policy, legislation and politics', *Immigration Review – Bulletin*, no. 39–40, April 2009, pp. 16–22.

30 Report of the Select Senate Inquiry into Ministerial Discretion in Migration Matters, Parliament of Australia, 2004, p. xix.

31 UNHCR, Submission to Senate Select Inquiry into Ministerial Discretion, 3 October 2003, p. 8.

32 https://www.findlaw.com.au/news/3168/cash-for-visa-inquiry-clears-ruddock---grudgingly.aspx

CHAPTER 9

Mandatory compassion?   2002–2007

U
nlike the 1998 election which was effectively a plebiscite on the Coalition's plan to introduce a broad-based consumption tax, the first election of the new millennium held on 10 November 2001 was not a poll of the border protection regime. Although more than 77 percent of Australians agreed with the Government's handling of the *Tampa* incident and handed the Coalition a third term in office with a slightly increased majority, the election result was determined by a number of other issues. The party that attracted the public's confidence in handling the nation's finances usually had the best chance of prevailing at the ballot box. The 2001 election was no different. Immigration had certainly not harmed the Coalition's vote. It could point to successive surveys revealing high levels of support for its approach but there was disquiet in some quarters about its management methods. Policies and practices that seemed harsh and draconian were justified on the grounds of precedent and necessity. According to the critics, this was an expression of the 'politics of cruelty'.

Detaining and deterring

The principal objection was mandatory detention. These two words symbolised everything that was wrong with what the Coalition was doing. Mandatory detention was arbitrary and indiscriminate, punitive and excessive. Clergy declared it was immoral and lawyers insisted it was illegal. Mandatory detention harmed children, destroyed families and was totally inappropriate for those who had fled torture and persecution. The whole regime was made even more egregious by the introduction of offshore processing. The advocacy organisation, Human Rights Watch, thought that Australia had 'shirked its own responsibilities to refugees' in using third party nations, such as Nauru and Papua New Guinea, as resettlement venues.[1] The United Nations (UN) High Commissioner for Refugees (UNHCR) was concerned that Australia was setting a bad example for other nations: 'Australia's actions are at variance with the 1951 UN Refugee Convention and have in effect jeopardised the proper functioning of the international protection regime. This responsibility-shifting move sets a negative precedent worldwide.'[2] Offshore mandatory detention was testimony to a complete lack of compassion on the part of the Australian Government. It was, the critics argued, utterly draconian and damaging to Australia's global reputation.

Mandatory detention was just one element of the Australian Government's policy. It had been endorsed by a majority of the joint Liberal-National party room and approved by the Cabinet. In the public mind, however, it came to be closely associated with Philip Ruddock. He outlined the policy and then defended it. In hundreds of interviews he explained why it was necessary and how it could not be avoided. Some commentators mistakenly thought he was the policy's architect and principal advocate, implying he gained a form of perverted pleasure from punishing people who presumed on his kindness and compassion. Cartoonists depicted him as either a cold-blooded sadist who was without any regard for those he had incarcerated or a hard-hearted bureaucrat who was indifferent to the anguish of those he had deprived of hope. Activists who opposed the Coalition's border protection policies, especially offshore detention, vented their fury on Ruddock. He had, they contended, the power to alleviate suffering and the prerogative to end misery but choose instead to prolong anguish and perpetuate sorrow. Their attacks were deliberately personal and they were intended to be painful.

Despite the campaign against him prompting the need for a constant police presence outside his home in Pennant Hills, Ruddock remained steadfast and he conceded nothing to the critics. His position on Australia's responsibilities under the UN Convention had not changed over the previous decade. In March 1994, he stressed that Australia has 'very important obligations in relation to refugees internationally; we have obligations to our fellow human beings.'[3] He noted that refugees were not only those who arrived in Australia seeking protection but desperate people 'in a multiplicity of situations around the world, and our obligations are universal'. While he had been 'very critical of the fact that people have been held in detention for as long as they have without their claims finally determined', he sought to ensure that 'Australia's ability to help those in real need is not compromised by allowing those people who want to exploit our compassion mischievously to do so'.[4]

In response to specific criticisms that the Coalition's approach was either illegal or unconventional, the Minister continued to assert Australia's entitlement to exercise its national sovereignty and defended the need for firm action to disrupt the people smuggling trade and prevent further loss of life at sea. In explaining that the Commonwealth's action was both legal and necessary, the Department re-issued a 'fact sheet' that was first drafted for the Keating Government in 1992 to refute the objections of refugee advocates.

> Australia's *Migration Act 1958* requires that all non-citizens who are unlawfully in Australia must be detained and that, unless they are granted permission to remain in Australia, they must be removed from Australia as soon as practicable. This practice is consistent with the fundamental legal principle, accepted in Australian and international law, that in terms of national sovereignty, the State determines which non-citizens are admitted or permitted to remain and the conditions under which they may be removed.[5]

These words would be echoed in the most memorable utterance of the 2001 election campaign and also perhaps of John Howard's political career: 'we will decide who comes to this country and the circumstances in which they come'.[6] The Government's determination was clear. Did this mean there was no place for compassion and, therefore, no scope for compromise?

Deliberate displays of indifference

Ruddock was never unmoved by human suffering. He had visited many refugees camps and knew the conditions were often intolerable, especially for women and children. But after five years as Minister for Immigration he had learned one thing: public displays of emotion hinting that the Government might consider altering its policy would invariably encourage moral blackmail, create precedents and embolden people smugglers. Those who profited from the 'people trade' saw compassion as weakness and charity as a vulnerability. He also noted the experience of other nations, especially Canada and the United Kingdom, and elements of Australia's own experience, that people whose claims for asylum were rejected would remain unlawfully rather than surrender themselves for deportation if allowed to remain in the community during processing. Failed asylum seekers would be hidden and supported by families, friend and supporters, and they would be exploited by employers willing to pay in cash if they accepted less than the minimum wage. The government wanted to avoid the emergence of an illegal resident underclass which would have severe social and economic consequences for the entire nation.

Nevertheless, Ruddock continued to speak of compassion as a guiding principle in his management of the portfolio. Australia was, he reminded observers, one of the ten countries that participated in the UNHCR's formal resettlement program. If the number of refugees resettled in 2000–2001 (13,750) were expressed on a per capita basis, Australia would be fifth on the list. Addressing the Anglican Church's General Synod in Brisbane in July 2001, he said that immigration policy was essentially a moral struggle.

> The good is extending our compassion and welcome to refugees who have no other option. The evil is against the exploitation by people smugglers of people desirous of a better life and the resultant abuse and distortions of the system that has been set up to support refugees. Only if we join together to do both will we restore to the neediest of refugees that quintessentially Australian right – the fair go.[7]

The policy still looked callous and its implementation was nonetheless seen as cruel. The press was never short of stories highlighting the desperation of detainees. Self-harm and suicide were said to be indicative of despair and disillusionment as the mental well-being of those in detention attracted national attention. How could this policy continue without major reform? How could these practices persist without any attempt to ameliorate the worst effects of prolonged detention? These questions were now being considered by a number of Commonwealth agencies that were independent of the government.

A report by the Australian National Audit Office, *The Management of Boat People*, was released in February 1998.[8] The Human Rights and Equal Opportunities Commission published its report, *Those who've come across the seas: detention of unauthorised arrivals*, three months later.[9] The Commonwealth Ombudsman looked at slightly different issues in *Administrative Arrangements for Indonesian fishermen detained in Australian waters* which was tabled in July 1998.[10] The Joint Standing Committee on Migration (JSCM) began inspections of detention facilities in August 1998. In September 2000, JSCM published its findings as *Not the Hilton-Immigration Detention Centres: Inspection Report.*[11] In November 2000, Ruddock commissioned a former secretary of the Department of Foreign Affairs, Philip Flood, to conduct an inquiry into detention procedures at Woomera after a series of complaints. Flood reported in February 2001, a month before the Commonwealth Ombudsman published his report into immigration detention centres. At the same time, the Human Rights Commissioner began a series of visits to the mainland immigration detention facilities announcing a 'National Inquiry into Children in Detention' later in the year.

In June 2001, a bipartisan report on immigration detention centres produced by the Joint Standing Committee on Foreign Affairs, Defence and Trade chaired by Liberal Senator Alan Ferguson, concluded that 'Australia's detention administration is appropriate and professional. It is currently handling the demands of unprecedented numbers of arrivals well.'

> While it does not believe that people smugglers should be tolerated, neither does the Committee believe that genuine refugees should be discouraged in their wish to settle here. There is a delicate balance to be achieved, and the Committee hopes that it has been able to assist in the process of changing the emphasis in the treatment of asylum seekers in the centres.[12]

The committee recommended a maximum of 14-weeks in detention and separate accommodation for families.[13] In what was becoming a familiar refrain, Ruddock was critical of the Committee's report which he said was naïve and devoid of 'life experience'. In contrast to his critics, and he was referring to some within his own party, Ruddock explained that he had been to many refugee camps and had seen the worst. Australian facilities were better than many if not most. The critics continued to think otherwise.

Human dimensions

On 14 August 2001, ABC television's *Four Corners* screened an investigation of the Villawood Detention Centre entitled, 'The Inside Story'. An academic clinical psychologist at UNSW, Dr Zachary Steel, summarised the findings of a study he and three colleagues had recently published in the British medical journal, *The Lancet*, showing that most asylum seekers at the facility were displaying signs of clinical depression.[14] One of his co-authors, Dr Aamer Sultan, was a Shi'ite from southern Iraq. As a physician, Sultan provided medical care to Iraqi Shi'ite rebels after the first Gulf War (1990–91). He later fled the country fearing reprisals for giving comfort to the adversaries of Saddam Hussein. Sultan was denied refugee status in Australia with Ruddock explaining to *Four Corners* that his case was 'thoroughly and exhaustively tested'.

Four Corners also reported on the case of Shayan Badraie, an Iranian boy aged six who was in a semi-conscious, near catatonic state after 17 months in a detention centre. Obviously traumatised, he needed to be drip-fed and re-hydrated. When asked about the case, Ruddock observed: 'Well, I'll simply say that the child is not the natural child of the mother – it's a stepchild'. He knew instantly that calling the child 'it' was a terrible lapse and regretted the choice of words. In the hundreds of interviews he had given to journalists over the previous five years, he had not made a mistake of this kind. This single mistake, of referring to Shayan as 'it', would be cited repeatedly as 'evidence' of Ruddock's intention to dehumanise asylum seekers.[15] He mentioned the existence of other factors which may have contributed to the child's plight but confidentiality prevented their public disclosure. He did say the boy was being cared for by his stepmother rather than his birthmother and inferred that it may have influenced his condition.[16]

Reviewing the *Four Corners* program in the *Courier Mail*, journalist Peter Charlton portrayed Ruddock as an affluent hypocrite, reminding his readers that Ruddock was 'educated by the Anglican Church at Sydney's expensive Barker College' and that he 'proudly sports an Amnesty International badge on his lapel'. This was gratuitously offensive commentary.[17] The Human Rights and Equal Opportunity Commission later determined that Shayan Badraie's rights under the UN's Convention on the Rights of the Child were breached. The Government did not accept the Commission's finding, the first such finding in Australian history, but still made an out-of-court settlement of $400,000 with his family.[18]

This case, and many others like it, gave the impression of callous disregard for the wellbeing of people who had already endured a substantial level of personal hardship, compounded by systematic failures within both the

Department of Immigration and the detention centres which were managed by commercial contractors. The media did not report the many instances in which Ruddock used ministerial discretion to assist individuals and families, the difficulties encountered by the Department in verifying asylum seeker claims and the behaviour of some detainees determined to have their way. Given the abundance of migrants and 'doctor's wives' in the Federal seat of Berowra, it was easy to imagine that the prevalence of negative reporting and the absence of positive reporting on the management of asylum seekers might have influenced the intentions of voters in November 2001.

When the ballot was declared there was no sign of a local protest vote against the Minister for Immigration. Ruddock received 45,575 first preference votes representing 58.57 percent of all votes cast. There was a swing of 4.1 percent towards the sitting member. This was another impressive result. The Labor and One Nation candidates suffered swings against them of 3.9 percent and 4.3 percent respectively. The Greens slightly increased their vote but managed to secure 5.1 percent of the first preference votes. The swing to Ruddock was consistent with the national average on a two-party preferred basis. Despite having much less time for local matters, the people of Berowra were evidently content with both the Howard Government and the Liberal candidate. The controversies associated with the Immigration portfolio did not turn the electorate against their local member who was now the 'Father of the Parliament' – the longest serving Federal parliamentarian. While he could take comfort from the swing towards him in Berowra, things were not about to get any easier for the Minister for Immigration.

The United Nations versus Philip Ruddock

In May 2002, Justice PN Bhagwati, United Nations envoy and former Chief Justice of India, visited Australian detention facilities (Woomera and the soon-to-be completed Baxter) and concluded that 'the human rights situation of persons in immigration detention in Australia is a matter of serious concern.'[19] Bhagwati identified the detention of children and unaccompanied minors, the length of time to process claims and the withholding from refugees of information about their rights, as the principal issues. Ruddock was critical of his commentary, saying it was emotive, subjective, fundamentally flawed and lacking credibility. Ruddock told ABC Radio:

He ignores the fact that people in immigration detention have either become unlawful or have arrived in Australia without lawful authority … Essentially our concern is that people would abscond. Experience here and abroad is that people who have received decisions that are adverse, who are being held for removal, if they were freed and in the Australian community they would not be able to be readily found.[20]

Ruddock complained that Bhagwati 'came with preconceived views … he spent all his time here talking to lawyers and advocates, he had one day to visit Woomera and he's come to flawed conclusions'. A joint media release from the Minister for Foreign Affairs, Alexander Downer, and the Attorney General, Daryl Williams, concurred with Ruddock's assessment of the report and its alleged flaws.

The United Nation was far from done with Australia. With Bhagwati still in Australia, a delegation from the United Nations Working Group on Arbitrary Detention, headed by the flamboyant French jurist Louis Joinet, arrived to conduct a parallel inquiry. The Working Group also expressed 'serious concerns' about the detention of minors and the use of contractors to operate immigration detention centres. Joinet referred to the emergence of 'collective depression syndrome' among detainees and privately told welfare groups that he had 'not seen a more gross abuse of human rights in more than 40 inspections of mandatory detention facilities around the world'.[21] In what appeared to be a carefully orchestrated campaign, the United Nations Children's Fund (UNICEF) issued a plea for the release of all children held in detention on the same day. Ruddock's substantial reserves of patience were rapidly ebbing away.

The United Nations was deliberately targeting Australia. Its agencies were worried that Australia's approach to asylum seekers might be adopted by a number of European nations, such as the United Kingdom, and endeavoured to weaken its appeal to prevent poorer countries without strong border control regimes facing an even greater refugee burden. The Geneva-based officials were also determined to deflect Ruddock's objections to the operation of the Refugee Convention and his arguments for urgent review. Ruddock rejected these concerns outright, arguing that human rights infringements were being concocted in the hope of dismantling the entire detention system. Ruddock advised Australian journalists: 'Don't dress up [these criticisms] on the basis that we treat people inhumanely when they come without lawful authority. We do not. We conduct a detention policy as humanely as possible with a high degree of amenity to ensure that people are available for processing and available for removal.'[22] The Working Group members were told they were actually part of the problem being addressed by the Government because their visits were being exploited by detainees who were willing to engage in self-harm in the hope of arousing greater public sympathy for their cause. Those who made the risky visit to Australia were, according to Ruddock, making a 'lifestyle decision'. He might have put this less provocatively by explaining they were seeking a better life for themselves and their families – an understandable aspiration. But this aspiration could not be pursued within the Refugee Convention.

The campaign being waged by the United Nations ended at the close of 2002. Although Australia was clearly unwilling to change its policy, the United Nations hoped it had sufficiently dissuaded other member nations from following suit. The new year heralded a series of tragedies that kept mandatory detention in the news. In February 2003, Habib Wahedy, a 46 year-old Hazara man who fled war-torn Afghanistan, received a letter from the Commonwealth offering him $2000 if he were willing to return to Afghanistan when his TPV expired. The emotional pressure was such that Wahedy committed suicide. When asked about the case, Ruddock replied: ' There is a range of support services ... and we are not going to be able to put in place systems whereby we have a counsellor beside every temporary protection holder, to hold their hand through the process.'[23]

The High Court versus Philip Ruddock

That same month, the Minister sought to deny asylum seekers access to the Australian legal system to prevent appeals against determinations of the Refugee Review Tribunal. The High Court ruled unanimously that a person held in immigration detention can appeal to the High Court, the Federal Court and the newly established Federal Magistrates Court. Their rights of appeal could not be limited by legislators.[24] This was a major setback for the Minister and his Department. Ruddock abandoned his long-held desire to remove the courts from administration of the Immigration program. He believed asylum seekers with weak or non-existent grounds for protection were abusing Australia legal processes and unnecessarily delaying their deportation. This was, he argued, a fundamental philosophical principle that the courts had consistently refused to accept in their reading of the Constitution. SBS reporter Mark Davis thought Ruddock's position 'represented a fundamental attack on the doctrine of the separation of powers'.[25] The issues associated with mandatory detention transcended departmental policy. They involved the foundations of state authority and the structures of public administration. Activists pointed to a crisis of compassion. To them, it was simply a matter of the minister selling his soul and the nation abandoning its conscience. The mandatory detention regime was an offence against Australian values.

Ruddock could have responded in a number of ways. He chose the most direct approach: the conduct of detainees was also contrary to Australian values. When detainees at the Woomera Detention Centre embarked on hunger strikes and others attempted suicide by swallowing detergent, Ruddock said these acts were 'something that offends the sensitivities of Australians'.[26] When several inmates sewed their lips together in symbolic protest, Ruddock responded: 'I've seen girls with pins through their tongues and through their nose'. This was, he contended, little more than intimidation and blackmail. The government would not make any concessions to such behaviour. He repeatedly made his position plain: 'We're not going to unwind the detention arrangements merely because ... of the potential harm that they may suffer. This is a situation in which they have placed themselves'.[27] He was, however, deeply affected by reports of actual and threatened self-harm during the 16-day hunger strike at Woomera in January 2002 and agreed to reconsider their applications and to study any new information the asylum seekers wanted to present. But mandatory detention would remain.

The activists were undeterred because they detected a shift in the national mood. There was growing disquiet about the consequences of detaining people in remote facilities. Medical practitioners and mental health experts were drawing attention to the physical and emotional harm inflicted on detainees. Some suggested the intention was to break the spirit of detainees in the hope they would agree to being returned to their country of origin. This was a form of psychological warfare. Ruddock firmly rejected claims that detention centres were 'concentration camps'. Referring to Villawood, he remarked, 'while I'd never describe it as a holiday camp or a hostel, I certainly wouldn't describe it as a gaol'.[28] Despite the obvious problems with over-crowding at Woomera and the difficulty of maintaining accommodation standards at offshore facilities, Ruddock continued to justify the policy on the grounds that asylum seekers needed to be 'available' for processing and deportation if their claims were unsuccessful. He was also adamant that people whose claims were rejected could and should be repatriated to countries that were damaged but not completely destroyed by civil strife or armed conflict. The sub-text was that asylum seekers needed to accept some personal responsibility for their actions and that detention was, indeed, meant to be a deterrent. Ruddock was open to exploring alternative arrangements, such as community housing for families, but the options were expensive and limited in the shorter term.

Liberal backbenchers versus Philip Ruddock

With public disquiet spreading, Ruddock was under pressure from members of his own party room to reconsider mandatory detention. He knew the backbenchers Petro Georgiou, Judy Moylan, Bruce Baird, Russell Broadbent and Mal Washer did not condone much of the Coalition's policy on asylum seekers. Christopher Pyne also sympathised with their cause. The foremost critic was Petro Georgiou who advocated discretionary detention in place of mandatory detention. He also wanted women and children housed in the community. His Liberal party room colleague, Sophie Mirabella, later referred to him as a 'political terrorist' although his personal involvement in immigration and multicultural affairs pre-dated that of Ruddock.[29] Baird, a former minister in the Greiner and Fahey Coalition governments in New South Wales, had known Ruddock longest. A close ally of Peter Costello during the growing leadership tussle with John Howard, Baird described himself as an economic 'dry' and a social 'wet'. Building on part-time employment with the Department of Immigration many years before he entered parliament, Baird had visited detention centres across the country, spoke to detainees about the conditions and was outraged by what he had seen and heard. He greatly sympathised with the uncertainty they faced as their claims were slowly processed, not knowing what the future would bring. This small faction, linked by a common concern for human rights, tried to interest their colleagues in detention issues and urged them to tour the facilities and speak to those most affected by the Coalition's policies. They were not alone in wanting the detention of women and children to end. Their campaign attracted veiled support from the judiciary.

In the case of an Iranian family who fled to Australia and were initially detained at Woomera, Justice Richard Chisholm ruled he did not have the legal authority to release the parents and the children from detention although they were 'in a serious state of mental health and distress' while their appeal to the High Court against deportation was considered. He thought the children would benefit from release into the community which the Minister of Immigration could approve. Justice Chisholm concluded: 'I express the hope that he will give careful and *compassionate* consideration to the urgent needs of this unfortunate family' [emphasis added].[30]

Ruddock, who was the most frequent visitor to detention centres across the country, thought this approach was mistaken. He argued that settling women and children in the community would encourage more men to bring women and children with them on a journey he, as the Minister, did not want them to make. He also believed that children were damaged in many alternative parenting arrangements and accepted that the detention of children could cause the same kind of harm to children. Surprisingly, he claimed not to have seen evidence that children were harmed by mandatory detention. He also insisted that children in need of care should receive that care but the provision would not include releasing them into the community. Individual issues had to be resolved within the wider policy framework. If a child was suffering in detention, the system needed to be addressed rather than the child released. After seven years in the portfolio, Ruddock was in no mood to change a policy he believed was serving the national interest.

Time for a change

By September 2003, Ruddock was the nation's longest serving Minister for Immigration, surpassing Harold Holt's previous record of 6 years and 310 days. He had also accumulated 30 years of parliamentary service and had been 'Father of the Parliament' for five years, having entered the House of Representatives nine months before John Howard. Friends and foes acknowledged his substantial influence on national affairs. Some thought for good, others for ill. He had certainly seized opportunity. Ruddock saw his role as overseeing the placement of some key building blocks for nation-building.

He had attracted the skilled people Australia needed but could not produce to increase economic growth and expand material prosperity. He expanded the working holiday visa program from European and Asian countries to supplement the workforce and boosted the overseas student intake bringing millions of dollars to the higher education sector. He believed that close family reunion expectations were met and Australia's international refugee and humanitarian obligations were fulfilled. Cultural diversity was being celebrated as a strong unifying bond. Australia was an example to the rest of the world.

Ruddock could also point to the significance of two figures published by the Australian Bureau of Statistics in 2003–04. The first was the overseas-born population was 24 percent. The last time it was at that level was during the 1890s. The second was that, for the first time in the nation's history, less than half of the new arrivals were from Europe. Prime Minister Howard remarked: 'Really, I think it demonstrates that we have run a truly non-discriminatory policy.'[31] It looked like he had prevailed over Pauline Hanson who was then in gaol for electoral fraud (a sentence later quashed).

Beyond the Coalition and its supporters, Ruddock remained the symbol of all that was wrong with the Howard Government. Sarah Stephen in the *Green Left Review* complained:

> In the seven years he has held the immigration portfolio, Ruddock has presided over some of the harshest treatment of refugees and asylum seekers in Australia's history. His demonising of refugees has contributed to an escalating climate of fear and suspicion. Ruddock's abuse of power has gone on too long. He has to go![32]

ABC Radio's *AM* program produced an extended profile to mark his 30 years in public office.[33] It began with the well-worn line from unnamed 'critics' who 'believe Mr Ruddock's lost the humanitarian principles of his earlier political life'. The segment featured file excerpts with verbal comments from a protestor: 'You're a hypocrite. You're a criminal'. The Indigenous leader, and now Labor Senator, Pat Dodson remarked that 'for a Minister of the Crown, that's supposed to have a responsibility for reconciliation, he's been terribly naïve and divisive'. Former colleague Fred Chaney thought 'it's a shame that Philip is capping a long political career with having to do a job that puts him at odds with some of the things which he has stood for, and courageously stood for.' When asked by the program's presenter, Linda Mottram, whether he had been changed by the portfolio and his experiences, Ruddock replied that neither his values nor his political philosophy had changed. He affirmed his commitment to individual freedoms 'within a framework of law and a framework in which the broader society at times has interests as well'. He defended the Humanitarian Program and insisted it was predicated on managing the nation's borders, a position the Labor Party endorsed when it was in office. He had no regrets about his time in parliament and no intention to retire: 'if you're contributing in a way which is positive and you believe useful, and you believe it is in the national interest … it's not something that you readily think about'.

New faces, familiar challenges
After a Cabinet reshuffle the following month, Ruddock relinquished the Immigration portfolio. Howard asked him to become the Attorney General, a post he held for the remainder of his time in Cabinet. Despite being Minister for Immigration for 7 years and 210 days, Ruddock had not sought a new portfolio and would have been content to remain in Immigration. As the new Attorney-General, he was one of only a handful of solicitors to serve as the Commonwealth's chief law officer. Ruddock later remarked: 'Howard came to a view that my predecessor [as Attorney General] had a number of difficult issues which were not being managed as well as he would have hoped. I was brought in to deal with a range of issues in which I was already on the edge.'[34] Ruddock had been involved in national security matters since 1999 when it was thought that 'migration may become the route for people of concern to access Australia'.

National security and intelligence issues were the most pressing issues in the new Attorney-General's portfolio, especially in the aftermath of the 2001 terrorist attacks in the United States and the Bali bombings of October 2002. While counter-terrorism legislation to enable ASIO, the nation's domestic security agency, to conduct interrogation of people of concern had been passed by parliament, the administrative arrangements, including the regulatory framework and appointment of judicial officers to approve warrants and supervise questioning, had yet to be implemented. These became Ruddock's first priorities. Warrants for searching premises, installing listening devices, phone interceptions and data interrogation could only be issued by the Attorney-General. This authority was exercised personally and could not be delegated. The Attorney was essentially the principal law officer executing domestic national security functions. ASIO itself was scrutinised by the Inspector-General of Intelligence and Security.

Ruddock found ASIO to be a highly professional organisation but one that was inadequately resourced and under-staffed. After considerable downsizing at the end of the Cold War and the contraction of its counter espionage functions, the agency needed to expand rapidly to address the growing counter-terrorism threat. An active recruitment campaign was launched under the new Director-General of Security, Dennis Richardson, a former Deputy Secretary in the Department of Immigration and a public servant well-known to Ruddock. Ruddock was determined, however, that national security would not become all-consuming and dominate his ministerial responsibilities. He wanted to achieve a number of important law reforms in the areas of defamation, personal property securities and family law. He also promoted Australia as a commercial arbitration centre and supported the expansion of Australian legal services in the neighbouring region.

Ruddock's successor as Minister for Immigration was the South Australian senator, Amanda Vanstone. She inherited two cases that would embarrass both the Howard Government and the Department in particular. Vivian Solon, a woman born in the Philippines who became an Australian citizen after marrying an Australian, was wrongfully deported to her country of birth in 2001 after Immigration officials mistakenly concluded she was an illegal immigrant.[35] Solon had been receiving psychiatric care and was unable to provide details of her identity. Although departmental officials became aware of the error in 2003, no action was taken nor was the Minister informed. In the second case, a German citizen and Australian permanent resident, Cornelia Rau, told police in North Queensland in late March 2004 that she was a German tourist.[36] She, too, was suffering from mental illness when she gave a false name. She was wrongfully held in immigration detention for ten months before her true identity was established and she was released into community mental health care. Both women received substantial compensation from the Government. A former Australian Federal Police Commissioner, Mick Palmer, was asked to review the two cases.[37]

When asked by journalists to comment, Ruddock conceded 'the outcome was very, very unfortunate for the people involved. We regret that it has happened.'[38] As more became known of the cases, he explained on 14 July 2005 that:

> In a country where we don't have a universal identifier, identification of people depends very much upon a high level of cooperation from those who are asked to provide their identity ... If that is not forthcoming, the task is always more difficult. The Palmer review will comment on how those issues were dealt with, whether they were dealt with well enough, but it shouldn't disguise the problems you have in dealing with the people who do not give accurate information about who they are and their background.[39]

Palmer's report was highly critical of the Department of Immigration. Shortly after its release, the Secretary, Bill Farmer, was appointed Ambassador to Indonesia, and the two deputy secretaries were reassigned to other positions. The removal of the Department's senior leadership was considered a substantial shake-up and evidence that its performance had been poor and its culture problematic. Howard defended Ruddock who was not aware of the Solon case until well after he became the Attorney General.

Vanstone's appointment to Immigration had initially been welcomed because she was considered a 'moderate' in the Liberal Party. She brought a different mood and work ethic to the Department of Immigration but did not change, nor seek to change, the Coalition's policy framework. This frustrated those in the Liberal party room who thought she might have championed reform to the mandatory sentencing regime. The crisis point for them came in August 2006 when the Government sought to amend the *Migration Act* to send all asylum seekers arriving in Australia by boat to offshore processing.[40] The amendment was a response to Indonesian anger at Australia's decision to grant protection to 42 asylum seekers from its province of West Papua where a long-running separatist movement continued to agitate for independence.

Parliamentary consideration of the Migration Amendment (Designated Unauthorised Arrivals) Bill commenced on 9 August. Georgiou, Moylan and Broadbent announced their intention to vote with the Opposition against the amendments which, they alleged, could lead to adults and children being held indefinitely. Baird reserved his right to cross the floor but ultimately abstained from voting. Georgiou described the bill as the 'most profoundly disturbing piece of legislation' he had encountered in ten years of Federal parliamentary service.[41] Moylan said it was contrary to 'our principles of justice' and a measure 'the citizens of this sovereign country' would never forgive. Broadbent explained: 'If I am to die politically because of my stance on this bill, it is better to die on my feet than to live on my knees'. The dissident members could not prevent passage of the bill through the House of Representatives. Their hope was in the Senate where Liberal Senator Judith Troeth had declared her opposition. Two other Liberal senators were reported to have misgivings while Family First senator, Stephen Fielding, indicated he would not vote for the legislation. The Bill was withdrawn when its defeat appeared certain.[42]

In a ministerial reshuffle in January 2007, Vanstone was replaced by the Victorian Liberal member for Menzies and former Minister for Employment and Workplace relations, Kevin Andrews. The 10 months that Andrews held the portfolio are usually remembered for the controversy generated by his decision to revoke the 457 skills visa issued to the Indian-born Dr Muhamed Haneef after the physician was granted bail on a charge of aiding terrorists.[43] When the Director of Public Prosecutions decided to drop all charges against Haneef, Andrews refused to reinstate his visa on the grounds that Haneef was distantly related to the terrorists involved in the Glasgow Airport bombing attack and therefore failed the mandatory 'good character' test. The matter was eventually resolved by the Federal Court which overturned the Minister's original action.[44] Andrews remained in the portfolio until the Coalition was defeated at the Federal election held on 24 November 2007. John Howard accepted responsibility for the result. There was no need for him to resign as Liberal leader; he had lost the seat of Bennelong to the Labor candidate, Maxine McKew.[45]

Reflection without retirement

As the Howard Government passed into history, News Limited columnist Janet Albrechtsen noted that, apart from John Howard, few politicians 'have been criticised, hounded and lampooned more than Ruddock'.[46] In addition to being derided and denounced, 'even his demeanour infuriated the critics. Grey and cadaver-like, they said, befitting the man who killed compassion in the country'. But she credited him with ensuring the Australian people accepted migrants and saw them 'as contributors, not freeloaders'. When asylum seekers began to arrive in boats, as 'vocal critics cried cruelty and lack of compassion', Ruddock was not swayed by 'hysterical emoting'. In increasing the annual intake from 67,100 new entries in 1997 to 142,000 in 2006 and securing the goodwill and support of the Australian people, she thought 'the fair-minded will call that a genuinely compassionate outcome'. In relation to refugees there were 'more compassionate outcomes accepted and supported by the community because they knew that Australia, not people smugglers, determined them'. After more than three decades in parliament, 'Ruddock's place in the history books as a politician with a clear moral compass is secure'.

He also enjoyed the enduring respect of his colleagues. Tony Abbott's assessment was typical of the mood in cabinet.

> Although Philip Ruddock had never been considered a close Howard ally, as immigration minister and then attorney general he turned out to be one of the most effective ministers of the government. His pro-digious administrative efficiency kept a series of complex and sensitive portfolios very well managed. Although his public presentations were steady and thorough, to the point of being long-winded, in cabinet he was concise and incisive and sometimes ended up clarifying issues that others had left confused. It was a terrible calumny to say that he had lost his conscience, let alone his liberal principles, in the administration of the government's border-protection and national security policies. It's easy for those who don't have to take responsibility for decisions to assume the best of people. Ruddock had to balance the rights of detainees against the rights of the Australian public. Unavoidably, he had to entrust the implementation of policy to a small number of officials and contractors, some of whom, inevitably, made mistakes under pressure. The ethical response to moral blackmail, such as the lip-sewing protests, was not to give in but to ensure that the process-ing system was working as quickly and as fairly as possible. It's often forgotten that long-term detention was invariably the result of appeals by people who wouldn't take 'no' for an answer.[47]

After the Coalition's election loss and the defeat of John Howard in Bennelong, Ruddock was the last remaining parliamentarian to have sat in the House of Representatives when Gough Whitlam was prime minister. Having served a record term as the Minister for Immigration and spending over four years as Attorney General, would he stay in parliament or would he go? Many presumed he had fulfilled his ambitions and would prefer a quiet life. They were mistaken.

Endnotes

1   Human Rights Watch, 'By invitation only: Australian asylum policy', chapter 3, 2002.
2   UNHCR, 'UNHCR criticises Australia for turning boat people away', Press release, 11 November 2003.
3   Ruddock, CDP (Reps), 15 March 1994, p. 2834.
4   Ruddock, CPD (Reps), 3 March 1994, p. 1681.
5   Department of Immigration and Multicultural Affairs (DIMA), 'Immigration detention', DIMA Fact Sheet 82, DIMA, Canberra, 2000.
6   https://electionspeeches.moadoph.gov.au/speeches/2001-john-howard
7   Philip Ruddock, 'Ensuring a fair go for those most in need', address to the Anglican General Synod, Brisbane, 27 July 2001, p. 10. Copy held by the author who was present.
8   https://www.anao.gov.au/work/performance-audit/management-boat-people
9   https://www.humanrights.gov.au/our-work/asylum-seekers-and-refugees/publications/those-whove-come-across-seas-detention
10 A copy of this report is not available on line but it is the subject of detailed mention in https://www.ombudsman.gov.au/__data/assets/pdf_file/0026/26297/investigation_2001_05.pdf
11 https://www.aph.gov.au/Parliamentary_Business/Committees/Joint/Completed_Inquiries/mig/report/hilton/index
12 https://www.aph.gov.au/Parliamentary_Business/Committees/Joint/Completed_Inquiries/jfadt/IDCVisits/IDCindex
13 The media's handling of the Committee's report was controversial with a story by Sydney Morning Herald commentator Alan Ramsey being deemed a 'Matter of Public Importance' by Senator Ferguson. See https://parlinfo.aph.gov.au/parlInfo/search/display/display.w3p;db=CHAMBER;id=chamber/

hansards/2001–06-27/0035;query=Id:%22chamber/
hansards/2001–06-27/0000%22

14   https://www.thelancet.com/pdfs/journals/lancet/PIIS0140673600045761.pdf

15   Richard Guilliatt, 'The making of Mr Methodical', *Good Weekend*, 27 April 2002, p.
     16.

16   https://www.abc.net.au/pm/stories/s643803.htm

17   Charlton, '*Tampa*: the Triumph of Politics', David Solomon (ed.), *Howard's Race*, p.
     91.

18   https://www.afr.com/politics/badraie-case-will-put-child-20050511-j6zlk

19   Reported in https://www.wsws.org/en/articles/2002/08/refu-a05.html

20   https://www.theage.com.au/national/asylum-seekers-would-abscond-if-freed-
     ruddock-20020801-gdugbb.html

21   https://www.smh.com.au/national/worst-ive-seen-says-un-asylum-inspector-
     20020606-gdfccr.html

22   https://www.smh.com.au/national/now-the-world-is-watching-20020608-gdfcjn.
     html

23   Ruddock quoted in the *Age*, 7 February 2003.

24   For a discussion of this case see http://www.austlii.edu.au/au/journals/
     FedLRev/2003/12.pdf

25   Mark Davis, *The Land of Plenty*: *Australia in the 2000s*, Melbourne University
     Press, Melbourne, 2008 p. 296.

26   Davis, *The Land of Plenty*, p. 220.

27   Margot O'Neill, *Blind Conscience*, UNSW Press, Sydney, 2008, p. 158.

28   O'Neill, *Blind Conscience*, p. 62.

29   https://www.smh.com.au/national/georgiou-the-party-conscience-to-quit-
     20081121-6e4w.html

30   AAP, 'Judge appeals to Ruddock to show compassion', *Australian*, 14 August 2003.

31   *Australian*, 20 February 2006.

32   Sarah Stephen, 'Cash for visas scandal: Ruddock must go!', *Green Left Weekly*, 25
     June 2003.

33   https://www.abc.net.au/am/content/2003/s950626.htm

34   Philip Ruddock, Hornsby Shire oral history, p. 10. Transcript held by the author.

35   https://www.smh.com.au/national/the-lies-that-kept-vivian-alvarez-hidden-for-
     years-20050820-gdlwu8.html

36   https://www.smh.com.au/national/cornelia-rau-the-verdict-20050718-gdlpe0.
     html

37   https://www.homeaffairs.gov.au/reports-and-
     publications/reviews-and-inquiries/inquiries/
     circumstances-of-the-immigration-detention-of-cornelia-rau-vivian-alvarez

38   ABC Lateline, Monday 23 May 2005.

39   https://www.smh.com.au/national/ruddock-defends-immigration-bungles-
     20050714 gdlocw.html

40   https://www.aph.gov.au/Parliamentary_Business/Bills_Legislation/
     Bills_Search_Results/Result?bId=r2559

41 https://www.smh.com.au/national/backbenchers-defy-howard-on-asylum-bill-20060810-gdo559.html

42 For a discussion of objections and the Bill's withdrawal see https://www.humanrights.gov.au/about/news/speeches/admission-and-exclusion-asylum-seekers-conference

43 https://www.heraldsun.com.au/news/key-events-in-the-mohamed-haneef-case/news-story/0fdc12fde17899a7432a4275d9b13b14?sv=3c9d7bd7948cf777fb6613dcd4f36254

44 https://www.afr.com/politics/andrews-has-no-regrets-20070806-jksw4

45 Margot Saville, *The Battle for Bennelong*, Melbourne University Press, Melbourne, 2007.

46 Janet Albrechtsen, 'Tribute to a moralist under fire', *Australian*, 17 September 2003.

47 Tony Abbott, *Battlelines*, Melbourne University Press, Melbourne, 2009, pp. 44–45.

CHAPTER 10

A crisis of compassion?

Political leaders are often obliged to be crisis managers. Natural disasters, external aggression, economic disruption and the unpredictability of everyday human behaviour often create situations that are frequently referred to as 'crises'. There is no universal definition other than the need for prompt action to avoid calamity. Refugee advocates thought the Howard Government's treatment of asylum seekers reflected a 'crisis of compassion'. In their view, Australia had failed to honour its international obligation to protect vulnerable people, undermining any claim to being considered a 'good international citizen'. The government was punishing people who arrived by boat before exploiting them for domestic political advantage by encouraging the worst kind of prejudice. This crisis revealed the moral failing of the nation's leaders, the ethical bankruptcy of Australian democracy and the craven duplicity of public officials. The refugee advocate, Klaus Neumann, argued that:

> Politics and compassion can hardly be separated, of course. In fact, what we have witnessed over the past 15 or so years is the rise of the politics of compassion: a politics that refers to compassion (rather than, say, rights) for its justification and draws on the language of compassion, and which increasingly informs policy making.[1]

Indeed, Neumann contended, 'it seems as if only compassion can trump politics'. He thought compassion was a marker of decency and a measure of humanity.

For the Howard Government's critics within and beyond parliament, this alleged crisis of compassion was a function of the political opportunism that had made Australia a pariah abroad. They complained that the nation's once proud record on human rights had been blighted and its enviable reputation for compassion had been readily abandoned by a government seeking only to maintain its hold on power. Lawyers, advocates and clergy condemned the Coalition for its reckless policy, criticised the inefficiencies of its heartless program and committed themselves to individual acts of kindness, including *pro bono* legal representation, community support and domestic hospitality. They wanted the world to know that the Australian people were still capable of compassion even if their government was not.

Those who opposed the Howard Government's immigration policies invariably singled out Philip Ruddock for censure. He was more than just the responsible minister of state. To some, he personally embodied all that was wrong with the Coalition's handling of immigration. He not only managed the program, Ruddock was its principal architect and chief apologist. According to his critics, Ruddock's worst failing was the absence of any apparent capacity for emotional connection with those he was detaining. The foremost lament was his lack of any compassion. Had Ruddock retained even an ounce of compassion, they asserted, he would not have become indifferent to the plight of asylum seekers nor would he have condoned a set of policies and practices that were cruel and callous. Compassion was crucial because it would have pointed him back to humanity and precluded an eventual slide into inhumanity.

There was no shortage of commentary on why he was wrong and where he was misguided. What were the critics expecting him to do? Were these expectations reasonable? In the following pages I ask these questions of a representative group of his detractors and a sample of their denunciations to determine whether Ruddock deserves the opprobrium he faced as the Minister for Immigration (or the 'Minister for Misery' as some called him) and which he continues to endure whenever the Howard Government's immigration policies are discussed.

Robert Manne

There are few critics more scathing of Ruddock than former La Trobe University academic, Robert Manne. In a series of essays, articles and book chapters, Manne was unrelenting in his condemnation of the Coalition's immigration policy and its implementation by Ruddock. Most of Manne's more strident writing dates from 2001 although he was always opposed to the mandatory detention of asylum seekers. Having convinced himself early that the Howard Government's policy was contrary to international conventions, Manne's chief objection was the Coalition's manipulation of public opinion against those who sought onshore processing of their asylum claims. He objected vigorously to Ruddock's inference that there were deserving and undeserving refugees. Manne attacked the highly conditional compassion implicit in Ruddock's choice of words as minister when introducing the Immigration Department's annual report, *Protecting the Border*, in April 2002.[2]

> The underlying premise – that for every boat refugee the government accepts it has no alternative but to reduce by a similar number its humanitarian program abroad – is self-evidently absurd. Australia's immigration program is not written in the heavens. It is decided by Cabinet. If the minister was really determined to help truly needy refugees, as he claims to be, he could argue for a decoupling of the onshore and offshore strands of the humanitarian intake and for a return to the situation that prevailed during the Labor years. Or again, if he was genuinely concerned with saving the lives of those whose needs are greatest, he could argue in Cabinet for special provision to help those refugees who are old and ill. At present it is almost impossible for refugees to gain entry to Australia if they are not fit and well.[3]

In essence, if Ruddock was genuinely moved by compassion, Manne thinks he would and should have done much more to help the vulnerable and needy. This criticism is unreasonable.

First, Manne had no knowledge of Ruddock's submissions to Cabinet on quotas and outlays noting the Minister for Immigration was not a member of Cabinet until after the 1998 election. For all Manne knew, as he noted, Ruddock *could* have pressed Cabinet repeatedly for an increase in the quota and outlays – which he did. Nor was Manne aware of Ruddock's success in countering pressures to have the quota reduced. It was wrong to single out Ruddock for individual criticism when dealing with a collective decision, especially when Manne was without any knowledge of the Cabinet's confidential deliberations. He mistook Ruddock's personal commitment to cabinet solidarity, a commitment which obliged him to explain and defend the government's policies, with a persistent failure to advocate for the needs of refugees. Ruddock was consistently the principal campaigner for a larger intake and additional funds. That the quota was not decreased or the departments' funding reduced was, in some senses, an achievement in itself. This was especially so during the first two years of the Howard Government when Cabinet endorsed a range of measures to eliminate the budget 'black hole' of $8 billion, and during the first six years when it strived to repay accumulated public debt of $96 billion.

Manne's criticisms were simplistic. Put simply, he argued that the Coalition should have done more for refugees. Presumably, Manne meant it should have provided more public money because there is a direct correlation between the number of refugees accepted for resettlement and the costs borne by taxpayers. Governments of all persuasions are always urged to do more, especially by opposition parties. Manne did not say how much more it should have done. There is no hint of what the annual financial outlay should have been, nor did he identify potential sources of funding. Governments like to do much more and, with more money they would, if only to boost their prospects of re-election. But governments must have priorities, especially when it comes to spending, and accept the inevitable retort that its priorities are mistaken. The Australian Government must set annual immigration quotas and, in relation to refugees, the quota must be cognisant of the substantial resettlement costs. Unlike skilled migrants, refugees receive considerable government support. The immigration quota must be determined against every other demand on the public purse. A more constructive and compelling critique from Manne would have compared and contrasted different areas of public expenditure and offered a more practical and persuasive means of determining the relative merits of immigration generally and the Humanitarian Program in particular.

The cost of resettling asylum seekers would, of course, escalate substantially if priority were given to refugees who are aged, infirm or disabled people or if the family reunion rules are relaxed. These people would impose significant additional burdens on the health care system and quite possibly, and very seriously, turn community sentiment against the Humanitarian Program. This is the chief flaw in Manne's argument. A government's first responsibility is to its own citizens while voters expect priority when accessing medical services and health care. Maintaining the electorate's goodwill and preserving community support is crucial to enhancing resettlement outcomes as well.

Manne's complaints about Ruddock were personal. His choice of words was intended to be demeaning. Manne might have called Ruddock's position on the refugee quota miserly rather than absurd because he (Manne) presumably acknowledges the number of refugees Australia can resettle is not limitless. Manne implied that he is warm-hearted and empathetic whereas Ruddock is cold and cruel. When he chastised Ruddock for exuding 'moral cant' in his attacks on 'the 'bleeding heart' liberals he has come to 'despise', and castigates Ruddock for waging a 'highly personal campaign … with remorseless vigour' against political refugees, he attacked Ruddock's character by attributing to him the meanest motivations and the lowest methods. This is neither argument nor assertion. It is *ad hominem* abuse which Manne attempts to obscure by claiming the high moral ground and asserting superior personal values. Manne also implied an ability to decipher Ruddock's public statements, an ability he apparently applied to reveal in the minister a dark disposition that was devoid of compassion. The only mitigation that Manne acknowledged was this: 'Mr Ruddock's punitive regime does act, to some extent, as a deterrent' to people smugglers. But any credit for hampering a trade that led to thousands of deaths at sea was clearly outweighed by Ruddock's flaws and failings.

Michelle Peterie

Michelle Peterie, a sociologist at the University of Queensland, also accused Ruddock of distinguishing between 'deserving' and 'undeserving' asylum seekers in a deliberate attempt to curtail the exercise of compassion. According to her, the minister depicted the former as passive, vulnerable and entitled to compassion while the latter were described as assertive, self-serving and liable for condemnation.[4] After criticising the government for promoting a binary discourse to suit its own ends, she offered a binary of her own: the government was deceitful and mercenary, refugee advocates were sincere and selfless. She contended that the government's 'discourses of compassion have functioned not as expressions of equality or solidarity', assuming that these things defined compassion, before portraying government statements as 'demonstrations of power' that unmasked hidden intent. There was no acknowledgment of either the place nor the importance of national sovereignty or democratic will in her discussion of these 'discourses', just a presumption that the government's line was 'contradictory and cynical'.

Peterie's article claimed to be focussing on words and their meanings but the text was marked by its own undisciplined use of language. It traded in generalisations and failed to consider either classical or contemporary accounts of compassion. Peterie cited Martha Nussbaum's interpretation of an Aristotelian account of compassion without acknowledging its flaws or answering any objections. Peterie's description of compassion, which she uses to chastise the government for employing the notions of deserved or undeserved compassion, suggests that compassion can be coaxed or con- trived. It makes no room for compassion to be spontaneous or surprising. Peterie has sought a definition of compassion that best fits the prosecution of her charges against the Howard Government. Her critique is a self-fulfilling argument. She interprets the motivation of government statements as entirely self-serving while anything that might be taken on face value is, according to Peterie, actually rhetoric when inconsistent with the overarching accusa- tion that the Howard Government was devoid of genuine compassion, as she defines it.

For instance, when Ruddock observed there were 'high levels of abuse of the asylum system in Australia', she counters by claiming the 'binary that it created acted to delegitimise all boat arrivals'. Really? She does not present any evidence from opinion polls or community surveys to demonstrate that this was so. Her claim is unconvincing. It is noteworthy in her analysis that Ruddock was apparently wrong to report that the onshore system was being rorted and that his remarks apparently implied the reverse (yet another binary), that none of those arriving by boat were legitimate. Ruddock did not say *all* and rejected the claim that he did. He was commenting on the method of arrival and not on specific asylum claims. Ruddock also insisted, virtually *ad nauseam*, that the Government's policy was to accept those 'in greatest need'. This was (and remains) a sensible approach. This policy did not infer that those coming by boat were unworthy of compassion but that the method of arrival, in and of itself, did not demonstrate or substantiate their claim for asylum. Ruddock never made this statement nor could it be reasonably inferred from his remarks. Neither the Refugee Convention nor the *Migration Act* mandated or required the exercise of compassion in such circumstances.

When the Government acted to prevent the drowning deaths of asylum seekers in northern waters, any claim that it was moved by compassion in taking preventative measures was, according to Peterie, cynical at worst and paternalism at best. She directs her anger primarily at the Australian Government rather than at the people smugglers. The latter were risking their client's lives in unseaworthy vessels for financial gain. What was the Australian Government to do in response to substantial loss of life at sea? Was it required to station naval vessels at the edge of Indonesia's search and rescue zone to rescue those taking passage in boats that could not complete the transit to Christmas Island or the Australian mainland? The only humane response was to prevent unseaworthy boats leaving Indonesia.

Yet, according to Peterie, this was no more than tokenism that disguised the Government's dislike for those who sought to arrive in Australia by sea. This 'model of compassion', which suggests that compassion can be made to conform to a preferred Aristotelian template, 'denies the equal humanity and similar prospects of even unworthy sufferers'.[5] Peterie seems enamoured with historic and contemporary accounts of compassion that focus on the relationship between the compassionate and those for whom they feel compassion. The underlying intention is unmasking power and privilege which she finds deeply problematic, especially when nationalism and sovereignty are involved. I am not convinced that Peterie is still referring to compassion. In losing sight of the Humanitarian Program's purpose and overlooking the validity of national interests, the machinery of government is Peterie's real villain. It cannot respond to human need as she thinks it ought.

Like Manne, Peterie simply disagrees with the Coalition's policies and dresses her political dissent in moral clothes to make the Government's conduct less defensible and her condemnation more severe. She is obviously untroubled by asylum seekers circumventing internationally agreed processes in their desire to enter Australia. They should not be impeded simply because 'they sought to take control of their situations, rather than allowing countries like Australia to control their destinies'.[6] Peterie forgets that it is not just the Commonwealth Government they are defying but the United Nations as well. She refuses to acknowledge Australia's sovereign rights. Perhaps she does not believe they are valid or legitimate. Her argument implies that the country's borders are essentially irrelevant when individuals are facing distress despite international order being predicated on the recognition of national boundaries and respect for domestic law. She is critical of Labor and Coalition governments when they assert Australia is a 'decent country'. In her view, 'underlying insecurities and need for control' make Australia far from decent. As every country is concerned with the global movement of people and no government ignores its duty to regulate national affairs, to suggest the Australian people are collectively insecure and the government is paranoid is a misunderstanding of how international relations really work. She is also implying the nation has all the capacities of a natural person. Nations are not people.

Like Manne whose critique is void of practical alternatives, Peterie does not propose any strategy for dealing with asylum seekers arriving by boat. Presumably, Peterie believes that Australia is obliged to process whomever arrives seeking asylum notwithstanding the cost of processing and resettlement to taxpayers. And if the method of arrival attests to their genuineness, everyone who arrives by boat should be accepted into the Humanitarian Program notwithstanding the need for annual quotas. Her article neither suggests nor endorses any limits on the global movement of people. She does not support the need for asylum claims to be thoroughly tested because, in leaving their countries of origin and accepting the inevitability of hardship, applicants are indisputably sincere and truthful.

Quoting an article that chided the Government's naivety in thinking 'that death at sea in an unsafe boat is the greatest peril that asylum seekers have to fear' – apparently there are worse fates – she thinks respect for the 'full humanity' of asylum seekers should undergird the Humanitarian Program. Ruddock could and should have extended care and compassion rather than question their motives and impugn their integrity. At no point does Peterie consider the root cause of the problem she wants to resolve: if genuinely vulnerable people were forced to pay hefty sums to people smugglers in order to flee persecution in their countries of origin, the UNHCR system is not working. The international conventions needed to be reviewed and reformed. Demanding the Minister for Immigration show more compassion was not the answer. The problems were, and remain, political and systemic. They are not personal and attitudinal.

Richard Devetak

Richard Devetak, a political scientist specialising in international relations at the University of Queensland, believes Ruddock's performance demonstrated the problems associated with prescribing an acceptable level of compassion. Without offering any data or methodology for measuring or tracking compassion, Devetak claimed that 'Australia's levels of compassion have been lowered'. This was because, he asserted, the 2001 *Tampa* controversy

> signalled a triumph of hard hearts. That was inevitable given the government's decision to turn people movement into a security problem. Security problems demand cold reason; after all, the very survival of the state is believed to be at stake.[7]

This was pure exaggeration of both government statements that asylum seekers might constitute a security threat and any valid assessment of the nature of the threat they may have posed. Ruddock never suggested the security of the Australian state was imperiled. On several occasions he expressed a concern for community safety. It was important that the government could establish the identity of those seeking to enter the country to ensure it did not admit criminals and terrorists. Government agencies need to manage actual threats to community safety as well as unfounded fears. Most fears do not materialise but they must be addressed. Handling of asylum seekers who attract adverse security clearances must be balanced against the community's entitlement to feel safe. This is an area of public administration where the electorate would and should tolerate risk-aversion. But the charge that Ruddock consciously exaggerated the risks that some asylum seekers might (and did) pose to national security suggests that Commonwealth agencies responsible for conducting background checks were complicit in the Howard Government's manipulation of public opinion by manufacturing threats that did not exist. By falsely implying that asylum seekers threatened national security and, indeed, the Australian state, Devetak argued the Australian Government was able to excuse itself from showing compassion. He thought the demands of compassion were conveniently set aside by bogus claims that state security was imperiled. In essence, Ruddock had manufactured an excuse for harsher policies and more draconian practices. Devetak also fell back on a persistent theme to validate his argument.

> By asking Australians to believe that asylum-seekers pose an existential threat to the nation, the government was exploiting the persistent fear, perhaps paranoia, in Australia's national psyche – one that extends from the *Immigration Restriction Act* of 1901 to the *Border Protection Act* of 2001.[8]

In other words, the Australian people had not transcended the racism of previous decades. They were still prejudiced despite building the most multicultural nation on earth.

With asylum seekers constituting a threat to national security they could be excluded from entering Australia on grounds that obscured the real reason for rejection of their claims: racial prejudice. This was yet another lazy argument. This contention was easily asserted because its truth was simply assumed. According to Devetak, differentiation of deserving from undeserving asylum seekers did not actually rest on rationing compassion, as Peterie suggested, but on racism. Australians could be compassionate but they were selective, if not preferential, in its application.

The suggestion that Ruddock provoked or exploited racism for personal political gain is a serious charge. The implication is that he was a racist or that he condoned racism. Racism is the antithesis of compassion. To level such a charge against Ruddock, who had campaigned tirelessly against racism, Devetak required evidence. In the absence of evidence he relied on the cliché that politicians cannot be trusted to tell the truth or to speak sincerely because their natural disposition is to propagate mistruths and obscure their insincerity. Ruddock's claims to compassion were either false or hyperbole. In the absence of evidence, Devetak assumed his readers needed no persuading that Ruddock deserved condemnation. The only question was calibrating the strength of condemnation with the paucity of compassion. As Devetak thought Ruddock was completely lacking in compassion, his work was little more than an attempt to provoke moral outrage. Rather than denouncing Ruddock, Devetak might have outlined a series of alternative proposals for dealing constructively with the legal, administrative and ethical challenges presented by the Humanitarian Program.

Frank Brennan

Father Frank Brennan, a Jesuit priest and lawyer, was one of the earliest critics of Coalition policy. In 1998 he alleged that 'the Australian government's treatment of asylum seekers arriving by boat has been a gross violation of human rights, endorsed by a parliament buoyed by populist prejudice against boat people and quarantined from effective judicial review.'[9] By the time he published *Tampering with Asylum* five years later, Brennan's criticisms were presented with less vehemence. His arguments related to the burden of legal responsibilities and the application of legal remedies to immigration problems. His principal objection to Coalition policy was mandatory detention which he believed was applied arbitrarily and unnecessarily and imposed without regard to due process or the inhumanity of its consequences. Brennan thought the problem had been exaggerated and the Government's response was wasteful. He did not believe 'we Australians are entitled to use a sledgehammer to crack this small nut because we are prepared to take 12,000 applicants a year through the front door.'[10] Brennan also disputed, rightly in my view, Ruddock's consistent assertion that 'detention is not punitive nor meant as a deterrent'. He contends that Australia needs to be 'a little more decent' to a larger number of asylum seekers and to ensure that children are never detained. Notably, Brennan does not ask for compassion but decency. He is, again rightly in my view, concerned with prolonged and, in some cases, indefinite detention because it goes beyond the requirement to ensure efficient processing of successful claims and deportation of unsuccessful claimants.

Elisabeth Porter

One of few Australians to consider the place and function of compassion in immigration during the Howard era is Elisabeth Porter who taught politics and international relations at the University of South Australia. She referred to compassion as 'an important emotion and a central moral virtue.'[11] In offering a prescriptive rather than descriptive account of compassion – what it ought to be rather than what it is – Porter claims three elements are necessary for the 'fullest expression of compassion' from a feminist perspective.

> First, the compassionate person feels the pain of another, and in experiencing some anguish becomes a co-sufferer, whether this is known personally to her or not ... Second, the compassionate person tries to

identify imaginatively with the other in order to understand the sufferer's viewpoint on her suffering and what might relieve her pain ... Third ... the compassionate person responds to the suffering and needs of the sufferer with compassionate practical wisdom.

This account is semantically unpersuasive and practically unrealistic. Porter's definition of compassion subsumed empathy and sympathy, kindness and generosity, and a range of other feelings and responses. It confused compassion with shared suffering and mistook solidarity for replicated pain. Drawing on a series of unexplained and undefended assumptions, Porter offered no explanation of why anyone *might* feel this way towards another and did not outline any imperative for why someone *should* feel this way. Her account relied too much on imagination and its dependence on emotional faculties some people do not possess or, if they do possess them, in similar measure. It was also maternalistic in presuming the compassionate person is called upon to dispense practical wisdom – whatever that might be – although she warned against 'presumptuous paternalism' which was a perennial problem with compassion.

In essence, her approach to compassion was this: 'I can feel a certain way about someone's sufferings but I might not be best, or even well placed, to know how they might be addressed or alleviated'. She conceded that 'realistically, there are many issues we cannot care for in a direct fashion because of distance, limited resources, or ignorance, such as knowing how best to care for the plight of people in war-ravaged nations'. Her response, 'caring about others is morally preferable to indifference', overlooked the range of possibilities at both the personal and political levels. In sum, feeling and doing something is clearly better than being indifferent and idle. Quite so. But this is only of limited utility in shaping public policy.

Drawing on her flawed definition, Porter accused Ruddock and Howard of 'actively fostering fear' of asylum seekers within the Australian population and she claimed most politicians 'refuse to imagine what it is like to be placed in mandatory detention camps in remote outposts with poor facilities'. Perhaps worse, 'the Australian government has failed to attend, listen, and react humanely to their suffering' and suggested that it needed to provide 'compassionate, appropriate, wise responses to particular needs'.[12] She claimed the

conceptual barriers that prevent the practice of political compassion
are significant but not insurmountable. Compassion is not too personal
for politics. Rather, it can be the emotion that helps prompt a critical
scrutiny of international structures; it is the driving force toward the
practice of compassionate justice; and, as an emotion and response, it
broadens political responsibilities.[13]

But Porter's account was so inclusive that compassion's distinct character
was lost and her depiction of compassion was so expansive that it lacked any
practical limit. What she might have conceded was compassion could also
be employed as a form of moral blackmail to compel officials with private
sensibilities to overlook their public responsibilities. She seems oblivious to
the philosophical difficulties of shifting from what are personal virtues to
their exercise as institutional values.

She acknowledges that 'we cannot assume responsibility for all suffering;
to do so is naïve. We can assume, however, some responsibility to try to alleviate suffering whenever we can'. This is the principal practical shortcoming
of her account of compassion. She never described how or when or where a
public official can be satisfied that they have responded adequately in terms
of exercising appropriate compassion. The devil is always in the detail when
it comes to challenges in public administration. Porter's insistence that we
show compassion 'whenever we can' is the problem. It is subjective and
indeterminate.

Nor was Porter able to explain why individuals have 'responsibilities
beyond our personal connections to assist whenever it is within our capacities and resources to do so'. Where does this responsibility originate? Who
(or what) imposes this responsibility and how are individuals made or kept
accountable? To say simply: 'we should care when it is possible' is inadequate
as a guide for the actions we expect of public officials, including the Minister
for Immigration. In being little more than wishful thinking, it presumes a
capacity among public officials for acting beyond self-interest, or even the
public interest, that is unrealistic. Had she dealt with the practical elements
of immigration policy and addressed the procedural complexities, she might
have been less critical of Ruddock and Howard, and given her readers a
few clues as to how the government should determine whether it has been
compassionate or, more controversially, compassionate enough. This is

the defining issue and one she fails to address despite condemning those accountable for the conduct of Australia's Humanitarian Program for failing to show compassion.

Peter Mares

Peter Mares, an ABC journalist and producer, researched a number of refugee stories for the Radio National program 'The National Interest' before publishing *Borderline* in 2001. Like most critics surveying Ruddock's political career, Mares overlooks his long-standing commitment to refugees and human rights. Mares focuses on August 1988, claiming it was 'an act of political bravery that deserves to be honoured'. At the time this was more a demonstration of personal principle than a display of political bravery but Mares nonetheless wondered whether Ruddock was 'still paying the price' more than a decade later. He claimed Howard placed Ruddock in an 'unenviable position' by offering him a ministerial post that left 'scant room to exercise any liberal instincts' relating to policy issues in which 'the prime minister and the majority of Cabinet are determined to show little, if any generosity'.[14]

Quoting an anonymous ministerial adviser who claimed Ruddock was 'incredibly ambitious', a view that is inconsistent with my knowledge of the man, Mares inferred that Ruddock was willing to abandon his principles rather than sacrifice his prospects after 1996. Worse, Ruddock was behind a campaign to vilify the people he once pledged to assist and was complicit, according to former Australian Democrats Senator Andrew Bartlett, in national misconduct: 'If we [Australia] are seen to be adopting such a destructive type of morality, conditional morality, it obviously makes it easier for other countries to deal with the problem in the same way'.[15] Mares then cites unnamed commentators who believed that Ruddock, like one of his Labor predecessors, Gerry Hand, was an independent thinker who had been 'captured by his department'. But Mares dismisses any suggestion that the department hid behind the minister. The minister was, he observed, more strident and adventurous than the department and its leaders.

According to Mares, the political sensitivity associated with the immigration portfolio is a function of deep-seated but usually veiled racist sentiment in the Australian community. He notes that many decades ago the major parties made an 'implicit pact' not to exploit this ugly side of the national character. But once the Liberal Party disendorsed Paul Hanson as one of its election candidates in 1996 (evidence that it did not share Hanson's views), she was free to give race a place in national politics it had been denied for so long. To his shame, Mares asserts, Ruddock conveniently exploited Hanson's willingness to foreground race in Australian politics. While Ruddock argued 'it is not scaremongering to look at the hard facts about the influx of unauthorised arrivals', Mares countered with a quote from the previous Minister for Immigration. Nick Bolkus claimed that of Ruddock's public utterances, 'every 1 time he says something positive about migrants, there's probably 19 times that he beats a drum that resonates with the One Nation electorate ... he's out there playing the tune that Pauline Hanson likes to hear'. Bolkus did not differentiate between Ruddock's comments on economic migrants and those seeking onshore refugee processing despite the differences. Without acknowledging any irony, when Mares' interviewed Ruddock's shadow from October 1998 to November 2001, Queenslander Con Sciacca, the Labor spokesman also referred to unauthorised arrivals as 'queue jumpers' and 'illegals'. While detention would have remained as a deterrent under a Beazley Labor Government and the Opposition pledged to maintain the Coalition's main policy settings if elected in November 2001, Sciacca claimed he 'wouldn't be out there playing the lousy wedge politics'.[16] The difference between Labor's approach and Ruddock's was not immediately apparent. It was a difference consisting more of practicalities than principles.

Similarly ironic was Mares' concession that the Government needed to impose a cap on the number of places in the Humanitarian Program. The country could not afford an unlimited number. Ruddock seized on this concession when he was interviewed by Mares who reflected:

> He knows that he had found the weak point in my position – a loose end that cannot be neatly tucked away ... would there come a point where I switched sides to join those calling for the pipeline to be blocked? ... deep down, I share some of the popular fear of invasion, if only on a subliminal, irrational level. But while the Minister makes a point of principle, his scenario is ultimately abstract and irrelevant.[17]

Mares dismisses his own admission too quickly.

The invasion scenario was neither abstract nor irrelevant. If there were not an element of deterrence in Australia's policy, the number of people arriving by boat would (and later did) increase exponentially and exhaust the nation's capacity to absorb new arrivals. Plainly, Australia's geographic location would not always work to impede the efforts of determined asylum seekers. But Mares is unmoved by the pressing practical dimensions of the issue and is unable to address the principal shortcoming in his own position: nations like Australia should not impose a quota. If 40,000 people arrived seeking asylum in one calendar year, according to Mares, 'Australia would then be obliged to offer them protection'.[18] One commentator, the New South Wales Solicitor General, Michael Sexton SC, is critical of those resisting annual quotas. They seem to offer

> no alternative other than a notion of open borders. How could this work when there are potentially millions of people in Africa and the Middle East who would like to live in the West? ... Historically one of the characteristics of any nation was that it exercised control over its borders. There is no obvious alternative to maintaining this position even in the face of the dramatic changes to population movements that have taken place in the past decade.[19]

Mares appeared to recognise the importance of borders yet was unwilling to say how many people should be resettled every year. It appeared that mentioning a number was akin to abandoning principle. If borders were important, a quota was required. Some people would need to be turned away. This was an unavoidable reality that needed to be faced. One of the few advocates willing to nominate a figure, former Baptist minister and World Vision CEO, Tim Costello, declared that Australia's 'fair share' of the world's refugees was 42,000 annually.

> I believe that from the *Tampa* on, we Australians have been paralysed in a toxic debate about refugees. It has damaged our national soul. Fear and hatred beget fear and hatred. We are a very successful multicultural society, but our hostility to boat people and their suffering is ugly and unworthy of an optimistic and caring people.[20]

It was one thing to condemn Australian attitudes; it was another to fund resettlement costs. Costello was advocating a three-and-a-half fold increase in Commonwealth outlays without identifying any budget offsets or approximations of the opportunity cost in terms of other areas of domestic spending, such as aged care and public housing.

In sum, Mares' position is untenable. Australia could not afford to resettle in excess of 40,000 people every 12 months without a range of existing government programs being drastically reduced. The Commonwealth must find ways to limit the number of people it can resettle, irrespective of its obligations under the UN Refugee Convention. None of the countries that have agreed to participate in the offshore refugee resettlement program are without strict annual quotas to which they firmly adhere. Australia is no different.

Acknowledging the controversy associated with immigration policy but not accepting the complexity of immigration practice, Mares makes no concessions or allowances in Ruddock's favour. Having overlooked Ruddock's pre-1996 advocacy work on behalf of refugees and migrants, Ruddock's experience and expertise in the field, and Ruddock's own desire to serve in a difficult portfolio and make unpopular decisions, Mares sides completely with Ruddock's critics who claimed the refugee's former advocate had become the asylum seeker's foremost adversary. The only explanation he could offer for Ruddock's change of heart was political gain. Thus,

> by vilifying boat people and other asylum seekers who arrive in Australia unlawfully, he puts the credibility of all refugees in question; he helps to burrow away at public acceptance of the resettlement program itself. He scratches at the wound exposed by Pauline Hanson, instead of applying a healing salve.[21]

When asked by Mares whether he agonised over difficult decisions, Ruddock replied: 'the simple answer is no and if I had trouble it would be enormously difficult to fulfil the responsibility. You have to be capable of taking tough decisions and being prepared to back your judgement.'[22] Mares was not persuaded by Ruddock's insistence that 'despite what people say, I am not a person who has changed or is lacking in compassion.'[23] While he disagrees with those who portray Ruddock as a modern Faust – the central character in a German fable who sold his soul to realise ambition – Mares offers no alternative portrait. Mares leaves his readers wondering why Ruddock became 'one of the government's frontline players in the shabby politics of division'. Leaving his motivation unexplained, Mares was nonetheless unequivocal about Ruddock's performance. His principal failure was the absence of leadership. He failed to 'offer calm words, to counsel moderation, to remind Australians of the international legal obligations we have signed up to'. He placed 'tolerance and understanding at risk' and threatened 'established legal principles'.[24]

Margot O'Neill

Another ABC journalist, Margot O'Neill, covered a number of stories relating to human rights and mandatory detention before she reflected on their interrelationships in *Blind Conscience* which was published in 2008. Its front cover carried the exhortation: 'this book shows what happens when politics gets personal'. Ruddock was the subject of several chapters including those covering the continuing detention of Australian citizens David Hicks and Mamdouh Habib by the United States at its military base at Guantanamo Bay, Cuba after the 2001 invasion of Afghanistan.

Like Mares, O'Neill was deeply dismayed by Ruddock's apparent lack of compassion for those subject to his administration. She asked whether he felt a 'little responsible' for the children who were damaged by their experience of detention. Ruddock's answer was simply 'no'. His job was to implement the Coalition's policies which he did according to law. In terms of the adverse impact of detention on children, he frequently spoke of the 'totality' of their experience from the moment they departed their country of origin to the time they entered detention in Australia. He was not prepared to accept responsibility when these children exhibited a range of post-trauma related emotions and behaviours. Ruddock asked: 'who put them in that situation? I'd say parents who put children on boats where they could lose their lives'. He stressed that Australia made no secret of its mandatory detention laws. Those seeking protection in Australia should have known they would be detained on arrival. Nor was Ruddock convinced that the apparent danger they were fleeing in their country of origin was greater than the perils they faced in making the long and hazardous journey across the seas.

As for exercising compassion in particular cases, Ruddock explained that could not make any determination until he was acquainted with the facts. He told O'Neill:

> My perspective is not that I am lacking in compassion for people who are refugees, I feel very strongly about refugees, I always have … we can't take the whole world's refugee population. In the end you have to make choices, and the difficulty about making choices is when you set criteria, if it is to be meaningful, in the end it means you have to be able to manage the process of selection. And if people say, 'well, we don't give a damn about your rules, we're coming whether you like it or not', you have to be able to respond to that and it's not easy, but it is important public policy and I think the great majority understand it.[25]

She was unpersuaded by his explanation. O'Neill could not see past what she considered his thinly-veiled opportunism. Ruddock's moral judgement had been clouded by his political commitments. O'Neill's readers were left to think Ruddock was unable to concede fault, unwilling to accept blame and devoid of compassion. He had perfected, she infers, a form of political amorality in which moral matters were reduced to mere practical considerations. Ruddock's conscience was blinded by what he deemed administrative necessity. Compassion appeared to take a distant second or third place to much less laudable considerations in her view.

★ ★ ★ ★

For more than a decade these, and many other commentaries, stood without reply other than from Ruddock's political allies who came to his defence. In contrast to his cabinet colleagues whose performance was the subject of critique, it was Ruddock's character that attracted the closest scrutiny. Were these assessments fair and reasonable? Were any of the commentators sufficiently well placed to know his motivations? Were any of the observers close enough to fathom the state of his heart? Did they understand what prompted his interest in immigration, multiculturalism and human rights? Did they have any insight into his brightest hopes and darkest fears?

Ruddock's critics presumed they had gleaned enough from his actions to conclude that he was obviously a hard-hearted man who was indifferent to human suffering. They came to this view because they thought he lacked compassion. And he lacked compassion because he was overcome with ambition. This was, they believed, an easy charge to sustain. Ruddock had the power to intervene in specific cases of incredible hardship but consistently declined. Report after report submitted to his office conveyed stories of mental anguish and deteriorating health. A compassionate person with the authority to intervene and the power to direct would, the critics complained, have moved swiftly to halt suffering and end pain. Instead, they lamented, Ruddock's only commitment was to address apparent flaws in government processes and unfortunate lapses in service provision. While activists were moved to tears by the plight of detainees, Ruddock was unmoved by their cries and stony-faced. Would nothing persuade him to reform the system, advocates asked? The more they protested, the less Ruddock listened. He had explained the policy and the need for processes. Nothing would compel him to act differently – not even public denunciations.

Concrete compassion

Unlike the activists, Ruddock was faced with the practical challenges associated with the global movement of people and the rise of people smuggling. As the responsible minister dealing with thousands of cases every year, Ruddock was committed to consistency in two ways. First, applications to enter and remain in Australia had to be treated in accordance with the law. He was opposed to preferential treatment for some and prejudicial treatment for others. Second, the movement of people across the nation's borders had to be sustainable. Nothing was gained by drafting policies and devising practices that required constant amendment. Australia needed a policy that promoted its national interests and a set of practices that ensured they were advanced.

Had Ruddock listened to his critics, the Humanitarian Program would have been inconsistent and, therefore, unsustainable over the longer-term. Officials would be constantly besieged by special pleading and demands for special exemption. Ruddock administered policies that were intentionally forceful. Such were the times and such were the needs, he explained. Did this mean that compassion had no place in immigration policy? This was the question that Ruddock's detractors consistently failed to consider. In reality, the *Migration Act* restrained compassion. It did not prohibit compassion but allowed its exercise only in certain circumstances. Plainly, compassion must be a matter of the mind rather than a murmuring of the heart for those holding public office.

The conduct of public administration is, of course, predicated on the existence and exercise of values and virtues, ranging from honesty to efficiency. Compassion is one of many sentiments that might animate the judgement of a public official. Unlike honesty and efficiency which are considered indispensable to effective public administration, compassion is not considered an absolute although it might be highly desirable in some areas of government activity. Compassion's relative standing as an imperative in decision-making is unclear. This means its exercise is open to negotiation. Is efficiency, for instance, more important than compassion when the number of asylum claims awaiting processing is so large? Would it better to assess more people more quickly than assess fewer people more slowly? If the procedural emphasis is on identifying the most 'compassionate' cases, are delayed determinations more acceptable to ensure those in greatest need of protection come to Australia first?

It is not enough for Australians simply to claim they are a compassionate people or that Australian society is compassionate. What are the defining characteristics of such a people? What marks out such a society? Is it within the capacity of government, even the most competent government, to deliver compassion in the management of a complex activity like immigration? When governments are chastised for lacking compassion and are censured for being callous, is the criticism of the policy or the people who administer the policy? Is this a judgement on individual attitudes or on the nation's culture? Do the majority of Australians really want their officials to act compassionately, and when and how? Can we determine whether public officials have indeed been compassionate and when they might have exceeded their mandate? Instead of acknowledging these tough questions and grappling with some of the unpalatable answers, the commentators turned on Ruddock and assailed his character.

Most refugee advocates, including those whose work is surveyed in this chapter, overlook the complexity of the principles and seem oblivious to the complications that are associated with the processes that have existed for more than two decades in Australia for dealing with asylum applications. Many of these advocates unnecessarily polarised the 'debate' by regularly accusing their opponents, principally Ruddock, of cruelty or, to quote former prime minister Paul Keating, a 'dark political heart'.[26] Conversely, the asylum seeker is routinely portrayed as courageous in fleeing oppression, motivated only by a longing for freedom, driven to despair by bureaucratic inertia in the decision to pay a people smuggler, never indifferent to the needs and wants of others, above resorting to distortion and deception in setting out their claim for protection and, of course, always deserving of care and compassion. Refugee advocates traded in stereotypes and often displayed either incredible naivety or amazing dishonesty. Activists tended to dismiss any suggestion that a particular resettlement case had been concocted to attract sympathy. There was an implicit fear that any concession of such behaviour would lead to the counter claim that every case deserving compassion was contrived as well. The mere suggestion that emotion could be manipulated by asylum seekers and their supporters was hastily rejected. This was an appalling insinuation because such behaviour was rightly considered contemptuous.

There was something troubling in the rapidity with which many advocates claimed for themselves the mantle of compassion. Similarly unsettling was their willingness to damn politicians and public officials for lacking compassion, implying that compassion is the principal virtue distinguishing moral from immoral people. There was an easy assumption that to be compassionate is to be moral and to lack compassion is to be immoral. While many refugee advocates and government critics condemned the Coalition for its lack of compassion, none offered anything more than a brief outline of compassion's place in the development and delivery of refugee policy. Its force and effect was asserted but never argued.

The contest place of national sovereignty

The prevalence of passion over persuasion masked ambivalence towards national sovereignty. For some activists, nationalism was an evil to be resisted and sovereignty a pretension to be overcome. For the Coalition, however, the assertion of national sovereignty was a key consideration across all areas of public administration. It was a virtually non-negotiable reality that needed to be strengthened rather than transcended. In explaining the need for the 'Pacific Solution' during the 2001 election campaign, John Howard spoke about

the future of the Australia we know and the Australia we love so much
... It's about this nation saying to the world we are a generous open-
hearted people ... but we will decide who comes to this country and
the circumstances in which they come.[27]

At a time when national sovereignty was being undermined and diminished by a range of factors, decisions to deter unauthorised arrivals were
a means of re-asserting the state's authority to secure the nation's borders.
The voters certainly wanted action. The nation's borders mattered and the
Australian Government should decide who crossed them. What may have
seemed a 'crisis of compassion' to some was considered a 'crisis of control'
to others. This was a disagreement about relative and not absolute values.
The Coalition decided that the national government's ability to control
the borders was more pressing. Without that control, the Humanitarian
Program was effectively imperiled. Compassion was deliberately afforded a
less elevated status. This was lamentable. For a national government, it was
nevertheless considered unavoidable in preserving the nation's capacity to
exercise compassion in the future.

Much of the criticism directed at Philip Ruddock was, therefore, unfair
and unjustified. It was unfair because he was compassionate at times and
in circumstances that were unknown to his critics and unfair because he
managed to maintain the Immigration program against its detractors and
eventually succeeded in raising the number of newcomers Australia was
prepared to take. It was also unfair because he was singled out for condemnation when he was obliged to operate within the dictates of the law, consistent
with his party's policy and Cabinet resolutions, and conscious of the comprehensive system of procedures and provisions he inherited from the Labor
Party which included mandatory detention. The criticism was unjustified
because he was required to manage a program with limited resources and did
so effectively; unjustified because he endeavoured to improve the detention
system while doing his best to promote offshore processing and resettlement;
and, unjustified because the system, even with its faults, continued to enjoy
the goodwill and support of the Australian people – whatever their views
of race and ethnicity.

These might seem minor matters to those who deemed the Coalition's
policies and procedures cruel or callous but they become more meaningful

in the context of community scepticism about the integrity of the immigration program in 1996 and the hostility towards immigration as a concept that accompanied the rise of the One Nation party in 1997. When Paul Hanson's party captured more than one-in-five first preference votes and secured 10 seats in the 1998 Queensland state election, the Immigration program was seriously threatened by ill-informed commentary and political paranoia. Ruddock managed to restore the program's overall integrity and to revive confidence in its management. Immigration was, he demonstrated objectively, a key element in nation-building. Throughout this period of heightened sensitivity to immigration, Australia continued to absorb around 12,000 people within the Humanitarian Program each year and an average of 90,000 migrants in the economic program. While advocates were unwilling to nominate what they deemed to be an acceptable humanitarian quota and were unable to identify suitable sources of additional funding to cover the additional cost to the taxpayer if it were increased, the Humanitarian Program in particular was under pressure and Ruddock was entitled to prioritise resettlement for those in foremost need of protection. Taking the time to identify those enduring the worst oppression and the greatest hardship was the most compassionate response. This was not the most convenient response. It was certainly the most controversial.

Giving every available place to applicants in detention centres would have placated the government's critics and made the issue disappear – for a few months. Before long, the number of people seeking onshore processing would exceed the annual quota and rapidly exhaust the government's ability to fund refugee resettlement properly. The government would lose control of the borders, community goodwill would evaporate and another cohort of critics, this time from the political Right, would demand action. It was possible they would have called for suspension or, perhaps, permanent cessation of Australia's participation in the UNHCR program. When the Rudd Labor Government decided soon after gaining office to abandon much of the Coalition's immigration policy and practice, what unfolded showed the practical good sense of Ruddock's approach.

Despite being frequently vilified, Ruddock never contemplated taking the path of least resistance or caving-in to pressure. He did not shy away from the consequences of his convictions. He visited detention centres and he spoke with detainees. He never claimed to be ignorant of what was happening and this made Ruddock a demanding opponent. He readily accepted that detention adversely affected people and he conceded government policies had led to misery. There was no point denying that the Coalition's approach was tough or implying a willingness to dismantle the measures in place. Shedding tears and promising reform would have conveyed a misleading impression to journalists and given false hope to asylum seekers. He was resolute: the system would remain. The refugee problem was a global one but local solutions needed to be sustainable. Australia would respond in its own way and Australians would hold the elected government to account for its decisions. As the minister, Ruddock would personally answer for his conduct as he accepted full responsibility for the actions of his department.

Echoes from Kakuma

Memories of the Kakuma camp in Kenya continued to shape his convictions and guide his commitments. Ruddock's vision of what the Humanitarian Program could achieve, if managed his way, did not impress critics. He was not distracted by what they thought. Believing that a systematic approach would bring better outcomes over the long term, he was misunderstood even by his more insightful opponents. They saw a man who was impassive and stubborn, lacking humanity and flexibility. They erred in not noticing a determined man who was deeply committed to his own objectives based on an acute inner sense of what he could contribute to the experience of all newcomers to Australia. His emotions were never on display, not because they could not be trusted but because he did not want them exploited. Those who attempted emotional blackmail, as he saw it, were destined to fail. He did not lack emotion. But he would not be deterred from a course of action that would secure the greatest net benefit for Australia and its people. Whereas the media, advocates and lawyers concentrated on tragic individual cases, Ruddock focussed on the entire program and the totality of human suffering. Responding to widely publicised criticism from daughter Kirsty that she found it 'hard to reconcile some of the things he's doing at the moment with some of the things he's taught me to believe,'[28] Ruddock remarked: 'I would like to think that I am still a very compassionate person in the administration of my portfolio and what I do.'[29] Indeed, Ruddock explained that 'sometimes compassion can be misplaced particularly if it means that you compromise on some broader questions'.

When asked to comment on specific individuals or particular families, he looked beyond them to refugee camps in Kenya and Thailand where thousands of people were enduring the most appalling conditions with little prospect of immediate relief. They were the main focus of his compassion. Their collective plight pressed much harder on his conscience than the individual circumstances of those attracting media attention in Australia. While being berated for persisting with mandatory detention and being blamed for its depravations, he continued to feel the burden of doing something constructive about those living without hope in squalid facilities far away. They had no voice, no sponsors and few seemed interested in their welfare. He was attacked for a lack of feeling. It was his feelings that prevented him from acceding to the pressure of critics, feelings that undergirded convictions he could not, and would not, deny.

Endnotes

1   Klaus Neumann, 'The politics of compassion', *Inside Story*, review article, 23 November 2017, accessed 29 January 2019.
2   See also Philip Ruddock, 'Hard Choices: The Asylum Seeker Challenge', Speech to the Commonwealth Lawyers' Association, London, 22 April 2002. Accessed on 10 October 2002 at www.minister.immi.gov.au/media/speeches/20020422_london.htm.
3   Robert Manne, *The Barren Years: John Howard and Australian Political Culture*, Text, Melbourne, 2001, pp. 176–77.
4   Michelle Peterie, 'Docility and desert: Government discourses of compassion in Australia's asylum seeker debate', *Journal of Sociology*, vol. 53, no. 2, pp. 351–66.
5   Peterie, 'Docility and desert', p. 361.
6   Peterie, 'Docility and desert', p. 357.
7   Richard Devetak, 'In fear of refugees: the politics of Border Protection in Australia', *International Journal of Human Rights*, vol. 8, no. 1, pp. 101–109, p. 107 quoted.
8   Devetak, 'In fear of refugees', p. 107.
9   Frank Brennan, *Legislating Liberty: A Bill of Rights for Australia?*, University of Queensland Press, St Lucia, 1998, p. 180.
10 Brennan, *Tampering with Asylum: a universal humanitarian problem*, University of Queensland Press, St Lucia, 2003, p. 11.

11   Elisabeth Porter, 'Can politics practice compassion?', *Hypatia*, vol. 21, no. 4, Autumn 2006, pp. 97–123.

12   Porter, 'Can politics practice compassion?', p. 111.

13   Porter, 'Can politics practice compassion?', p. 109.

14   Mares, *Borderline*, p. 153.

15   Mares, *Borderline*, p. 154.

16   Mares, *Borderline*, p. 158.

17   Mares, *Borderline*, p. 151.

18   Mares, *Borderline*, p. 152.

19   Michael Sexton, 'Open borders invite chaos', Australian, 17 July 2019, https://www.theaustralian.com.au/commentary/open-borders-invite-migrant-chaos/news-story/5795031fd35122e8633df3f4cdc5e6e3

20   Tim Costello, *A Lot with a Little*, Hardie Grant, 2019, quoted in the *Weekend Australian* magazine, 27 August 2019.

21   Mares, *Borderline*, p. 160.

22   Mares, *Borderline*, p. 146.

23   Mares, *Borderline*, p. 158.

24   Mares, *Borderline*, p. 160.

25   O'Neill, *Blind Conscience*, p. 231.

26   Paul Keating described the Minister for Home Affairs, Peter Dutton, as 'mean spirited' and called on voters in the electoral division of Dickson to 'drive a political stake through his dark political heart'. See Richard Ferguson, 'Paul Keating calls on voters to 'drive stake through Dutton's dark political heart', *Australian*, 14 May 2019.

27   https://electionspeeches.moadoph.gov.au/speeches/2001-john-howard

28   ABC Radio interview, https://www.abc.net.au/am/stories/s677000.htm

29   https://www.theage.com.au/national/ruddock-tells-daughter-i-care-too-20020917-gdulld.html

CHAPTER 11

Delayed vindication?

P hilip Ruddock continued to be closely associated with the Immigration portfolio long after he relinquished the post in October 2003. He did not interfere in the affairs of his former department but was always willing to defend its people and processes. The approach to managing asylum seekers that he devised, delivered and defended had worked and was retained by his successors. With the policies in place, Amanda Vanstone and Kevin Andrews refined rather than recast the procedures that gave the Coalition's priorities practical expression. The statistics told a powerful story. In 1998–99, 921 asylum seekers came to Australia in 42 boats. The following year the figure was 4175 and, in 2000, 4141. From 1 July 2000 to 31 May 2001, 3196 people arrived in boats and applied for protection visas. The number of people arriving by boat had escalated quickly. Processing their claims had become unmanageable. The MV *Tampa* controversy in August-September 2001 was the catalyst for more decisive action. Between the implementation of the 'Pacific Solution' in early 2002 and the defeat of the Howard Government in November 2007, only 300 asylum seekers arrived in Australia by boat. The Humanitarian Program continued but the allocation of places was not affected by the large number of unexpected arrivals on the nation's northern shores.

The Rudd Labor Government took no time dismantling the Coalition's border protection regime and abandoning the 'Pacific Solution.'[1] It had campaigned strongly against Coalition policy and practice, promising a more compassionate approach to asylum seekers. It was deemed to have ended in early February 2008. As a number of observers predicted, Ruddock among them, new arrivals increased dramatically from 161 people in 2008 to 17,202 in 2012. A total of 31,000 people arrived by boat in less than five years. More than 1000 people were also thought to have died at sea undertaking the perilous journey to Australia in leaky Indonesian fishing vessels. Labor's changes were disastrous but it had been warned. A decade earlier Ruddock explained:

> you'd have to be very naïve to believe that millions of people are not interested in coming to Australia. There are finite numbers that any country can accommodate ... Lobbying in relation to immigration issues is evidenced by the fact that I get something like 40,000 letters a year. I mean I have compassion for everyone but I can't help everyone. Compassion is felt according to a hierarchy of need.[2]

Those who argued that Ruddock's predictions of a rapid influx of asylum seekers were excessive and inflammatory were obliged to reconsider their position. There was no major social or political change in the countries from which asylum seekers came and no reason to think they would not come again if efforts to disrupt the people smuggling trade were wound back.

After she replaced Kevin Rudd as prime minister in June 2010, Julia Gillard identified border protection as an area in which the Rudd Government had apparently lost its way.[3] The Gillard Government then proceeded to rein-state policies and processes she had condemned on moral grounds when in Opposition. Although she had once said that offshore processing was 'wrong in principle', by the end of December 2012 Labor had revived offshore processing.[4] The Government had to find an alternative to Nauru given Gillard had previously condemned its use. When it increased the number of humanitarian places to 20,000, the announcement encouraged the flow of asylum seekers and subsequent family reunion applications from successful applicants.[5] Plainly, the 'Pacific Solution' had worked as a tool for managing unauthorised arrivals. It may have been harsh but Labor's policy mistakes proved that it was necessary. Those critical of mandatory detention were at least consistent in their views.

Dennis Atkins writing in the *Courier Mail* condemned both Rudd and Gillard for moving to 'extreme Right positions on asylum seekers' and expressed near incredulity that Gillard would propose excising the entire continental mainland from the migration zone. Atkins accused Labor of embracing more extreme policies than the Howard Government in attempt-ing to shore up its declining political support.

> At some stage Labor is going to have to look to its soul and answer
> some existential questions. What kind of party is it? What does this
> lurch to the Right mean? Can it maintain its social justice principles
> after this decision?[6]

Labor had chastised Ruddock for his performance but it found immigration
no less difficult to manage.

With its election loss in November 2007, the Coalition conducted a review
of the campaign and the result, and concluded that immigration policy had
not contributed materially to its defeat. Although Labor was abandoning
the 'Pacific Solution', the Coalition saw no reason to change its policy during
the years the Liberal Party was led by Brendan Nelson and then Malcolm
Turnbull. After replacing Malcolm Turnbull as Leader of the Opposition in
December 2009 and coming close to winning the August 2010 election, Tony
Abbott made a pledge to 'stop the boats' a central pillar of the September 2013
campaign.[7] It resonated with the electorate. When the Coalition regained
office with a 3.6 per cent swing and 18 seats changing hands, Abbott fulfilled
his promise with the launch of *Operation Sovereign Borders*.[8] It would led
by the Australian Defence Force. After 12 months, the number of arrivals
had dropped from 2629 in November 2012 to 207 in November 2013. There
were no arrivals in the first six months of 2014.[9]

By this time the fate of so-called 'moderates' in the Abbott Government
was attracting widespread media attention. Commentators thought the
prime minister was purging his party of non-conservatives and pushing the
Coalition towards the political Right. Liberal Senator Judith Troeth, a well-
known moderate, differed from her colleagues on the handling of asylum
seekers. She told Fairfax Media: 'I don't see how anyone could be devoid of
compassion on this. Particularly in the lead-up to the last election, it was a
race to the bottom between the two parties as to who could put forward the
most punitive policy and I find that very shameful'.[10] Troeth lamented that
the renewed emphasis on Coalition parliamentarians being team players had
meant that individual dissent was a costly exercise. It was difficult for those
sharing her views in the Liberal Party to prevail because the treatment of
asylum seekers was not a domestic issue that touched voters in the way that
health or education did. Voters might oppose the Coalition's approach to

asylum seekers but not to the extent of changing their vote to Labor or the Greens. But were other countries doing any better? Not really.

The forced displacement of people and the resettlement of refugees had become a challenging area of public policy for most First World governments. By the end of 2018, the UNHCR estimated there were 25.9 million refugees with a further 3.5 million people seeking asylum. In 2018, 92,424 people were resettled in third countries, representing 0.4 per cent of the refugee population. The United States, Canada, Australia and, to a much lesser extent, Norway and Sweden, take the bulk of refugees who are resettled each year. Countries such as Spain, which resettled only 830 refugees in 2018, and Japan, which took just 22, have been unwilling to lift their quota.[11] Using a range of measures, such as national Gross Domestic Product, Canada has been considered more generous and welcoming than Australia. These comparisons are largely meaningless because they overlook numerous relevant considerations but they are politically useful in pressing for change. But even Canada has sought tighter regulation of its annual intake. In April 2019, the Canadian Government, led by the progressive liberal Justin Trudeau, quietly introduced new legislation which would prevent people from making a claim in Canada if they had unsuccessfully sought asylum elsewhere. Trudeau explained the legislation and justified greater investment in border security on the grounds of being 'fair' to everyone. The Canadian prime minister was personally condemned with a parliamentarian from a rival party commenting: 'humanitarian leaders do not shut their borders to asylum seekers during a refugee crisis'. The head of the Canadian Council for Refugees described the legislation, which was designed to stop 'asylum shopping', as a 'devastating attack on refugee rights'.[12]

Advocates and activists remain critical of what they see as Australia's mean-spirited approach to the global refugee problem and its treatment of asylum seekers. They want their own country to do more in the face of international inactivity. Lifting the annual quota, as Tim Costello suggested, to 42,000 would not make much of a difference to the millions of people unable or unwilling to return to their homes. It would, of course, make a world of difference to the additional 30,000 people who could make a new life in Australia but the global problem will continue to exist. The Australian people are unlikely to be that collectively altruistic. As for the treatment of asylum seekers, former

High Court judge Ian Callinan concluded a review of the Administrative Appeals Tribunal in July 2019 and recommended a series of measures to ease the backlog of migration cases arising from the continuing high number of appeals. He observed that the avenues provided by Australia to challenge migration decisions were 'no less, and probably more' generous than those offered by comparable countries. Callinan thought criticism that 'Australia does less than other common law countries to provide review of applications made by foreigners to enter and remain in Australia are not well founded'.[13]

Following 15 years of discussion and debate, pronouncements and protests, there was growing acceptance that offshore processing and mandatory detention were the only avenues for Australia to exert the control over its borders that the electorate seemed prepared to accept. The country remained deeply uneasy about 'boat people' and wanted decisive action. Writing in 2016, former ABC television producer Jonathan Holmes, conceded:

> Though I agree with almost everything [Waleed Aly] and other refugee advocates have to say about the practical evils and the moral bankruptcy of 'off-shore processing', I don't believe one should pontificate about a policy unless one has some vaguely practical alternative to propose ... I still see the opposition to boat people dismissed by refugee advocates as 'racist'. That's a fundamental misunderstanding. Australia is rightly proud of its immigration program. It has created one of the most diverse and successful multi-ethnic nations in the world. The reason the boat people had to be stopped was that – justifiably or otherwise – they were undermining Australians' belief in a fair and orderly immigration program.[14]

After noting the large numbers of people who had drowned making the perilous journey, the *Australian's* national security editor, Paul Maley, reached a difficult conclusion.

> This is the dreadful fulcrum on which this debate has always turned: is it better to be tough on asylum seekers and stop the smuggling trade or show compassion and open the floodgates to even worse forms of suffering? Anyone who refuses to answer this binary question is a moral coward. Anyone who thinks the refugee lobby has a lock on

compassion is a scoundrel. In my experience, immigration ministers understand better than anyone the weight of their decisions. There may be a dozen ways to stop the asylum trade without inflicting hardship on good people. We know of one that works. I hate it as much as you do, but the alternative is worse.[15]

The Minister who knew most about the weight of this particular office and who had argued most vigorously against these alternatives was about to retire.

After the Coalition's election defeat, Ruddock made clear that he was staying in parliament. His desire to serve the nation was undiminished. Notwithstanding his seniority in the Liberal Party, Ruddock chose not to seek a shadow ministry, opting for a mentoring role and for involvement in committee work, including the Joint Standing Committee on Foreign Affairs, Defence and Trade, the Joint Standing Committee on Intelligence and Security, and the Privileges Committee. The new party leaders, first Brendan Nelson (2007–08) and then Malcolm Turnbull (2008–09), appreciated his experience and sought his expertise. With Tony Abbott's election as Leader, Ruddock was appointed Shadow Cabinet Secretary. After the September 2013 election, he was appointed Chief Government Whip until replaced by Scott Buchholz in February 2015.

Three months later, Ruddock was asked to work with the then Parliamentary Secretary for Social Services, Senator Concetta Fierravanti-Wells, on the National Consultation on Citizenship. Their report, *Australian Citizenship: your right, your responsibility*, made 15 recommendations designed to strengthen the requirements for citizenship.[16] Ruddock also remained an advocate for human rights, chairing the Human Rights Sub-Committee of the Joint Standing Committee on Foreign Affairs, Defence and Trade and the Joint Standing Committee on Human Rights Scrutiny (March 2015 to May 2016). The latter's role was the examination of draft legislation for its compatibility with Australia's international human rights obligations under the seven treaties to which Australia was a party. He also renewed parliamentary interest in campaigning for the international abolition of the death penalty, becoming co-chair of Australian Parliamentarians Against the Death Penalty. This group was re-invigorated by the execution of reha-bilitated Australian drug traffickers Myuran Sukumaran and Andrew Chan in Indonesia. Ruddock's penultimate parliamentary speech in May 2016 followed tabling of the report on 'Australia's Advocacy for the Abolition of the Death Penalty' prepared by the Human Rights Sub-Committee of the Joint Standing Committee on Foreign Affairs, Defence and Trade.[17] After 42 years of service to the parliament, the people and his party, it was finally time for him to leave.

In a valedictory speech delivered on 3 May 2016, Ruddock mentioned the dozens of people with whom he had worked and to whom he owed a debt of thanks. He commented briefly on his ministerial service, beginning with immigration.

> I believe that we have to be always as humane as possible in the way in which we deal with people. But I also believe that, if we do not manage our borders, we cannot manage an immigration program in the national interest. It is extraordinarily difficult. It is important for Australia and its cohesiveness that we manage those issues with compassion. I welcome the prime minister's desire to get children out of detention and to resolve issues where it is possible, but I know the enormous challenge and difficulty.[18]

He then spoke of his new role as Australia's first Special Envoy on Human Rights and his main task: 'trying to get Australia elected to the United Nations Human Rights Council … if we are able to influence around the world many of the issues about which I feel strongly, I believe I may have played an important part'.

The Prime Minister, Malcolm Turnbull, responded to the hour-long speech with praise for Ruddock's humility and many contributions to national life. With that, Ruddock left the House of Representatives for the last time – the second longest serving Federal parliamentarian in Australian history. He was still some way behind the longest serving. Billy Hughes had served for 51 years and had changed his party allegiance five times. Ruddock had represented three electorates but remained a loyal Liberal. The media said he was 'retiring' from parliament but his family and friends knew he would not, and perhaps could never, retire.

With his appointment as the Human Rights envoy set to end with Australia's election to the United Nations Human Rights Committee on 16 October

2017, Ruddock announced in August 2017 that he would be a candidate for mayoral office at the next local government elections. He was elected Mayor of Hornsby Shire on 9 September 2017.[19] He was again following in his father's footsteps. Max Ruddock had been the Shire President, as the office was then known, 60 years earlier. Two months later, Prime Minister Turnbull asked Ruddock to chair a review of religious freedoms in Australia following the Australian Marriage Law Postal Survey producing a majority 'yes' vote in favour of same-sex marriage and the introduction of a private member's bill to amend the *Marriage Act*.[20] On 26 February 2018, Ruddock was elected President of the New South Wales division of the Liberal Party after the 2017 annual general meeting, scheduled for November, was delayed while factional disputes were resolved.[21]

Although well into his 70s, Ruddock's strong sense of duty and continuing enthusiasm for public office remains undiminished. He continues to work as an advocate for ethnic communities and human rights organisations, delivering speeches on immigration policy and the dynamics of nation building while making time to attend conferences and being interviewed by academic researchers. Ruddock is always generous with his time and seems never to lack energy. Although he has enjoyed a privileged life with many comforts and consolations, he has chosen to promote the interests of those who face disadvantage and hardship. He was never obliged to travel to the world's most wretched places. He was not compelled to visit the most desperate refugee camps on the planet. Ruddock decided without any coercion or even encouragement to make the plight of people who would never vote for him or his party a personal cause. He pursues improvements in their safety and welfare notwithstanding the frustration and anguish that comes with being an advocate for people the world would rather forget. And when others might have suffered from severe compassion fatigue, Ruddock continues to find the time and gather the energy to raise awareness of what might seem intractable problems. Even in 'retirement', he is devoted to causes that others – including his one-time critics – have long forgotten. A life of public service that is motivated by conviction and propelled by compassion shows no signs of ending.

Endnotes

1   https://www.smh.com.au/world/pacific-solution-to-end-on-friday-20080206-1qkv.html

2   Philip Ruddock, 'The Gatekeeper', ABC TV Australian Story, 10 September 2002.

3   https://www.smh.com.au/national/labor-party-was-losing-its-way-under-rudd-gillard-20100624-z10q.html

4   https://www.hrw.org/news/2012/08/17/australia-pacific-solution-redux

5   https://www.aph.gov.au/About_Parliament/Parliamentary_Departments/Parliamentary_Library/pubs/rp/rp1617/AsylumPolicies

6   Dennis Atkins, 'Party Games: Labor goes where even the right fears to tread', *Courier Mail*, 31 October 2012.

7   https://www.theguardian.com/world/2013/sep/07australia-election-tony-abbott-liberal-victory

8   https://www.abc.net.au/news/2013–09-17/angus-campbell-to-oversee-abbotts-border-protection-plan/4963732

9   https://www.aph.gov.au/About_Parliament/Parliamentary_Departments/Parliamentary_Library/pubs/rp/rp1819/Quick_Guides/BoatTurnbacksSince2001

10 Bianca Hall, 'Liberal Wets hang out principles on asylum-seeker policy to dry', *Sydney Morning Herald*, 23 February 2014.

11 https://www.unhcr.org/en-au/resettlement-data.html

12 'Canada to end asylum shopping', *Australian*, 12 April 2019.

13 Nicola Berkovic, 'Migration, social security appeals face crackdown in wake of Callinan report', *Australian*, 23 July 2019.

14 https://www.smh.com.au/opinion/the-brutal-fact-of-the-pacific-solution-is-that-we-need-it-20160502-gok4sf.html

15 Paul Maley, 'Being 'compassionate' only causes asylum seekers more harm', *Australian*, 22 October 2018.

16 https://www.homeaffairs.gov.au/reports-and-pubs/files/australian-citizenship-report.pdf

17 https://www.openaustralia.org.au/debates/?id=2016–05-05.16.1

18 https://parlinfo.aph.gov.au/parlInfo/search/display/display.w3p;db=CHAMBER;id=chamber%2Fhansardr%2F2f71294b-3aa4-45d8-ae01-c94dbd36aa02%2F0108;query=Id%3A%22chamber%2Fhansardr%2F2f71294b-3aa4-45d8-ae01-c94dbd36aa02%2F0128%22

19 https://www.hornsby.nsw.gov.au/council/noticeboard/media-releases-archives/2017/its-official-philip-ruddock-is-our-new-mayor

20 https://www.theguardian.com/australia-news/2018/oct/11/ruddock-religious-freedom-review-what-is-it-and-what-do-we-know-so-far

21 https://www.thecourier.com.au/story/5252010/ruddock-elected-nsw-liberal-president/

POSTSCRIPT

There are many different reasons for writing a book. They range from the task being a professional obligation to a personal quest. For me, this book started as one and ended as the other. As an academic employed to research the Howard era (1996–2007), I began this volume as a standard study of Coalition policy and its influence on national affairs. It would differ slightly from similar projects in focussing on one minister and one attribute. I realised not long after commencing that it would be different to the book I had envisaged. The personal dimension needed to be more prominent.

I first met Philip Ruddock during September 2001 in the Great Hall of Parliament House in Canberra after a national memorial service for the victims of the '9/11' terrorist attacks on Washington and New York. I had conducted the service as the then Anglican Bishop to the Defence Force. As I spent more time with Philip and reflected on the familiar accusation that he lacked compassion and was indifferent to suffering, I recognised how little I knew (and his critics knew) of the inner man. I was also conscious that my thinking about compassion barely transcended vague and unexplored notions of charity and kindness. As I thought more deeply about Philip's temperament he became more, rather than less, mysterious. He was difficult to know and even more difficult to comprehend. He seemed to defy labels; his actions resisted generalisations. And in thinking more expansively about compassion, I struggled to find a stable place for the exercise of compassion in human affairs beyond the realm of inter-personal relations.

Despite these tussles, I hope this book has at least done two things. The first is showing that the beliefs and values that animated Ruddock's political outlook on entering parliament in 1973 changed very little over the ensuing forty years. They were modified, but only slightly, for changing circumstances. Those who think he became hardened or callous with the passing of time have understood neither his personality nor his political vision. There is remarkable consistency in how he approached the issues that demanded his attention between his maiden speech and his valedictory address. The second is identifying some of the practical complexities and philosophical controversies associated with making compassion the defining element of Australia's immigration program. The word compassion has been used indiscriminately and without precision to turn political censure into moral condemnation. Along the way, I have canvassed the difficulties and dilemmas encountered by a man of genuine compassion who had to manage a portfolio on behalf of a nation with contrasting views on immigration and diverging opinions on humanitarian concern.

I must also confess that writing this book left me feeling uneasy and, at times, inadequate as both an Australian and as an academic. I was troubled by some of the things the Howard Government did in pursuit of the national interest; I was saddened that many desperate people had perished attempting to reach a country whose peace and prosperity I have long taken for granted. I also felt deficient in being unable to interpret many of the things that Ruddock said and did to either explain or to defend the Coalition's management of the immigration program. Was the Government merely playing the politics of self-interest or acting with sincerity to preserve the integrity of the nation's borders? The Coalition's opponents claimed it was the former; the Coalition's supporters said it was the latter. But motives are difficult to decipher because individuals and institutions can fake sincerity and disguise dishonesty. Was simply doing the absolute least to fulfil Australia's moral and legal obligations Ruddock's overarching objective? Were his personal convictions subordinated to political obligations? Did moral dilemmas cause existential angst when he was away from the parliament and beyond the gaze of the press? Considering these questions imposed a heavy burden on the consistency and cogency of my own beliefs. The answers would unavoidably draw on my values and sense of virtue.

As the manuscript took shape I felt the need to consider the Good Samaritan story featured in chapter 10 of Saint Luke's Gospel. I have read it many times. But reflecting on its message while writing this book was unsettling. Saint Luke writes:

An expert in the law stood up to test Jesus. 'Teacher,' he asked, 'what must I do to inherit eternal life?'. Jesus replied: 'What is written in the Law?' he replied. 'How do you read it?'. The expert answered, "Love the Lord your God with all your heart and with all your soul and with all your strength and with all your mind'[a]; and, 'Love your neighbor as yourself'. Jesus then said: 'You have answered correctly. Do this and you will live'. But the expert wanted to justify himself, so he asked Jesus, 'And who is my neighbour?' In reply Jesus told a story.

'A man was going down from Jerusalem to Jericho, when he was attacked by robbers. They stripped him of his clothes, beat him and went away, leaving him half dead. A priest happened to be going down the same road, and when he saw the man, he passed by on the other side. So too, a Levite, when he came to the place and saw him, passed by on the other side. But a Samaritan, as he traveled, came where the man was; and when he saw him, he took pity on him. He went to him and bandaged his wounds, pouring on oil and wine. Then he put the man on his own donkey, brought him to an inn and took care of him. The next day he took out two denarii and gave them to the innkeeper. 'Look after him', he said, 'and when I return, I will reimburse you for any extra expense you may have'. Jesus then asked him: 'Which of these three do you think was a neighbor to the man who fell into the hands of robbers?' The expert in the law replied, 'The one who had mercy on him'. Jesus told him, 'Go and do likewise'.

The story concludes in a most unexpected way. Jesus offers no measure or standard of compassion. There is no universal benchmark to which individuals must aspire. The compassion is open-ended both in terms of its depth and duration. The compassionate person can always do more in response to pressing need. The story is an invitation to strive for the maximum obligation not the minimum response. It prevents anyone from readily or easily claiming to be compassionate; it works to deflate pretension and expose hubris. This teaching is intended to be a template for right relations between people. It is a guide for those who seek nobility and strive for moral excellence. It is not just a message for the religiously inclined although, for the followers of Jesus, it has the force of an exhortation.

As a Christian, this story tells me that the sincerity of my faith will be assessed by the quality of my actions. I am instructed to be compassionate to those who suffer because they have *become* my neighbour. I have entered their experience. When I think about immigration and refugee policy, my spiritual convictions and my political commitments (and I do not mean party loyalty or voting behaviour) do not converge. Australia welcomes skilled migrants with the knowledge that many of them leave communities with a greater need for their expertise and experience than we do. Immigration enriches this country even as it potentially impoverishes another. Part of me finds mandatory detention excessive and repugnant; another part concedes it is necessary and defensible. My reactions and reflections propel me in different directions. Reactions and reflections are not opposites. Intuition and cognition are not adversaries; one is not more appropriate than the other. I recognise both are informed by ideas and shaped by ideals. They foreground different values. Reactions and reflections are susceptible to distorting factors that make them either inaccurate or unreliable as guides to what is right, let alone what is necessary. In coming to an opinion on immigration policy, I am relying on information that I have sought from a range of sources with varying levels of accuracy and reliability. This information is not without an ideological dimension given this area of public policy is so thoroughly contested.

I readily admit that my conclusions are unsatisfactory. I am unable to demarcate for compassion a clear place in the development and delivery of public policy. This is mainly because I am not confident institutions can be compassionate notwithstanding the disposition of their leaders. I look to individuals and not institutions for compassion. Without compassionate people there is no compassion. Making compassion a prerequisite for public office is impractical and unrealistic. There is a big difference, however, between showing compassion and being compassionate. The compassionate person will not limit the expression of their compassion nor be concerned with whether they have been compassionate enough.

It is far from fanciful, however, to invite the exercise of compassion. An action often instils an attitude. When a person is implored to acknowledge the suffering of others, they are encouraged to transcend self-centredness and embrace altruism – and many do. In the famous 'quality of mercy' speech

(Act 4, Scene 1) in Shakespeare's play *The Merchant of Venice*, the exegesis of mercy, and the exhortation to show mercy, might equally be applied to the exercise of compassion.

> The quality of mercy is not strained.
> It droppeth as the gentle rain from heaven
> Upon the place beneath. It is twice blest:
> It blesseth him that gives and him that takes.
> 'Tis mightiest in the mightiest; it becomes
> The thronèd monarch better than his crown.
> His scepter shows the force of temporal power,
> The attribute to awe and majesty
> Wherein doth sit the dread and fear of kings;
> But mercy is above this sceptered sway.
> It is enthronèd in the hearts of kings;
> It is an attribute to God Himself;
> And earthly power doth then show likest God's
> When mercy seasons justice.

As with mercy, those who show compassion and those who receive it are both blessed. If nothing else, compassion serves as the last resort when justice has failed in a civilised society. Sadly, much public discussion of immigration is entirely pragmatic while political debate overlooks many of the ethical principles associated with immigration. Most participants engage in special pleading and emotional posturing in the face of what remain complex ethical questions and complicated moral dilemmas.

I believe Ruddock was compassionate and, in resorting to ministerial discretion on more occasions than anyone who has ever held the office, he showed compassion. But there were times when he could and should have visibly shown more concern for the plight of people caught up in mandatory detention. There were occasions when he might have been more vigorous in pursuing and promoting less harmful alternatives. While I reluctantly accept the need for certain actions in relation to the management of asylum seekers, these actions remain deeply disturbing. That anyone finds mandatory detention distressing is neither trivial nor unimportant. We rely on emotions to elucidate the values and the truths that give our lives purpose and direction.

Elements of the Humanitarian Program produce an emotional reaction. This reaction needs to be reconciled with an intellectual response to deep philosophical questions about nationhood and sovereignty. The emphasis is on reconciling reactions and responses. One should not be subordinated out of existence. Respecting reactions and responses ensures we take a whole-of-person approach to an issue, allowing our hearts and minds to speak in unison.

Consequently, we should not consider people with different views to be men and women of defective character. Assuming the high moral ground comes with the temptation to denigrate those with 'lower' views. Eventually they will be deemed lesser people. Australian attitudes to immigration are a shifting amalgam of preferences and prejudices, hopes and fears. There will continue to be different views and consensus will be difficult to find. The greatest danger, however, is losing perspective.

Although separated by vast expanses of water from other countries, Australians do not live in isolation from the rest of the world. Some Australians strongly prefer, however, that we did. Hence, vehement reactions to the arrival of 'boat people'. In addition to being a reminder of what the world is really like for millions of its inhabitants, 'unauthorised arrivals' are emblematic of diminishing control and crumbling order. With its vast coastline, Australia will always struggle with border security. A relatively small population inhabiting a vast continent fears being overrun. This anxiety is irrational. The panic is excessive. Australians want the borders controlled but they would prefer to remain oblivious as to the means: out of sight means out of mind. The electorate does not want to take responsibility for the demands being made on public officials who implement border control policy. It is easy to talk tough when the consequences are unseen, especially the human toll. Those who have carried responsibility for the implementation of immigration policy know that tough talk comes with its own set of problems.

Ruddock has administered immigration policy for longer than any living Australian. He has devoted countless hours of his personal and professional time to refugees and those denied basic human rights. He was not obliged to do so. In representing an affluent electorate with First World concerns, he could have ignored refugees and been indifferent to their plight. He wasn't and he isn't. His sense of compassion led him into politics and, on many occasions, to make zealous speeches about causes in which he believed deeply.

Unlike many others who claimed to be concerned about refugees, Ruddock retained a sense of proportion. This made him an effective advocate.

In an important essay on politics as a vocation, the pioneering sociologist Max Weber concluded that passion needed to be tempered with proportion for a politician to be effective.[1] Proportion was, according to Weber, the 'decisive psychological quality' for a politician: 'his ability to let realities work upon him with inner concentration and calmness'. Conversely, a lack of distance was 'one of the deadly sins of every politician'. The challenge was how 'warm passion and cool sense of proportion [can] be forged together in one and the same soul'. The best political personality possessed 'qualities of passion, responsibility and proportion' to prevent over-excited responses and superficial posturing.

If politics is fundamentally a 'contest of ideas', compassion is a thoroughly contested idea. While there is considerable disagreement about what being compassionate entails and what showing compassion demands, leaders and their followers ought to think about the convictions that undergird an understanding of compassion and the call to be compassionate. This is the most compelling message I have taken from examining the life of Philip Maxwell Ruddock.

Endnotes

1   http://polisci2.ucsd.edu/foundation/documents/03Weber1918.pdf

INDEX

www.ingramcontent.com/pod-product-compliance
Lightning Source LLC
Chambersburg PA
CBHW070401100426
42812CB00005B/1591